TIME

WILL

TELL

TIME

WILL

TELL

A TRUE STORY OF ABDUCTION, SURVIVAL AND RECONCILIATION

YEMI ELEGUNDE

Matador
9 Priory Business Park
Kibworth Beauchamp
Leicestershire LE8 0RX, UK
Tel: (+44) 116 279 2299
Fax: (+44) 116 279 2277
Email: books@troubador.co.uk
Web: www.troubador.co.uk/matador

ISBN 978 1783061 945

British Library Cataloguing in Publication Data.
A catalogue record for this book is available from the British Library.

Printed and bound in the UK by TJ International, Padstow, Cornwall
Typeset in 11pt Aldine401 BT Roman by Troubador Publishing Ltd, Leicester, UK

Matador is an imprint of Troubador Publishing Ltd

In Loving Memory of my dad Lekan Elegunde.
God be with you till we meet again.

ACKNOWLEDGEMENTS

When I started the project of writing the manuscript in June 2005 which eventually became the published book "Time Will Tell", never in my wildest dreams did I think that I would attract so many readers, I never thought that I would talk to the media, appear at seminars and even pick up an award for the book.

It started out as a project for me, I knew that I had a lot of thoughts that I couldn't let go of, and some that I wanted to make sure I never forgot. In the beginning I kept my thoughts to myself but later I found that I was more willing to open up to some people and talk about the events that eventually became the story. I took my time writing, in fact, it took six years. There was no deadline; there were no targets and I had no real intentions of it becoming a published book. In fact I didn't even realise at the time, the depth of the ongoing issue that is *International Parental Child Abduction*.

Before the book I didn't know anyone else who had been through experiences similar to mine, so it never crossed my mind that this was a global issue and one that needed more publicity. According to research released by the United Kingdom Foreign and Commonwealth Office (FCO**) in 2011, every other day a British child is abducted by a parent to a "non-signatory "country (one which has not signed the Hague Convention on international child abduction). In practice, this figure is likely to be even higher as many cases are simply not reported. Figures from the United States are even higher. New figures reveal that the number of parental child abduction cases dealt with by the Foreign Office has risen by 88% in under a decade. It is now a worldwide issue with the Foreign

Office and Reunite International working on cases that relate to 84 different countries.

Understanding the effects that parental child abduction has on the families involved financially, mentally and emotionally as well as the long term scars left on the children involved is low. The long term objectives and results of parental child abduction vary vastly and ultimately unless the complex situation is resolved amicably and quickly, no one wins. Not the abductor, the left behind parent or the child or children caught up in it.

"Time Will Tell" helped me in many ways: the writing was somewhat therapeutic for me, and somehow it made me feel a little more at ease with things that had really bothered me and played on my mind for close to thirty years. The book also opened many doors for me, it helped me start something that I had always wanted to do, which is to support other kids, and parents who find themselves thrown into similar situations.

I have met and worked with Reunite International, Abducted Angels and various other charity organisations that specialise in International Parental Abduction issues, I have worked with experts on case studies focused on the psychological effect parental abduction and alienation can have on a child, I have also met many parents of various ages, from all over the world. These people had one thing in common: their child or children had either been abducted to a foreign country or they feared that their child could be abducted by the other parent at some point.

In this revision, I have attempted to answer most of the questions that readers of the original book asked, including the biggest question of all, in my father's own words, why he took us away without our mum's knowledge or consent. I have also tried to fill in some of the missing gaps that people wanted to read about including how I actually spent my early years rediscovering myself in England. I have also attempted to bring the book up to date. In the original version I focused loyally on the events through my own eyes as were relevant to the whole story, hence leaving out some peripheral stories, here I have tried to bring the audience up to date beyond the initial reconciliations between me and my parents, but also to the continuous reconciliations with myself, getting to know my parents better and becoming a father.

I wrote "Time Will Tell" from my early vivid memories, it would seem a lot of things are stored almost permanently in our minds. Occasionally, while chatting with friends, colleagues or even strangers the topic of my sister and me having been smuggled away to Nigeria while we were kids would crop up. I would have to elaborate on this topic a little more and my audience would always be intrigued. Time after time the same suggestion would come up "You should write about this" they would say and I would say "Yeah, maybe one day".

Gradually I began to realise that I did, in fact, have a lot of memories and thoughts about the years I spent in Nigeria, so when Jo Larsen, the wife of a colleague, urged me for the umpteenth time to put my memories to paper, I realised that perhaps I should take her advice more seriously. So In June 2005 I began to type and re-type, only to delete and start all over again. Slowly but surely the pages started piling up.

A lot of people have helped me along the way, some just by telling me to write about my experiences and by saying how much they would love to read my story. Others kindly read my manuscripts, some, more than once. Some really pushed me to keep feeding them with more pages; collectively they pushed me all the way to the end of this book.

I would like to thank the following people in no particular order for their insight, feedback, time and encouragement. Kristina Savytskaya ; Yulia Kharchenko; Isolde Fischer; David Sanford; Stephanie Ferrero; Frank & Jigs Awuah; Darren Awuah; Lorraine Reid; Clare & Aaron Tebbutt; Brian Emmanuel; Lanre Elegunde & family, Angie Ruiz Martin; Lisa Holding, Lindsey whitehead, Louise Springall, Ima Scotney and Lisa Davidian.

My thanks also go to Sean Felton and the staff of Abducted

Angels, Alison Shalaby and the staff of Reunite International, My Child Abduction Meet up group members Jonathan Banjo, Jean-Christian Cattin, Sabeena Sumrust, and the many other left behind parents I have met along the way, My step-Dad Owen Powell, My Uncle & Aunt Charles & Erika King, my cousin Oliver King, my step-brother Bola Ogunkoya and My beautiful sister Bisi Ogunkoya (with whom I shared most of these experiences and who kindly read it all to authenticate and remind me of some important events and dates).

I would also like to thank my parents Florence Powell & Lekan Elegunde who both read the original book and willingly helped me with a lot of facts in this revised version. The message from my father is that sometimes it becomes impossible for parents to live together, but to take a child away from the other parent without the knowledge or consent of the other parent or to restrict the other parent from seeing their child can leave long term scars for all.

Shaya my daughter, you are loved, thank you for coming into my life and making me a complete man. Finally, my gratitude also goes to Lucy Mellersh my editor on this revised project, who in spite of the first-hand experience she had gone through as a result of parental abduction, still read my book and manuscripts numerous times and kindly carried out the editing.

This book is dedicated to the memories of Tunde Adeaga and my brother Damian "Chisel" Powell. I would also like to dedicate it to my mother who I now see as my true hero, for all the things she has gone through in her life.

Yemi Elegunde
February 2013

PROLOGUE

When I returned from Jamaica late in November 2004, I was returning from probably the worst time of my life, but when I got back home to Luton, UK and sat down to reminisce, one small irony hit me. Although I did not see them in the same country let alone at the same time, this was only the second time that I had physically seen both of my parents in the same year since I was seven years old, back in September 1973.

I had seen Dad in April of that year in Nigeria it was kind of a home coming trip, then, in November, tragedy brought me to Mum in St. Elizabeth, Jamaica.

The significance of seeing both my parents in the same year, albeit seven months apart, could be easily missed, especially under these circumstances, it dawned on me that my sister hadn't even managed that, and it made me realise that this was something that may never happen again.

My parents live at least 9,203KM apart on different continents, Mum lives in Jamaica in the West Indies while Dad lives in Nigeria, West Africa, they have neither seen nor spoken to each for well over 30 years.

For me, this was the year that I had finally closed the door on 31 years of soul searching, pain, and a host of emotions. 2004 was when I decided to stop fruitlessly searching for the answers to my questions. To be honest, the answers probably wouldn't make me feel any better now.

I decided it was time to move on with my life, I had to give my daughter a better beginning than I had. It was time to let go of the lost years that I could never get back and appreciate the roller-coaster years that I experienced instead. I have been both lucky and unlucky to experience life the way that I have, I fought a lot of battles with my emotions as well as with other people. I made a lot of friends along the way. As a result of my experiences, and what I have seen and done, some people say it made me a better or a stronger person. I disagree: better or stronger than what?

Who really knows how I would have turned out had the events of 1973 never happened? What I do know is that I am a strong person, most people will say that I smile through almost any circumstance and I truly appreciate what I have and the life that I have been given.

If I had a choice, I wouldn't have chosen to be where I ended up in September of 1973 nor would I have chosen to go to Jamaica in November, 2004 but this is all part of my destiny.

I have always been a firm believer that everything in life happens for a reason, we all end up in the right place at the right time, and sometimes we are just not lucky enough or perceptive enough to know it.

Destiny plays a role, as do our individual choices. No matter how bad life seems to be, you only have to listen to the news, look across the street and so on, and there is always someone, somewhere, having a day or a year that makes yours look like a blessing.

Still, we all have a story to tell, some of us have lived very sheltered lives others have bigger wilder experiences. Here's my story...

CHAPTER ONE

WELCOME TO NIGERIA

Bisi and I held hands tightly as we walked along the muddy, bumpy clay road. We were trying to keep up with Dad who was a few steps ahead of us, hauling a couple of large suitcases. It was a warm night in September 1973, there was a light drizzle falling and it was mostly dark along the road.

We both looked up to Dad for reassurance; we knew something unusual was going on, but no one had taken the time to explain anything to us. Dad just looked at us and smiled.

It was past 9pm, there was very little light about, a few of the small houses we could see had candles flickering in the wind, some had kerosene lanterns and occasionally we would walk past a house with electricity.

Bisi and I had never been to this place before. We continued to walk along the muddy path, as the light drizzle now turned into slightly heavier rain, none of us had a raincoat or an umbrella, so we had to walk faster; I wiped away a bead of rain from over my eyebrows as I glanced over to my right where two boys were playing ping-pong in the rain with just a dull fluorescent light hanging above the table.

I could see little chicks scurrying across in front of us chasing after their mother hen, there was a pig burying its nose into the smelly damp soil and I also noticed little kids running around barefoot with nothing but a pair of pants on. What I still didn't know was where we were.

"We're nearly there now" Dad said. We both nodded, as we had done countless times over the last few hours. It had already been a very long day and now it was getting weirder. What had started as a nice surprise earlier that September morning, was now looking very strange. Of course, I didn't know it then, but this was going to be the turning point in my life, the point that would define the rest of my life. That fact wasn't even in my wildest dreams that night. I was only 7 and Bisi 5.

As we approached the little house, one of the few painted ones that I had seen so far, Dad's excitement grew. Then suddenly a young lady came running out of the little house, she was ecstatic as she ran screaming and beaming at Dad. She gave him a massive bear hug as some more people came rushing out of the house. She was now talking, almost yelling to him speaking in that dialect Dad usually uses only with a handful of uncles at home. "Hello, hello" she shouted towards Bisi and me, as more people came out of the house, some taking Dads bags off him and carrying them through into the house.

We walked in; I didn't recognise anyone in the room. I felt rather tired and nervous as I am sure Bisi did too. We sat down still holding each other's hands tight; you would have needed a chisel to ply us apart. Dad had gone into another room, Bisi and I looked at each other quizzically. The windows were all wide open now and there was dozens of kids all staring in and talking excitedly in the same language that neither of us understood. We just sat there without a clue as to what was happening.

Suddenly, a jolly woman, larger than life, with a huge smile on her shiny face came into the room and handed us a bottle of Coca-Cola and a pack of zoo crackers each.

She was really excited and was trying her best to communicate with us. But we just sat and stared at her as the commotion carried on all around us. "Eat …e nice" I heard her say; as she tried to encourage us to try the biscuits. I kept wondering where Dad was. It was getting more confusing by the minute; we just sat there, silent and bewildered. "Eat…e…sweet…e…nice" but we just held hands, the kids at the windows were still loud and there was at least 15 people in the little room.

After what seemed forever, Dad came back to the little living room. "You alright?" he asked, we nodded, I think we were too confused at this point to find the right words.

Soon we were both too exhausted from the whole weird day that we crashed out right there, where we were sitting, in spite of all the noise around us.

The next day, I woke up in a small room, it took a few seconds to understand my bearings; it must have been very early in the morning because everyone else was still asleep. I glanced up at the grey ceiling, in one corner of the room I could see a wall gecko, on my left side I could see someone else was asleep right beside me and on my right I could see Bisi who was still deep in sleep. I sat up and counted at least eight other children all asleep some on the bed with Bisi and me but most of them on an old shabby straw mat on the floor.

I got up, and manoeuvred around the legs and arms sprawled all over the mat, I walked out of the room into a dark narrow corridor, it was all quiet, I turned to the right but all the doors were locked so I turned back, there was a row of rooms on both sides and I could see people asleep in some of them. I made it back to the living room where we had sat the previous night; Dad was in there sitting at a desk, at the other side of the room. He was busy writing, I went over to him, "Good morning Dad, what are you doing?" "Writing a letter" he responded. "But where's Mum" I asked. It had now been close to 24 hours since we had last seen her. Dad replied "I am writing to her right now, do you want to tell her that you are OK?" "Why?" I inquired, "why not just go back home instead?" then the words that will live with me forever were uttered. "She's still in England; we are in Nigeria so we won't be seeing her for a very long time".

I was only 7 years old, up until this point, the only thing I knew about Nigeria was that it was my dad's country, I had never even seen any photos of the country. At that moment though, the only thing I could hear in my mind were Dad's words. In my heart, I understood what Dad had just told me but I didn't understand how this could be happening. I was looking for a reassuring sign that Dad was just joking but there was no such sign.

The chilling reality was there for me to see. The previous day we had unwittingly boarded a plane from England, we stopped briefly in Ghana, then caught a connecting flight to Nigeria later that night.

I continued to press Dad, I wanted to know exactly when he thought we would see Mum again "you will see her again one day soon, you may not understand right now but when you are older, you will understand". Bisi was awake now and had found us in the living room; she could see the tears in my eyes and the flabbergasted look on my face.

Dad invited Bisi to join him in writing his letter to Mum; eventually I conceded and joined them too. I asked that he tell Mum that we were fine and well and I asked her to send me my wristwatch. It was my first real watch, a present from my birthday back in February of that year. I had always been obsessed with watches so it was the perfect present and one that I did not now want to be without. I wore it whenever I was going out with Mum or Dad and had I known that I was never going to see it again I would have tried to go back home to get it before we left.

As it turned out Bisi and I left England in exactly what we had worn to Mrs Brown's in the morning, Dad didn't pack a suitcase or any of our belongings whatsoever as he didn't want to arouse any suspicion. On the day we left, not only had he pretended to go off to work, he must have waited around till he knew Mum had left the house and then gone back in and packed everything he needed, including two passports that he had secretly applied for and acquired for Bisi and me. The passports and the clothes we wore that day were the only possessions that Bisi and I took from England to Nigeria.

We finished the letter, the only content of which I remember

4

was my little paragraph about being OK and the request for my wristwatch, as for the rest, I was not interested and could not care less.

It seemed everyone in the house was awake now and wanted to come into the living room for a chat. We still had the language barrier of course, and now I was beginning to feel that I wanted to be left alone with my thoughts, it was a feeling I was going to get again and again in the coming years.

It was amazing to see how many new cousins I had in just one house. Uncle Joe was the oldest of Dad's nine brothers and sisters. It was his house in Agege that we had arrived at, and were now living in. He had a big family of his own, his wife the jolly lady who had offered us the crackers the previous night I only ever knew as "Maami", which roughly translated meant "my mother" but not only did all her children address her by that name so did most of the children in the neighbourhood and eventually so did Bisi and I.

Between them they had six children; the oldest Dipo was only a few years younger than Dad so he would have been in his late 20's when we first met him, next was his sister Bolaji, then a brother Lanre followed by three girls Bolanle, Yetunde (the young girl who had rushed out to greet Dad as we approached their home the previous night) and the youngest one Abake. Abake was only a year younger than me so eventually she was the one that I was closest to and the few words of Yoruba that I learned in those early days were courtesy of her especially as she spoke no English at all.

I remember Dipo used to be a goalkeeper for his local team and would take me to a few of his matches. Lanre spoke the most English whilst Yetunde and Abake hardly spoke any at all.

They all lived in one of the biggest houses on their street in Agege. It was a bungalow. The living room was the first room you came to as you walked in through the main door. It was sparsely furnished; there was an old piano in one corner, two old armchairs and a three-seater surrounding a centre table, above which was an old dusty ceiling fan.

5

The living room had two doors, the main entrance and the other door which led to a long hallway. Five doors on each side of this hallway led to bedrooms which some of the older ones like Dipo and Lanre used as bedsits. The first bedroom on the left was the largest and this was Uncle Joe and Maami's.

The hallway led on to the kitchen which was at the other end of the house, it was a big room and the walls had been plastered but not painted so the room looked dull and dark. The kitchen also served as a kind of storage room for kegs of cooking and drinking water and sacks of rice, beans & gari a traditional staple meal made from cassava. The kitchen had two twin kerosene stoves and was the busiest room in the house always full of women cooking, cleaning black eyed beans or rice from a tray or pounding yam or cooking one of their various delicious-smelling pepper soups whilst chatting in loud and excited voices.

There was a door from the kitchen which led outside to an unkempt garden and a shack built from aluminium which, to my horror, was the toilet. I had never seen or heard of a pit latrine in my life. Even more horrifying for me was his explanation of how to clean myself after squatting over the hole in the ground, there was no toilet roll, instead there was a lime scale filled old plastic kettle, I had to remember to fill it with water before using the toilet. While I still stared at him with my jaw dropped, he reminded me to thoroughly wash my hands afterwards. "You mean I run this water over my bum and wash my dudu off with my actual hands?" I asked. "Yes, with your left hand" was the reply.

I left the commotion of the living room and went outside where I sat on a step in front of the house, I watched some ants busy carrying pieces of food in a well organised queue, past my feet and into a crack near the step I was sitting on.

I was still very upset I tried to wipe away my tears, but they just kept welling up in my eyes and streaking down my cheeks, I remember Yetunde trying to comfort me, but I wasn't about to be friendly, instead I was getting angry and more confused.

Bisi came out and sat down beside me on the step, she was only five years old. She had recently joined my school, St James Norland School in Shepherds Bush West London. I had been looking forward to being a big brother at school for so long. As it turned out, she only got the one day at school and now we were never going back. I am sure she understood even less what was going on and just needed to know that someone was there for her.

I sat there thinking, It was already getting hard for me to take, difficult for me to see how what had started as a normal day had managed to turn into a nightmare scenario so quickly and without Mum or us having any idea what was coming.

So how did we get here? How did two children unwittingly end up leaving Holland Park in London that September morning and arrive in a small suburban town called Agege in Lagos State, the then capital city of Nigeria, that night without our mum, or indeed anyone, suspecting a thing? How did Dad convince us to leave home and board a plane from Heathrow? Even now, I don't have all the answers but here is what I do recall.

There were two little clues in it for me, just two minuscule but unusual things happened that morning, one of which was enough to make me raise a question but nothing more.

We lived on the 15th floor of a 22 storey building in Holland Park West London, called Norland House, the building still stands tall and proud today. It wasn't our first family house but it was where I had lived for the most part of my life. Our regular nanny Mrs Cross was a very fat white lady we called her Aunt Mary, she had a son of her own, Peter, who was a couple of years older than me. Her husband Sam who we called Uncle Sam was always great fun to be around. Peter and I spent a lot of our time watching TV. We were both Batman & Robin fans, although my favourite TV character at that time was actually 'Joe 90'.

If the Cross's couldn't have us for any reason or if Mum and Dad didn't need us to go all the way over to the Cross's, then Mrs Brown was the alternative. She was good friends with Mum and they also lived in Norland House, just above us on the 16th floor.

Mrs Brown's daughter Beverly was about my age and we were pretty much best friends. We loved playing 'doctors & nurses'. Once I was in from school, I couldn't wait to see Beverly.

On this September morning, I don't recall Beverly being at home, I think she was at school, but we weren't, for some reason, instead we were with Mrs Brown while both Mum & Dad were at work.

The first clue that this wasn't a normal day was when Dad came back home rather early from work to everyone's surprise, no one was expecting him back just about a couple of hours after he had left to go to work! But here he was.

The second clue was that he wanted to take both Bisi and me to the barber's! That was strange to me because Bisi had never been invited to the barber's with us before. It had always been a boy's night out, never a family afternoon outing, besides, I didn't even need a haircut, both points of which I was quick to raise, but Dad was even quicker with his counter, explaining that we couldn't leave Bisi by herself and how another cut would be just right for school, oh, "and don't forget Kentucky Fried Chicken as usual". That sold it to me and to Mrs Brown, so we said our byes and left. We went straight to the lift and down to the ground floor; there was no stopping at home to get our coats or anything else.

Another strange thing was that Dad didn't have his car! "Stupid thing broke down on my way to work". He said. Years later, I would find out that he had in fact sold the car to a friend of his that morning and had only gone out earlier that day to deliver the car and pick up his money.

It was no major surprise to see Uncle Taiwo waiting downstairs, he had been round to see Dad quite often recently. I don't think Mum liked or trusted him much, especially since whenever he visited Dad at the flat, they always spoke in a language that none of us understood. We all got into Uncle Taiwo's car and headed off, past every barber shop I knew, past every KFC we knew, and on we went.

Finally we arrived at what I later realised was Heathrow Airport; the sight of planes was fascinating. Bisi and I were already tired after the long drive, so the sight of planes was a great distraction.

I don't quite remember how or why we boarded the plane with Dad, apart from maybe the excitement. I can't say I recall any part of the actual flight either, but I do remember stopping en-route in Accra the capital city of Ghana, I remember looking around me in awe at these people all dressed in different coloured clothes, there was so much noise around.

For some reason, I have always remembered Dad saying "this is Ghana". It's imbedded in my brain now, yet it meant absolutely nothing to me at the time. We must have boarded again from Ghana for the short flight to the International Airport in Lagos Nigeria. Perhaps I slept on both flights all the way to Nigeria, perhaps I was just bewildered by the whole unusual day, or maybe it was just the 100% trust that we had in our dad, for whatever reason we boarded both flights without much objection.

Still perched on the step with Bisi, I continued to wipe away my tears and looked around me, at the muddy derelict clay roads full of massive long cracks in the middle of the road and pot holes everywhere, the little brick houses, some missing windows, others missing roofs and most of them not painted, the pigs, billy goats, pot-bellied goats, hens and ducks wandering everywhere, the smelly gutters, the half-built hospital next door to us which now served as a play area for kids, the old woman bent over with a long straw broom sweeping the dirt off the clay path to her house and the kids running around barefoot and I wandered how this could be home.

Dad spent the next night with one of his other brothers, Uncle Tony in another part of Lagos, leaving us alone in Agege. Living away from Dad was a pattern I would have to get used to for most of the years I spent in Nigeria.

Although it was clear that we were not going back home to Mum that day, it hadn't sunk in yet that I wouldn't see her for a very very long time. I always believed she would come and get us one day. I held on to that dream for many years.

As it gradually dawned on me that I was not going back to England for now in spite of whatever strop I threw, I had no choice but to try to get used to my new life and my new extended family. Dad was already looking around for suitable schools, so in the meantime, I slowly started adjusting and adapting to my new environment.

∞

It wasn't too long before I had learned how to stand on the edge of a well and pull up a bucket of water by hand and rope only. The wells were a luxury source of water that only a few of the richer people in the neighbourhood could afford. Uncle Joe had a well for his family, but he also left it open to the neighbourhood so that anyone could fetch a reasonable amount of water for free to take back to their households.

The wells looked very much like the pictures I had seen in my nursery rhymes of Jack & Jill but they didn't have the wheel and handle that would conveniently lower and raise your bucket, instead you had a soft small bucket made from rubber with a thick long rope tied to its handle. As there was no wheel it required someone to lower the bucket into the well, fetch the water and pull it back up.

Now you could stand on the ground beside the well and lean over and lower your bucket but this required extra strength and because the bucket of water would scrape and bang against the edges of the well as you pulled it up, it also meant that you only got half a bucket or less of water at a time due to the continuous spillage as you dragged it up. So it would take longer to fill up your main bucket or tub.

The logical and easier if more dangerous way to fetch a bucket of water was to actually balance yourself on the edge of the well then fetch your water, this way the bucket went straight into the middle of the water, tilted sideways quicker and therefore sunk and fetched a full bucket of water. Then, because you were balanced precariously on the wall of the well, you could pull the rope up rarely knocking the sides of the well and requiring less attempts to fill your main bucket or tub whilst also increasing the life-span of the fetching rope.

If you were unfortunate enough to lose your grip of the rope and allow the bucket and rope to fall into the well, the rubber bucket usually floated for a while so you would have to climb down to retrieve it or find someone willing do it for you.

Sometimes you could retrieve it with another bucket and rope if there was a spare one about, other times if there had been a dry spell the well might dry to mud at the bottom of the well and you would find your lost buckets and could fetch them if you were brave enough to climb down the well.

The bucket was a luxury commodity and had to be retrieved. That was the bottom line.

Amongst other things, I learned how to hand wash my own clothes with a bar of soap in a small tub. I got used to dipping my hand into the same bowl as up to eight other children during meals, I learned to eat or at least try a whole new variety of local and traditional meals, some that I liked and others that I never ever liked but ate nonetheless. One such example was a meal called amala. The name alone put me off, the looks didn't help it was a dark thick mash and to me it didn't taste any better than it sounded.

Bisi was a bit more resolute here. She hated most of the meals and refused to even try them. I don't know how she survived; she hated most of the traditional dishes, she hated black eyed beans she even hated eggs.

I adapted to life in Nigeria a lot quicker than Bisi did, but it wasn't too long before I started rebelling, I started refusing to learn the things they wanted me to learn, I refused to play happy families and refused most of all to learn the local Yoruba dialect.

In those first few days, Bisi was very quiet and reserved while I tried my best to communicate with my new cousins in spite of the obvious language barrier.

I remember going out for a walk one morning in a pair of flimsy slippers it was less than a month since we had first arrived in Nigeria. I was getting used to the various short cuts and other bushy roads when I suddenly felt an excruciating pain in my foot. I tried to move my foot, but could barely lift it due to the pain.

I took a closer look, I could see a lot of blood all over my slipper, and I started crying as I tried to lift my foot slowly off of the piece of wood I was standing on. I realised that I had placed my foot firmly on a six inch nail. I limped back home and watched my foot begin to swell. Yetunde was the first to spot me, she realised what had happened before I could even try to explain it to her in our usual mish-mash of languages. She washed off the blood with a damp cloth, cleansed the wound with some TCP and applied a plaster. That was the one and only treatment my foot got. I could not believe the pain I endured for days to follow. I watched my foot swell parts of it turning yellow and then I saw it finally begin to heal.

This was another sharp lesson and a reminder of the environment I now lived in. Although it was a lesson learned, it wasn't something I could avoid. It would happen again on a few more occasions, but at least I was better prepared for the pain.

Getting used to our new home and to our new life was a battle full of many incidents and lessons along the way. Our first few weeks in Nigeria were spent in Agege at Uncle Joe's, Dad mainly stayed in Ikeja with another brother of his while Maami looked after us.

CHAPTER TWO

THE PRIMARY SCHOOL YEARS

The first school we went to was "All Saints Preparatory School"; Ikorodu in Lagos State, Dad chose this school because the proprietor and his wife had both lived in England for many years before returning to settle down in Nigeria. His feeling was that they would understand and help us settle in quickly.

A few weeks after arriving in Nigeria, we were on our way to All Saints Primary. It was a boarding school, and so it was a shock to see Dad waving bye to us as he left us at our new school/home. Even though we had been prepared for this day, it still came as a rude shock to us. Everyone had told us that we would be going to a boarding school about 30 miles away from Agege where we were still residing. We had even been out to the markets to stock up on provisions for boarding school life but nothing was enough to prepare me for the reality.

The essential provisions to survive boarding school in those days included tooth-brush, toothpaste, bars of soap for showering, a box of blue detergent powder for washing clothes, a big tin of powdered milk, Ovaltine, tins of sardines, tins of mackerel and some biscuits. We also needed essentials like pillows, mattresses, sheets and, most importantly, a mosquito net.

On the evening before joining All Saints' Primary, we had packed our suitcases full of all our provisions and new uniforms as well as our spare clothes, neither of us were excited. It was strange being here in Nigeria, stranger that we didn't live with Dad anyway and even more bewildering that we were now going away to boarding school, quite a few miles away from the place we now called home. I found it hard to believe that I was actually going to miss Maami as well as my cousins Yetunde and Abake.

The long drive along those part tarmac and part dusty roads was a quiet one apart from the constant clatter of metal and springs as we rode over pot holes in the road. I wasn't looking forward to boarding school at all. In spite of time passing by I was at a point where I didn't talk much to anyone anymore about my true emotions. I liked my own company, I kept my concerns to myself and most nights, all I did was cry in bed and wonder why my Mum had not come to get us yet.

Instead, here we were on our way to live even further away from Dad, and he wanted to tell us how great this experience would be!

We drove in to the school grounds through the large white metal school gates; they imposed a big barrier for kids of our size. I immediately felt like I was being locked away in a prison barracks. As we approached the main building I could already see kids in the playground in their grey uniform.

I carried my suitcase and followed Dad who was carrying Bisi's case. We walked up to reception, met the proprietors, Dad had a brief chat and signed a couple of forms, then before we knew it, Dad was heading back to the car without us. He told us he'll be back up to see us in a fortnight. I just stood there perplexed and a little petrified. Dad drove away waving as if he knew everything would be alright while we both cried.

Once we had settled down a little, a matron showed me round the school, first the boy's hostel which was a slightly dark long room with rows of double bunk beds on either side, I carried my case in along behind her, and she showed me to my new bed which was the bottom of one of the bunks. I placed my mattress on the metal springs; I then got my sheet and blanket out, and made my bed. The matron then showed me how to tie a corner of my new mosquito net to each corner of the bed above me; she showed me how to pull down and tuck the mosquito net around my bed for bedtime and how to tuck it away during the day.

The matron showed me the toilets and bathroom which was one long room, again it looked quite dark as usual the walls were plastered but not painted. The bath area was one big open area with aluminium buckets all over the place, there were a few taps spread around but nothing else. On the other side of the bath area was a row of six toilet cubicles; I was relieved to see that they were not pit latrines.

∞

I had only been at my new school for an hour and I was already homesick, I could not understand why Dad would leave us alone in a boarding school. Later on I went outside to the playground where I found Bisi, She was still very upset. The matrons were patient and understanding it seemed, they spent some time with us and kept trying to calm Bisi down. She looked more bewildered than I felt.

I walked on the sandy part of the playground and sat down on my own at the base of a shiny silver metallic slide. Suddenly I could hear two boys giggling and calling out towards me…"Oyinbo".. I didn't understand what they were saying, but they kept repeating the same word "Oyinbo, Oyinbo" I looked at them, and then the shorter one of the two came over to me and asked if I was the new boy from London? I nodded, "I guess so" I told him, he then introduced himself as Festus and his friend the taller light skinned boy as Augustine.

Festus and Augustine seemed genuinely inquisitive and friendly. I told them my name and asked them what they had been shouting out to me, Festus explained that "Oyinbo" means white person, a term usually used to refer to white foreigners, so I laughed as I assured them that I wasn't white, I thought it was ridiculous that they would call me a white person, but I could see the funny side too, they had a good sense of humour. I immediately felt at ease with these two lads and followed them as they showed me round the school.

It turned out ironically, that Festus and Augustine were both from Eastern Nigeria and the word "Oyinbo" was a Western Nigerian Yoruba word. Not even their own language!

Festus was quite dark skinned, he had a very cheeky smile and was the more talkative, he carried a small afro comb around and he loved combing his hair. Augustine was much lighter skinned than me, nearly as light in complexion as Bisi, he was one of the tallest kids in school and probably one of the more muscular too, he was about 9 years old, Festus was 8 and I was still 7.

Of all the kids the teachers might not have wanted me to meet and acquaint myself with straight away, these two were probably top of the list, they were loud, cocky, and confident they also seemed to boss just about every other kid at the school around. They also spoke in what I later learned was "broken or as they called it Pidgin English" I found it fascinating, "where are you going" became "where you dey go"; "what are you doing" became "wetin you dey do"; "Do you want to play" became " You wan play" it was just great!

The teachers called me in on numerous occasions, reminding me how beautifully I spoke and asking me not to copy Festus and Augustine, they wanted me to help teach the other kids good English, they also wanted me to learn Yoruba at lessons in school, and so my rebellion began. Within the first month, I had become so fluent in Pidgin English that it became the only way the three of us communicated. I helped them both at lessons, arithmetic, English, literature etc. and they taught me more and more cool slang!

In February the following year I turned eight, it was my first birthday in Nigeria where we had now been for five months. For the first time in my life, neither Mum nor Dad was there to celebrate it with me. The school dressed me up in some native attire at Dad's request for a photo shoot. They placed a dozen or so cupcakes in a pile in front of me and gave me a knife to cut through them as everyone at school sang "happy birthday" I remember it so vividly. I was so miserable and refused to smile even once for a photo.

Academically, it was all going well, I was doing great in every class and when we did our mid-term exams I was 1st overall in class, I had passed every single subject including, to my dismay, Yoruba!!

The teachers were so pleased with how well I had done in learning Yoruba and had started telling me how they would help me progress further, they promised that next time I would be top of the class in Yoruba too, the more they smiled, the more disappointed I became. I felt as though I was letting myself down by adopting a language when I didn't even want to be in Nigeria in the first place. And so I started to lose interest in Yoruba classes, I would drift away, and I would do my best not to listen or learn. On the other hand, I sharpened up on my Pidgin English.

Festus, Augustine and I were best of friends, we spent a lot of time in the play-grounds talking about our families and the different ways we had grown up, I learned a lot about Benin and the tradition of the people. Festus family home was still in Benin, but his parents thought that the best schools were in Lagos, so they travelled over 230 miles to enrol him into All Saints School. He also had a little brother who still lived at home.

His parents were friends with Augustine's, they lived in the same neighbourhood and so Augustine also ended up at All Saints. They were both obsessed with cars and soon so was I. One of our favourite games was to sit on the sand and look over the fences at the busy main road and count the different brands of car going by. We would pick a brand each and whoever spotted the most, won the game. It soon became clear that whoever chose Peugeot would probably win the game. There were so many Peugeot 404s and 504s. You had a chance with Volkswagens, Datsun's or Toyotas but Peugeot would, more often than not, be the winner.

Sometimes we would play spotting only Peugeots and choose between 504, 404 and 304 just to make the game a little less predictable.

Dad had kept his promise: he visited us fortnightly on a Sunday evening, he would leave us some pocket money for emergencies and top up our provisions each time. Bisi always got a little extra as a bribe in the hope that she wouldn't cry too much when dad left. Of course it never worked.

On one of his fortnightly visits, there was a problem. The proprietor was not happy with my academic progress. I was still top of the class in every subject, but I had gone from being one of the top in Yoruba to absolute rock bottom and I knew it. Bisi had long since overtaken me in Yoruba classes, she was doing quite well. Dad was disappointed and told me so, he told me I had to improve but I really didn't care. I stood in front of him listening and watched him as he broke into a kola nut, threw a bit on the ground next to the small wooden stool he was sitting on, and ate the other half.

The kola nut is indigenous to West Africa, it's a very sour tasting nut which men like to chew to diminish sensations of hunger and fatigue as well as to aid digestion.

By the time Dad left, I was pretty upset, Bisi came over to console me and we talked for a long time, we then walked back to where Dad had been sitting earlier that evening and I picked up one of the pieces of kola nut still scattered on the ground and started to eat it, just like I had seen Dad do. It was foul, and very bitter, but I chewed it all up, Bisi just had a tiny bite but spat it out in disgust.

Later on that night, I began to complain of stomach cramps, and soon it got worse. I was vomiting constantly and had diarrhoea as well. My pains and condition continued to worsen, eventually, I decided to go and see a matron and through a flood of tears I explained my problems to her. She took me to one of the head matrons where they then decided to rush me to hospital. We boarded an old bus and sped off towards the local hospital. By this time I was in such a bad state, I was in severe pain, still vomiting and crying. By the time we got to hospital I had passed out.

I spent the next couple of days at hospital recovering from food poisoning. It turned out that the kola nut had nearly killed me!

When I finally returned to school, Festus and Augustine came straight round to see me, we went back outside to the play area for a round of spot the cars. I had missed them a lot. Soon everything was back to normal. I was still top of the class but my Yoruba was not improving at all. Soon both Dad and the proprietor were fed up with my Pidgin English and my refusal to learn Yoruba.

The final straw came soon after that. The proprietor had a daughter called Nike who was always on the school premises, she helped look after the kids, and did some of the teaching as well. She also loved speaking in Pidgin English so Festus, Augustine and I got on well with her. She was about 16 or 17 at the time.

One day I was asked to stay behind and help Nike clean up one of the classes, it was late in the evening. We started cleaning away and chatting: as it got darker, Nike went to sit down on a mat underneath one of the tables, she then called me over and asked me to lie down, she lay down beside me and started talking while she held my hand, and soon she was undressing me and touching me. I didn't understand what was going on but I must have been enjoying it and it seemed like fun. So I didn't complain. I remember her sitting on top of me and play fighting. Soon we were all dressed up and headed back to the hostel, she asked me if I had had fun and I responded "yes" so she said we should do it again and we can keep it our secret.

A few days later I felt this burning sensation when I tried to wee, it stung real bad, so bad that I had to force myself to stop. I tried again a few hours later and this time the burning sensation was so bad I started to cry, but I could not stop myself from urinating this time. This carried on for the whole day.

Finally the next evening as I tried to wee again, the burning was so unbearable that I collapsed to my knees and cried and cried, it still burnt even after I had stopped weeing so I stayed in there crying. A teacher must have heard the sounds and found me on my knees crying, I tried my best to explain what was wrong while he pulled up my shorts and carried me out to see the school doctor. I still couldn't stop crying, eventually we headed off to hospital and a message was sent to Dad who was at the hospital by the time we arrived there. I was still in pain, during the examination, I remember one of the doctors asking me if I had had sexual intercourse with anyone recently, as I didn't know what he meant, I naturally said "No".

The doctor left my bedside, but I could still hear him talking to Dad and the teachers, they laughed and all said they believed me, I must have come across really innocent, but they knew what had happened and who might be at fault.

I stayed in hospital overnight as a precautionary measure; I had a couple of injections and was soon feeling well again.

That was the final straw, both Dad and the principal agreed that they couldn't keep us at All Saints any longer, so just one year after joining we were on the move to a new school.

The next school we went to was called Ifako International Primary School; Ifako was a small village just about two miles from Agege in Lagos. It had a primary and a secondary school campus. We were at the Primary, while the Secondary school was just across the road. It was another boarding school; we were relocating all over again. We had bought all our provisions as usual and new school uniforms. I had three pairs of blue shirts with the biggest white spots, blue shorts and white socks and I also had a pair of "Cortina" branded school sandals. Bisi had three long blue dresses with big white spots and pairs of white socks and the same sandals. I also had a few sets of khaki brown shirts and matching shorts which were for wearing on the school premises after classes. You had to have a uniform on at all times.

Once again Dad was saying his good byes to us; Bisi was upset again, while I was nervous about meeting new people all over again. As it turned out, things were a lot smoother, I wasn't pushed to learn

Yoruba this time, instead I was encouraged to join the debating society, the drama club, and to keep learning science, a subject that I had loved back in England. As a result things went well, I was soon top of the class in every subject and I even began to understand and talk a little Yoruba without ever going to a Yoruba lesson. They did ask me a few times if I would like to attend a lesson but I always declined.

Things were going so well, that I was soon on national TV with Bisi and another boy Michael who had recently joined the school, his parents had recently moved back to Nigeria from England. We appeared on a Variety show, where we sang a few songs and I told a few jokes.

For Christmas that year we had two school plays, one was the usual nativity play where I played one of the three wise men and the other was a one man show where I was the star, playing all six characters in a short story about a boy who would not tell his parents the truth. That show went down very well I got a standing ovation from all the parents and teachers as well as my fellow pupils even Dad and some uncles and aunts were in the crowd.

Every day after lessons, we would have to go back to the dormitory, get out of the blue and white spotted uniform and change into the khaki uniform, then we would all get into bed for an hour-long siesta. This was a very strict routine, we had matrons marshalling the dormitory, you had to be silent and observe the siesta. After we would go out to the playgrounds until the bell rang for dinner time.

A lot of kids used to hang around one of the huge iron gates speaking to people from the senior school across the road, a lot of them had brothers, sisters or friends there who would always come to the gate and hand them sweets, money or other small goodies. I remember being near the gates once waiting for a friend who was meeting his brother, when this tall man called over to me and asked me to come nearer. I obliged, when I got nearer to the gate, he introduced himself, his name was Tunde and he told me he was my cousin and he would make sure that everyone looks after me at school, he explained how we were cousins, later I got to understand how we were related.

Dad came from a large family; his dad was named Yemi and His mum Bisi. Hence our names, his dad had four wives who together gave him 10 children in total. Dad was the ninth of ten and Tunde's mum Aunt Joko was one of Dad's older sisters she was the third oldest of the siblings. My Uncle Joe with whom we had lived with when we arrived in Nigeria was the oldest.

Tunde was excellent from the moment I first met him, he was quite a tall skinny young man; he wore glasses and had a very soft voice almost like a half whisper. He talked to me for a long time, he reassured me that everything would be OK here at Ifako and he encouraged me to keep writing to Mum.

At this point, I had written to her more than six times and had only seen one reply from her. We had already been living in Nigeria for nearly two years. I guess my enthusiasm and optimism that eventually Mum would come and get us encouraged me to keep writing even if I rarely saw a reply from her.

Tunde came round to the gate as often as he could and always brought me anything I asked for. Things were still going well academically too, I had been moved up a year so, for the first time since arriving in Nigeria, Bisi and I were going to be in different years at school.

Two years later, I had turned 11 and it was time to start getting serious, start planning for secondary education and to start deciding which school I would like to go to. Dad's visits were now getting very irregular, it was no longer fortnightly, sometimes three or even four weeks would pass before we saw him, and even the school holidays were spent away from him.

Dad sat me down during one of his visits to school and told me that he didn't think that Ifako would be able to offer me the best level of education to help me pass the national exams and choose a good secondary school. He felt it was time to switch schools once again for the last year of my Primary education. He had a school in

22

mind. Mayflower Junior School, I had heard of Mayflower, they had Mayflower Senior school as well, which was one of the very top schools in the country, they were always winning National School Quiz competitions and debates.

So it sounded like a good idea to me. Dad also told us that we would be in good hands, as Uncle Tony's ex-wife Mary was the Nurse and head matron at the junior school and Uncle Tony's son, Ade was also at the school. Uncle Tony was another of Dad's brothers who we knew very well from England. We had never met his wife or son before.

In retrospect, it was amazing that Dad felt so confident about moving us to Mayflower. It was over 90 miles away from him and worse still, he didn't have a very good relationship with Uncle Tony's ex-wife. In fact, he was quite wary of her, but still felt that she would be good to Bisi and me. Mary had a bad reputation, it was rumoured that she had once tried to kill both Uncle Tony and Dad before. She was well feared in her local village with many believing that she was very powerful in witchcraft also known as juju. Of course, Bisi and I didn't know this at the time.

It was the end of school term and I knew I would not be coming back to Ifako, I wasn't sad. I said my final goodbyes to the teachers and friends that I had made and then got into Dad's car. As he pulled away I glanced round and took one last look at the big iron gates as they closed behind me. I was getting used to moving around.

Dad told us that we would all be spending the first night of the holidays at Uncle Tony's house. This was refreshing, as it seemed that we were always away from Dad even during school breaks. When we got to Uncle Tony's house, Tunde was already there, he was staying over too. He came running out to meet us and carried our suitcases inside. We said our hellos to Uncle Tony who then introduced us to another cousin who was also staying over at the house. His name was also Tunde, I called him T. jnr. I thought that I might have seen him somewhere before, then Tunde told me that

Jnr. was also a student across the road from my soon to be old school.

Dad, Uncle Tony and a friend of theirs were all going out for the night; Tunde was in charge of looking after us whenever they were out as he was the oldest. They briefed him on what food to cook for dinner and how to lock up securely.

Uncle Tony had a successful business at Holloway Motors and he lived in style, he had two Merc's and a nice house in one of the more luxurious parts of Ikeja in Lagos. I wandered around the house which had a sparse living room and a nice kitchen; it only had two bedrooms, so how were three grown men, two teenagers and two kids going to share it I wondered. As it wasn't a problem for me to sort out, I went outside to play. There was a dirty old Hillman car behind the house, I climbed inside and sat in the drivers' seat, Bisi sat beside me and I began pretending to drive. We played for ages until Tunde called us in for dinner. After dinner, we had a wash and went to bed. Bisi and I shared the double bed in the spare room. While Tunde & Tunde Jnr. shared a mat in the living room.

It must have been around 2am when Dad, Uncle Tony and their friend staggered in; they had been out celebrating all night. I heard them come in and Dad popped his head round the door to check that we were OK.

A few minutes later, I was startled by a loud smashing noise, then a few thuds against the adjacent walls, within seconds there was a lot of shouting and more banging against the walls, Bisi woke up too, but we were far too petrified to get out of bed and have a look at what was going on. Suddenly, our bedroom light came on, and three big rough looking men barged into the room, all holding long knives, they looked around the room and then one of them, still snarling headed towards us, Bisi started crying and was about to scream, I put my now shaking hand over her mouth and cuddled her while I kept looking at the man who was now leaning over the bed. He started tugging at the bed sheet we were lying on, he pulled viciously then one of the other men pushed us the other way so that they could pull the sheet right off the bed from underneath us. Once they had the sheet, they ignored us and proceeded to fill the sheet with ornaments and clothes from the room.

There was still a lot of screaming and banging from the living room, there was glass smashing and I could still hear thuds against our bedroom wall. Bisi and I lay still in bed, she was still crying, I was scared too, but even now, I still cannot explain why I lay there in bed so calm that night. Perhaps it was because I wanted to be strong for Bisi, although I think it was more a case of never having seen anything like this before and therefore being scared out of my wits.

Suddenly it all went quiet, we stayed in bed, for a few more minutes, then Tunde came into the room, he lifted Bisi out of my arms and asked if I had seen Dad, I told him I hadn't. I got out of bed and followed him into the living room, it was an absolute mess with broken glass all over the floor, furniture turned over, and the floor was all wet. Uncle Tony was sitting on the floor, his shirt torn to shreds and he was bleeding from his head and from a long gash on his right arm.

We had just been burgled by 12 thieves all armed with knives, the two Tunde's had got out the house through the toilet window and hid round the back of the house, Dad's friend had run out of the kitchen door at the rear of the house, he joined the two boys in their hiding place and Dad had barged his way straight past the incoming robbers, he ran straight out the house wearing just his boxer shorts. Uncle Tony stayed in the house, undeterred by their knives he tried to fight them all and amazingly, he seriously injured one of them. The injury to one of the robbers scared the rest so much that they left with what loot they had managed to gather whilst dragging their battered colleague along.

Dad was still nowhere to be found; I sat on one of the sofas dumbfounded, shaken and in disbelief, watching while someone wrapped a makeshift bandage around Uncle Tony's injured arm.

About 10 minutes after the robbers had left, the police turned up and right behind them was Dad. Within a few minutes, Bisi and I were dressed and Dad was driving us over to Agege our first home in Nigeria.

It was close to 4am when we arrived at the house in Agege, the whole household was up; they already knew about the burglary and were expecting us. Dad asked if we were OK, he explained that Bisi and I would have to spend the rest of the night here, he said goodbye, and headed back to Uncle Tony's.

Dad was back at Agege by the time I woke up later that morning. Everyone was still telling me how brave I had been, it made me feel a little proud, but I knew in my mind that I had only done the one thing that came to my mind. My reward was an extra bit of pocket money for breakfast. Breakfast was usually a case of taking what money you had been given and deciding what you wanted to eat. The choice was not exhaustive; the most popular choice was the rice kiosk across the road.

When we arrived in Nigeria back in 1973, Yakubu Gowon was the Head of State, he had taken power after a military coup seven years before and would be ousted in another coup a couple of years later. Nigeria was rising up on its newfound oil wealth and because of this, Gowon was able to invest money into reconstructing the former Eastern Region, also known as Biafra. His successor, Murtala Mohammed was installed in a 1975 counter-coup sparked by a postponement of civilian rule and perceived corruption in the Gowon regime. Murtala Mohammed purged the administration, civil service and judiciary of people suspected of involvement in corruption, focussed his policies on reducing inflation and began moving the country towards a civilian government. He was assassinated in 1976 and succeeded by Olusegun Obasanjo, who completed the plan of an orderly transfer to civilian rule by handing power to Alhaji Shehu Shagari on October 1, 1979.In 1960 Nigeria gained its independence from Great Britain.

The Nigerian currency was the Naira, the exchange rate was 2

Naira to 1 Pound in the 1970s. The equivalent to the penny was the Kobo, there were 100 Kobo to one Naira. Thirty Kobo was enough to get a kid a small portion of cooked rice and a couple of tiny pieces of meat from the small "bukateria" stores you would find on every street. Some kids would go all the way and sacrifice one portion of meat for some beans to go with the rice. As for me, I needed food; I wasn't bothered about meat so with my 30 Kobo I would usually buy a larger portion of rice and a small portion of beans for a much more filling meal. Today however as a reward for my bravery, I had 50 Kobo, to everyone's surprise; I came back with a larger portion of rice and beans but still no meat! I needed something filling.

∞

After breakfast that morning, I decided to send another letter to Mum, I hadn't heard from her in over a year, so I stepped out for a brief walk to gather my thoughts after such a hectic night. I looked around me, things had not changed much in the three years since we first set foot in Agege, hardly any of the houses on either side of the street were painted, water was still a rare commodity and power failure was still a regular thing.

I walked along the familiar red dusty local streets while I gathered my thoughts and decided what to write, it was all clay, bumpy and full of pot holes, running parallel on either side of the road was a gutter full of dirty, stagnant water, there were planks of wood across the gutters for people to get across to their houses or to the multitude of shops that lined the street. A lot of the houses were incomplete, some without windows others without electricity and most without water.

It was still quite early but already noisy in the neighbourhood, there were kids running around laughing and playing, there were a few loose chickens and other animals running around while women and the occasional young child would walk by calling out at the top of their voices as they tried to attract attention to the goods they had to sell. Goods that they carried around for miles delicately balanced in a large tray on their head with just a piece of cloth to act as a cushion between tray and head.

I was amazed at how far some of these traders would walk and how long some of them would work every single day. Some of the women would also have their babies strapped to their backs with a scarf which served both to keep the toddler tight to its mum's back as well as a support to keep it from sliding down her back.

Mother, child and balanced tray would then travel up and down the neighbourhood in the usually baking sun selling all sorts of items including bread, yam, washing powder, water, plantain, cooked meals such as rice & beans, daily household commodities and so much more. Some had regular customers, for example on a Tuesday the woman who sold rice & beans would come calling outside our house in Agege knowing that a lot of us kids had pocket money for hot food.

I missed Mum and England so much, I still remembered some of the friends I had made, I remembered and missed my school in West London, I missed Norland house and I kept picturing my bedroom there with all the Jackson five and Osmond's posters, most of all I missed and still wanted my wristwatch, Mum and Dad had bought it for me on my 7th birthday, I loved that watch and really wanted it back.

I had come to accept my new way of life but I still hated parts of it. I would still find myself a quiet spot away from anyone once in a while and I would reminisce and cry, remembering every detail of the way things used to be in England.

After a nice refreshing walk I went back into the house, sat in the small living room and started writing my letter to Mum. I used Mayflower Junior School as my new correspondence address, I told her we were moving school again, and how much I missed her, I asked again if she was ever coming to get us and told her how much I wanted to go back home. I also asked her if she could send me my wristwatch. Dad took the letter and posted it for me.

A few weeks later, it was time to head out to our new school. Bisi and I squeezed into Dad's little car and settled ourselves down for the long drive to the town of Ikenne in Ogun state where the school was located.

We drove along the bumpy and dusty red roads for a few miles. It was a very hot day. Bisi and I were relatively quiet; I guess it was the nerves again in anticipation of yet another start at yet another new boarding school. This time around we had to buy a few extra items along with the usual food and hygiene provisions. These included a sort of machete, a hoe, a metal bucket and our own mattresses; we also had our new school uniform and a new khaki uniform for after lessons.

After about half an hour, we left the bumpy urban roads and joined a new motorway which they called an expressway. Expressways were very fast roads, officially there was a speed limit, unofficially, the worst that could happen was a bribe to the traffic enforcement officers. The expressway was busy with all shapes and sizes of vehicles, some really old rickety ones too. As we sped along, we also saw some old trucks in the middle of the expressway which had been involved in accidents and then abandoned right in the middle of the busy road.

It seemed to take forever but we eventually came off the expressway and headed down some very dusty narrow roads with bushes whacking against the windows from either side. We carried on through a busy little village which Dad told us was Ikenne. We must have carried on for another six miles beyond Ikenne village when I finally spotted the big signs "Welcome to Mayflower Junior School".

We drove through the gates and pulled up in front of the school clinic. Dad hopped out of the car while we waited, a few minutes later, he walked back with a woman who he then introduced to us as Head Matron and Uncle Tony's ex-wife Mary.

She wore a nurse's uniform and a pair of thin round glasses, but looked younger than I had imagined her to be, she was still in her Mid-30's she had a nice bright smile and encouraged us to step out of the car and follow her into the clinic. She introduced us to a couple of staff she had working with her, and then spoke to Dad in Yoruba for a while; I couldn't understand what they were talking about.

Two of the matrons helped me with my bags and mattress while I carried the machete, hoe and a few other things, they showed me the way to the boys' dormitory and pointed out where the girls' dormitory was. It was quite a trek away from ours; I just wondered how Bisi would cope. I walked into my new dormitory and noticed a few boys sitting down on some of the beds chatting and playing. Just like all the other dormitories I had been to; it was rows of bunk beds as far as I could see.

The matron showed me to my new bed, again it was the bottom bed of the bunk. I just hoped I would be sleeping under someone nice. It had no mattress, so now I understood why we had brought our own. I laid my mattress on the springs, got out my bed sheets and made my bed, then I put up my mosquito net and folded it up above my bed. I changed into one of my new Khaki uniforms and headed back out to say bye to Dad. Bisi was very upset this time; she really didn't like this change at all. Dad told us that he wouldn't be able to visit fortnightly especially as this school was so far away from home and because of his own work commitments; he said he would try to see us as often as he could, but reassured us that we were in good hands; after all, we were with family. She still bore the name Mrs Elegunde on her Identity badge, plus we also had another cousin here, her son Ade.

Dad drove off and Bisi bawled her eyes out, she was inconsolable for a long time, finally I took her away from the clinic and told her that I will always be there for her, asked her not to cry, I told her that we will always be together and it seemed to calm her down.

A matron took Bisi and me along with all the other new students on a tour around the school premises, it was a very large school on a few hundred hectares of land, it was the biggest of all the schools I had attended in Nigeria so far.

There was grass everywhere, miles and miles of it. We walked along the playgrounds which were vast. There were two slides, a few swings and not much else. There was also a large football field.

∞

We carried on past the playgrounds towards two long blocks of classrooms, there was one on either side of the path, they were both painted red and each block had about 10 classrooms. Each classroom on average sat around 30 children.

Around the back of the block of classes to my left was the dining hall, it was massive, it had over 100 long tables with each table able to sit up to ten children. I could already smell dinner cooking.

The toilets were the same as I had seen nearly everywhere else I had been so far in Nigeria aside from Uncle Tony's house. There was about ten aluminium doors in a row near the boy's dormitory, in each one, there was a five inch wide hole in the concrete floor and a wooden lid cover to pull over the hole and they stank. I really hated them and I knew that my feelings could worsen here as Mayflower had much more boarding students than either of my previous schools.

∞

We had a look at the assembly hall, again it was massive, with a huge stage in the front and rows of wooden chairs below the stage that filled the whole hall. The matron told us that this is where we would assemble on Monday morning to meet the school principal and his staff.

The school bell started ringing, the sound was from near the dining room, it was about 5pm and time for dinner, Bisi and I walked over to the dining hall with a few of the other new students all looking nervous. There was already a long queue of kids waiting patiently to go in and get seated, so we joined the queue. As we moved forward, there was a bit of shoving from behind and some of the bigger boys barged their way into the front of the queue.

I also noticed one rather bigger and older person in the queue, he also had Khaki shorts on, but not sandals like the rest of us, instead, he wore a pair of big sneakers. He did have a Khaki shirt on but it wasn't tucked in like the rest of us, in fact, his shirt was wide open with just one or two buttons done up. I kept trying to catch a better look at him, he looked fairly old, but he was in the queue for food with the rest of us, so he must have been one of us I thought. I saw him being served, the cooks were laughing and joking with him and then he walked away to one of the tables and I lost sight of him.

I eventually got to the head of the queue where I was given an old shiny aluminium dish and a spoon that I could break with very little effort, I then looked around for somewhere to sit. I found a table which already had about six other kids around it and a massive aluminium pot in the middle of it.

I took my seat and said hello to the other boys at the table, once everyone was seated, one of the matrons made an announcement, welcoming all the new students and she told us some of the ground rules which included meal times, class times, siesta and bathroom procedures. We then said a short prayer "Bless this food oh Lord, for Christ's sake Amen" one of the matrons then opened the pot of food on our table and dished out some food to each of us around the table.

It was one of the local Yoruba delicacies called "eba" it was made from ground and dried cassava and the first time I ever saw it was in Agege and it reminded me then of a blob of glue. I never really liked it but I ate it anyway.

At bedtime I tidied my bed sheets and pulled down my mosquito net as usual all around my bed and tucked it under the mattress. I still hadn't met my cousin Ade, his bed was empty he was one of the few students still missing from the dormitory.

We were allowed about 20 minutes to use the toilet, get our pyjamas on if needed and then get into bed. Once the 20 minutes was up the matron in charge would announce that she was about to switch off the lights, a few seconds later the whole dormitory was pitch black and it all went quiet apart from a few whispers.

A matron would stay in or nearby the room for up two hours after lights out making sure that no one sneaked out of bed and to try to prevent whispering.

In the morning, the school wake up bell went off at around 7am, it was Sunday morning, the day before our first classes. I got out of bed and had a long stretch and yawn. A matron started banging on the metal beds waking people up. I folded up my mosquito net and made my bed, I then got my bucket which was padlocked to the springs underneath my bed and followed the line of boys with buckets outside.

We walked into an open yard which had a wet concrete floor, there were at least four matrons standing there. I had my towel wrapped around my waist and was wearing no top, most of the boys were dressed in the same way although one or two of them had shorts or just pants on and no towel. The matrons showed us where to fill our buckets with water; it was a large aluminium tank. I got my bucket of water and found a place to stand, got my toothbrush and toothpaste and brushed my teeth first then, like everyone else, I hung my towel on a piece of wood and started having my wash while the matrons supervised. I had a little bowl which I dipped into the bucket and then poured cold water over myself. The cold water always made me jump initially then I would get used to it. I got my sponge which looked like a ball of thick hay and scrubbed myself clean, then threw bowls of water over myself to wash the soap away, leaving just enough water to rinse off the soap from my sponge with more bowls of water till the bucket was empty.

Once I was dressed and ready for breakfast, I went straight out and headed for the girl's dormitory to find Bisi, she was on her way over to look for me. We held hands and walked to the dining hall together just as the breakfast bell started ringing. There was already a long queue which we joined and waited for our turn. I looked around for the man I had seen in the queue at dinner the previous night, but I couldn't see him. Again, we had separate tables, this time, the food was already served out in the little aluminium plates with about 10 children around each table. We said our prayers and tucked in.

The rest of the day was a taste of boarding school life at Mayflower School. Bisi and I stayed together throughout the day; we played together, walked around and avoided the school clinic. We went to our separate dormitories for the hour long siesta, but as soon as siesta was over, Bisi was outside the boy's dormitory waiting for me. This was our usual pattern for our entire time at Mayflower, we were almost inseparable.

I finally met Ade on Monday morning; his mum brought him into the dormitory just before bath time. She introduced him to me as my cousin, he was eight years old, quite skinny and I could see immediately that he was the spitting image of his dad. His mum emphasised to me the fact that Ade would have the top bunk. I didn't really care but I did wonder why it was so important that this boy who was smaller and three years younger than me had to climb to the top bunk.

∞

I had the usual wash, and an earlier breakfast. Then we headed to the assembly hall as the assembly bell continued to ring. Once we got there, we were told to go around to the side of the hall where there were numerous queues forming. We had to queue up according to our class year and in your year according to your height, with the shortest at the front of the queue, I had always hated this part at all my previous schools, because I was always one of the shortest and my luck hadn't changed at Mayflower either. I was very slow to shoot up in those early years.

We sang some songs as well as the national anthem and said a prayer, this time The Lord's Prayer, all the while; we were still standing outside the main assembly hall. Then the head teacher introduced himself and all the teaching staff to us. He also introduced the head matron and school nurse. Mrs Mary Elegunde. We all shouted good morning to everyone. Finally one more introduction, the proprietor of the school and his wife came out, and they were introduced to us by the head teacher as Dr Tai & Sheila Solarin. I kept staring at the proprietor thinking I had seen him before, I kept racking my brains, I was certain I knew him or had seen a picture of him somewhere before, then I heard the kid behind me whisper in Yoruba to one of his friends: "That's the same man who was in the Khaki shorts the other night at the dining hall when we queued for dinner."

I realised then, that it was indeed Dr Tai Solarin the proprietor of Mayflower International School who I had seen the other night in the queue with us. For the first time since I arrived in Nigeria, I was truly impressed and began to think that I may actually enjoy my year at this school.

Dr Tai Solarin was famous in Nigeria as both a social critic and an educator. Affectionately known as "Uncle Tai" by his admirers, he was usually found wearing sneakers, shorts, and a khaki hunting cap, inspiring some to remark that he looked more like a "village eccentric" than a great intellectual. Although there were several people and organizations in Nigeria and Ghana attempting to educate the public about secular humanism and its ideals, Tai Solarin was by far the most interesting of them all.

Tai was often jailed for his public remarks, even in my year at Mayflower; we all knew that he had been in and out of detention.

He was a man who spoke up for what he believed in and I respected and liked the thought of being a Mayflower student just because of Dr Tai Solarin.

The Nigerian government did not like him to express his views and so he was repeatedly arrested and detained, sometimes for months at a time.

Loved or hated, there can be no mistake that Tai was among the best known citizens of Nigeria. He was so well known that a friend retells a story where an Englishman mailed a letter addressed only as "Tai Solarin, Ikenne, Nigeria," and it quickly found its way to Tai's house.

Tai and his English wife Sheila, who he married in Manchester, England in 1951 came back to live in his home town of Ikenne where they founded Mayflower Junior School, which at the time was the first and only secular school in the country. Tai was a well-known humanist and atheist who opposed the ownership of schools by churches in Nigeria.

Dr Tai Solarin was indeed very forward and rebellious in his thinking and he was not afraid to voice his opinions. He died at the age of 72 in 1994, his wife continued running the school until her death in October 2012

CHAPTER THREE

A NEW PRIMARY SCHOOL

Things started out very well for me at Mayflower, I liked the classes and there was never an issue of me taking subjects that I wasn't interested in, especially as this was my final year before secondary school.

My favourite teacher was Mr Kip Smith; he was our history and literature teacher. But he was also a fountain of knowledge, he had so many interests that fascinated me. He was a white South African, who always wore sandals and a native top; he had long flowing ginger hair and a ginger beard to go with it and he looked like a hippy in his faded blue jeans with rips at the knees.

He aroused my interest in the world of stamp and coin collections, he introduced me and my class to the classic film "Roots" he also gave Bisi and me so many interesting books to read. I always read them so quickly, returned them to him and collected the next book.

Academically, I was doing well once again, I was top of my class, but this time around I was also trying to help lots of friends with different subjects.

The other thing was that for the first time, I began to develop an interest in the opposite sex. The girl in question was the most attractive girl in class, her name was Bukki. She knew that I liked her, I spent a lot of time studying with her and I sat directly behind her in class. I really liked her, but I also began to realise something else about myself. I was shy, too shy to ask her to be my girlfriend. So someone else eventually beat me to it, we stayed best of friends throughout that year, but lost contact as soon as I left Mayflower.

Bisi and I were closer than ever, we were almost inseparable, we would meet up after every class, every siesta and every morning we would be outside the dormitory waiting for one another and then we would walk around holding hands. I remember someone once telling us that we wouldn't be able to stick together forever, I just laughed it off as impossible, as far as I was concerned, we had been taken away from our mum, but no one was ever going to keep Bisi and me apart.

Within the first couple of weeks of school we started to realise that things were not going to be easy with our aunt, the head matron.

I remember being woken up by a lot of noise and commotion one night; Ade was upset, I could hear him moaning in the bunk above me and then I felt a little drop of water come through my mosquito net. A matron approached our bed, got him down and asked him to take his clothes off. Through my half open eyes as I pretended to sleep, I could see that his clothes were totally soaked.

A few seconds later, while he was getting changed into dry clothes, his mum arrived; she had her own quarters situated less than half a mile away from the school grounds. Clearly someone had sent a message to her, I heard her ask one of the matrons in Yoruba to wake me up, the matron duly obliged, I still pretended that I had been deep in sleep and opened my eyes slowly, taking time to stretch and yawn, I was still trying to get my head right when I heard head matron Mary's voice ordering me out of bed immediately. I jumped out, and stood up beside Ade, looking at the matrons, I could tell that some of the other boys in the dormitory were also half awake and listening in.

I then watched as one of the matrons took down Ade's mattress and replaced it with mine! I was then told to get back into bed on his wet mattress. I was so tired and could not believe what had just happened. I just got back into my now wet bed, and slept on the very edge as far away from the big wet patch as possible.

When I woke up in the morning to the noisy wake up bell, I noticed that I had rolled over into the wet part of bed overnight, the bed had pretty much dried out, but I jumped out of bed nonetheless recalling what had happened that night.

One of the rules in the morning when you wake up was to get out of bed, fold your mosquito net up and then stand by your bed; the matrons would then inspect everyone's bed while they asked if anyone had wet their bed. You had to own up straight away if you had wet your bed otherwise you could get punished not only for bed wetting but also for being a liar. The matrons would do a random check of a few usual suspects, so it was no surprise that someone checked Ade's bed, the surprise was that for once they wanted to check mine as well, as expected my mattress was a little wet and I was announced out loud as having wet my bed. The punishment was a few strokes of the cane.

Let me take time out here to explain caning. First of all, in my time in England, if we were ever naughty, Dad would take the palm of our hand and smack it hard with his two index fingers, Bisi and I would bawl out loud as if we had been shot. In Nigeria I got to meet three new forms of smacking, two were beatings either with a cane, which was any long tough piece of a tree branch that could withstand a good impact and would bend freely; they were usually about three feet long and would fit into your palm quite comfortably. I had seen these used only at my previous schools a couple of times and it looked painful, something I was determined to stay away from.

The other form of beating was by use of a whip, the whip was between three and four feet long, made out of dried up and toughened sheep skin, so it was a form of hard leather in the shape of a horse whip, I had only ever seen that at Uncle Tony's house, he had used in on both the Tunde's before and that looked terrifying to me. It left parts of their flesh exposed and bleeding sometimes.

The final form of smacking was Uncle Tony's speciality, he would form a fist, and while he spoke to you, he would whack you on the head with his knuckles. The thud from the impact was sickening and I absolutely hated that the most. Not just because it hurt but I just found it insulting and annoying.

On this particular day it was the cane, I was quite upset and protested my innocence, but even as I made my stance, I was pulled by my arm and felt the lashes on my bum. I was so mad that I did not cry, instead, I glared over at Ade and told him he would pay.

For days afterwards, I found it hard to believe what had actually happened, so did a lot of the boys who witnessed it. The one person I thought was there to protect me had drawn first blood.

I found it hard to report the incident to anyone else. I did tell Mr Smith about it and he was kind enough to make an enquiry, but he was soon told in no uncertain terms to concentrate on his classes.

Things would gradually get worse between me and head Matron Mary. The next incident was almost immediate. Ade was still feeling smug about what had happened a few days earlier, so I taunted him into a fight and beat him up, which brought me back face to face with his mum and her cane.

I was growing fast, we had already lived in Nigeria now for just over four years, I had learned that I had to get mentally and even more importantly, physically strong, so I started working out, doing sit-ups, press-ups, skipping and running. My inspiration came from reading an autobiography of Muhammad Ali. He remains my ultimate hero, I love everything about the man, I didn't just watch his fights; I studied them in the same way that I studied his out of ring antics. I loved the fact that he was rebellious and wasn't born to conform to people's expectations.

I remember back in 78 when I was still only 12, a lot of the family was round Uncle Tony's, watching the "Rumble in the jungle" Ali v George Foreman fight, as Foreman hit the deck and was counted out, Dad leapt up and started shouting "fix" everyone agreed with him except me, I tried to explain to them that Foreman had punched himself out, just as I had been telling them during the fight while he was pummelling away at Ali. No one seemed to understand, they were happier to believe the fight had been fixed.

I worked out very hard I found a level of discipline and determination for exercise that surprised a lot of my fellow pupils. I was also determined to be the best in anything where people expected someone not born in that environment to struggle. One prime example was in the way I learned to excel at grass cutting.

I had always wondered what the machete and hoe that we brought with us were for and if we would really need them. It didn't take long to find out.

Saturday mornings were dedicated to grass cutting: every student would be given a plot about 8 feet wide and up to 300 yards in length and you had to cut the grass down to an acceptable height. Some students were much faster at this than most, the quickest time to finish your plot in the glaring sun was about two hours, and the longest, about five hours.

Some of the boys would work at breakneck speeds to finish their allocation, either just to show off or so they could offer some of the girls a hand. It was unbelievably tough for me the first few times around, I had constant blisters in my hands, and the heat didn't help, but I was determined to improve so I worked away and never gave up till I was among the fastest.

One of the new subjects that I took up was agriculture; this also involved a lot of machete work, and some ploughing with the hoe. I enjoyed planting corn, tomatoes, okra, cassava and a host of other crops, also through working on my farm plot, I had my first encounter with a snake, this one was a Green Mamba, and fortunately I was not alone! The first thing I recall was all the screaming and the petrified faces running past me then before I could even ask, I saw the big long snake slither over my plot and into the bushes, it was amazingly fast. Some kids had been trying to kill it, they had sticks and stones, but this snake got away. I wondered then why they wanted to kill the snake, I have never liked snakes but I didn't think people would want to batter one to death either. I soon learned though, that they were a very dangerous pest and you had to kill them. Prevention was far better than being bitten by a snake and we had many species of snake there. Cobras, Mambas, pythons, Constrictors, Grass snakes you name them. The most dangerous time of each year was the hottest part of the year, the period between March and October.

I remember receiving my first letter from Mum addressed to Mayflower School, I knew straight away, the moment I saw the letter that it was from Mum, I was so excited, and she did not let me down. The letter was not as long as I might have liked, and she did not say anything about coming to get me, but she told me she was OK, and that it was great to read my letter and how much she missed Bisi and me, she also sent me a few stamps and coins from all over the world for my collection; and she promised to send me my watch.

I read the letter over and over again; I also showed it to Bukki the girl I liked in class and to Mr Smith. I then proudly put my new stamps & coins into my collection books.

That year Mr Smith suggested I keep a diary, he told me to write a few words about significant events each day while I was growing up in Nigeria. It seemed like a good idea, so I got myself a big exercise book and started writing half a page for most days, just keeping track of my daily life. This turned into such a great idea, that I kept sellotaping more exercise books together and I kept my diary throughout Mayflower, my secondary school, and even the first year of my A-level life.

My diary became something that I had to fill in and keep safe, I wouldn't show it to anyone except Mr Smith. Most people knew I wrote personal things in this book so I had to keep it safe.

∞

I had never been in any major fights during my first four years in Nigeria, until the confrontations with Ade. He would try to fight me, but I could always deal with him easily but things were getting worse between us. His mum knew that whenever she harmed me I would get my own back by taking it out on Ade, so she raised the bar.

She decided that every weekend from Friday through Sunday, Bisi, Ade and I were to spend our time at her school quarters apartment, it meant we didn't stay at the hostel over the weekend.

Things deteriorated from the very first night we spent there, it was clear she wanted pay back for the times I had beaten Ade up, she wanted to teach me a few lessons. We were never really made to feel welcome, Ade showed us round the small apartment which was a very short walk from school.

That evening when dinner was ready, Mary called Bisi and I in to the kitchen to pick up the food and take it into the boy's bedroom, while she left Ade to sit and wait for us to serve the food, I initially thought that this was because he was the youngest, so I carried through a tray while Bisi brought in a jug of water and some plastic cups. Ade sat there waiting, once we had laid everything down on the straw mat, we sat down on the floor either side of him.

He said the prayers over dinner, and then Bisi went to dish her portion of food out of the big bowl in front of us. Suddenly, Ade Started shouting at her, telling her to drop the spoon right away, we were both stunned, so she put the spoon down and we both watched as he began to serve each of us a portion, Bisi had the smallest, while he had the largest and best bits. Naturally, I was not impressed and tried to re-balance the shares, but Ade started screaming again till his mum came in and told us that this was Ade's house, she questioned my audacity to try and take over and made it crystal clear that Ade was boss here. He just sat there with a big smirk on his face that I was determined to wipe off.

I had a little dinner that night, I had lost my appetite. The following morning at breakfast, we went over the same routine as from the previous night, I went to take a piece of bread as I reached across, I saw Ade's hand from the corner of my eye as he smacked my hand and then asked me what I thought I was doing! I was so shocked, that I was lost for words, I got up in a rage and shoved him across the room, he tried to fight back, but I was too mad and strong for him.

Soon he was crying. I always had this weakness, whenever Bisi and I would fight, once she started crying, I always felt bad and wanted to console her. It was the same this day, but as I went to apologise to Ade, he fought back and screamed louder until his mum came in. I tried to explain what had just happened, but she was not interested.

Her solution was simple. She took Ade out of the room, she then sent me directly across the road from the apartment, where there was a bush of trees, and my errand was to break off a fine branch that would make a good strong cane. I duly obliged, took it back into her and then got flogged about 10 strokes on each wide open palm. This time I didn't cry in front of anyone, I don't even think the strokes hurt me anywhere near as much as my pride.

So as soon as I was alone, l found a quiet spot round the back of the house and wept. I missed Mum, and all the things I had left behind, I continued to weep and think. I could not wait to get away from the quarters and go back to the school hostel. Bisi came out to find me, she came over, sat down beside me on the dirty ground full of shed leaves and twigs and then she cuddled me, that made me cry some more.

I had learned a lesson, I now knew that I could neither trust nor rely on Head Matron Mary or any of the other matrons. I also decided that every time I suffered at her hands, I would continue to take retribution by beating Ade up. This became the pattern for at least six months of my year at Mayflower School.

Bisi really hated this period of our lives in Nigeria almost more than any other. Even today she looks back and recalls that as one of her darkest times in Nigeria. We tried to tell Dad on his few visits to the school, but for some reason he refused to believe us and was convinced that we had to be exaggerating.

We only saw Dad once a month now, if we were lucky. Yet during these rare visits, Matron Mary managed to spend more time with him than we did! Whenever Dad came out to visit, he would park outside the school clinic and then go straight into the clinic to say hello to Mary, she would sit him down with a drink and proceed to give him an overview of our development. In the meantime, some of the other kids who had recognised Dad's car, would search around school for Bisi and me and tell us that our dad had come to visit, then we would head to the clinic to say hello.

Unlike a lot of the other kids, we never looked out for him at the weekend since we never knew when he was going to visit. The only one who did know was Mary and she kept it to herself.

Between Dad and I, there was neither an embrace nor a hand shake, just a hello, he would hug Bisi and he always fondly called her his "only daughter". I was used to him calling her that, it was just something he loved to say to her in an affectionate way to make her feel good. I didn't mind at all as I knew he only had two kids.

The problem was that the relationship between Dad and me was beginning to get cold. I always tried to find a few personal minutes with him during his visits, so that I could tell him what was really going on between Mary and us. Sometimes I would manage to tell him, but he would dismiss it all as exaggeration, suggesting that I just wanted to change schools again. As much as possible, Mary would always interrupt and make sure I didn't spend too much time alone with him.

So perhaps after half an hour or so, she would tell me to go back out to the playground while Dad spent the rest of his visit at the clinic speaking to her. It was harder to get rid of Bisi because she would cry; she always did at the end of Dad's visits.

The consequence of all this was that I could no longer confide in Dad, instead, I had begun to fear him, anytime I tried to tell him how bad things were getting, he would bark back at me, Mary would tell him I had been naughty, wetting my bed, disobedient etc. and when I tried to say "no Dad…" he would bark "Yes" he wouldn't give me an opportunity to explain myself and he would not give me the chance to start an argument with him. He had to have the final say and make sure that everyone around knew that. I started to feel that I was being shown up, and even when we were away from school at holidays, the relationship between Dad and me remained the same. I could never seem to get my point across anymore.

Another thing Mary would do was make sure that any weekend Dad was coming over to visit us, we stayed on the school premises rather than over at her quarters, he knew that we did visit her quarters, but I don't think he knew at that point that we spent most weekends there.

My whole demeanour was changing slowly but surely. I became quiet at school, I kept to myself quite a lot, and I was also growing shyer. Academically, all was still OK; I had chosen my favourite classes and was preparing well for the upcoming exams. All my life, I had wanted to grow up to become a doctor, that was still the case, so I took science, Geography, agriculture, English literature and the compulsory English language and mathematics.

I still did a lot of exercise, I jogged around the school block as often as I could, I still helped my friends in class, but on the playground, I was a loner, I kept to myself most of the time. I would sit in the quietest parts of the grounds where no one could bother me, for a while Bisi was the only one I trusted and let close to me.

Bukki, came over to sit beside me one day after a visit from Dad, she told me that she knew what was going on between Mary and me, she told me how she felt bad for me, she put her arm around my shoulder and we sat there talking for ages.

She asked me about England, what my school had been like, about my mum, my friends and how I felt about being torn away from it all and then we talked about her and her family. We must have been talking for over half an hour when someone ran over to us and told Bukki that her mum had come to visit, she got up really excited and asked me to come along with her to meet her mum.

I ran after her across the football pitches towards the girls' dormitory, and then she sped up and ran straight into her mum's arms, her mum picked her up and they hugged for ages, while I stood and watched from a few paces further back. It looked beautiful and at that moment, I realised what I was missing.

Bukki looked round and called me over, she then introduced me to her mum; she told her mum that I was the boy from England that she had told her all about. I stayed with them for a few more seconds then I told Bukki where she could find me and I walked back to the playground.

I felt really privileged that Bukki had invited me to meet her mum and also for the conversation that I had with them both and I kept imagining how it could be with my mum and me, it made me smile.

I went back over to the playgrounds where a ladies' football match had just started; there was a small crowd so I joined them. It was an Inter-School match and the Mayflower girls were putting in a good performance, so I joined in the support and chants for Mayflower.

I was amazed at one girl in particular, her name I never forgot was "Biodun" roughly translated from Yoruba, her name signifies she was born during a festive period, in her case it was Christmas day. What caught my eye that evening was how powerful and direct she was, none of the other girls could cope with her strength, she was fast, and even good in the air, she scored three goals as Mayflower came out worthy winners.

Everyone celebrated, jumping for joy, some of the teachers and matrons were there too, later I went over to Biodun, introduced myself and told her that I thought she had played really well, she thanked me and said that she knew who I was but had never said hello as I was always far too quiet.

We agreed to catch up later, I walked away to look for Bisi and bumped into Bukki who, in the meantime, had waved her mum goodbye. She was really happy, she told me how she now had a locker full of new provisions and even offered me some. I spent most of that evening with Bukki and Bisi.

My determination not to be hurt by any of the Matrons actions strengthened, sometimes I would be stubborn in the hostel and argue back at them, but most of the time, I remained quiet and reserved and took any punishment or decisions without crying in public. At the weekends, our routine remained the same at Mary's quarters, but I had got used to her beatings, I began to realise that she couldn't hurt me as much as she thought, so sometimes I would pretend that her strokes hurt me more than they actually did.

I still took retribution on Ade on a regular basis, I was determined that this would continue as long as she and Ade took their problems out on Bisi and me.

It turned out to be a good thing that I had met Biodun as well. The next time I saw her was at another inter-school function, this time it was athletics, I also ran for the school, I was useless at sprinting, but quite good at middle distance running; I always finished in the top half of my group, without ever winning a race. Biodun was amazing once again. She won the 100m girls race, the 400m and also 110m hurdles. I just stood there amazed at how good she was.

After the athletics evening was over, I went over to Biodun to say hello again, this time she was with the head matron of the girls' hostel who turned out to be Biodun's mum. Biodun introduced I me to her mum before we walked away together.

We had a good long chat about sports and how proud her mum was of her, I remember her telling me that she wanted to grow up to be a head matron just like her mum, and I teased her saying no kid would be able to run away from her at least.

I didn't tell her about my problems with Mary, I rarely spoke about that with anyone any longer, but in the end Biodun's mum would be the one who helped me.

For now Biodun and I became good friends, we learned from each other, she jogged and trained with me, while I revised with her and helped her in science and a few other subjects.

One of the other things we did together whenever we could, was take the two mile walk from the school grounds through the bushes towards a stream, where all the older kids went to fetch buckets of water for drinking and the next morning's wash. We would walk down a very narrow dusty and eroded path with bamboo and a few other bushes on either side of us which would twang at you or poke you. As you walked towards the stream, you would also see other kids on their way back to the hostel carrying or balancing their buckets of water on their heads and struggling back uphill.

Some of them were really skilled: they would roll up a small cloth into a ball to serve as a cushion between their head and the metal bucket and balance the bucket on their heads without using their hands for support. Others, like me, would balance it on their heads but need to have both arms up on either side to support it.

Like a lot of the others, I usually splashed more than half my bucket of water all over myself during the long and bumpy uphill walk back to the hostel. It took a long time for me to learn to carry those buckets back without spilling.

I had even seen kids trip over and lose their entire bucket of water, get up, dust themselves down and then go back to the stream to start all over again. At first I wondered why nobody seemed to just carry the bucket by its handle all the way, but I soon found out that it was nearly impossible to carry a bucket that far by its handle, it was much easier to carry it the same way everyone else did.

Once you got to the stream, it was divided into two sections, one each for the girls and boys, this was useful, because you could get your first bucket of water in the morning, have a wash near the stream and then take back another bucket so you didn't have to come back down the next morning. That was my style, not everyone wanted to have a wash in the bushes but I saw the logic.

On the way back to the hostel, Biodun and I would again walk back together, one ahead of the other up the narrow path, she was really good and rarely spilled a drop, I was really determined, but I could never keep my neck straight, I had to bend my head at an angle.

One day, as we came back from the stream, there seemed to be a lot of commotion at the school, Biodun and I parted for our respective hostels, hid our buckets of water under our beds and then met up again to find out what was going on. It turned out that the school head priest "Reverend Mellor" had died. He was a white English man, but I had never spoken to him, I just knew him from going to the school chapel. His funeral was a big affair, and every student, and member of staff filed past his coffin to pay their last respects. I had seen dead bodies before, mainly littered on side roads or on the Express Roads just left to swell up and then decompose and rot away, but Reverend Mellor's death was the first time I can recall, where I had known someone who died.

In my last few months at Mayflower, I had forged a strong friendship with Biodun and Bukki, Bisi and I were still inseparable, and I had joined my class's football team. I was getting excited about the imminent exams and the fact that I would soon be able to leave Mayflower.

Dad did not like me playing football, in fact he didn't encourage most extracurricular activities, all he wanted was for me to study hard and get good grades so I could have a choice of the best Secondary Schools available. But at that stage, I didn't have to study much; I felt very confident and was surrounded by good teachers. I still had to keep it a secret from Dad that I had joined my class team.

For some reason, perhaps a mixture of being shy and a lack of confidence, I took a long while before getting up the courage to ask if I could join the team. I could play a little bit of football at that stage, but I was definitely nothing special. My main weapon was that I had a powerful shot, I learned from an early age to kick right through the ball so few keepers were brave enough to get in the way of one of my shots. I was soon given the nick name "Hot Shot Hamish" from the old "Tiger & Shoot" comics.

I still struggled to make the starting 11. This was because I wasn't assertive enough during play and I was far too quiet, also I was still one of the shortest in school, but I enjoyed being part of the team and did get a few chances to show what I could do.

There were three holiday breaks that year and three half-term breaks as well. On the first holiday break, Dad came to pick us up as usual; I stayed at Uncle Tony's while Bisi stayed with another of our aunts, Aunt Lola.

Aunt Lola was a very lovely, generous and caring person, her first son Akin lived in America but we had met him many times back in England. He still lived in the States but visited Nigeria once in a while. She looked after Bisi as if she were her own daughter. Initially Bisi didn't mind going there, it was a breath of fresh air, but just like me, she wasn't enjoying the whole Nigeria situation.

Still Aunt Lola was very good to her and even though I wasn't as accommodating as Bisi, she was always good to me too.

I stayed at Uncle Tony's new house, he had moved from Ikeja to another small town in Lagos; it was a bigger house, with more bedrooms and a larger living room. Neither of the Tunde's were there this time, Ade stayed with his mum over in Ikenne. So there was only Uncle Tony, Dad, a live in house helper and me.

I spent most of my time playing football downstairs on the concrete grounds whenever Dad and Uncle Tony were out, I also took up a new hobby, "skipping" I enjoyed skipping and went downstairs in the front of the house every morning to try and reach a higher number each day.

Part of my responsibilities when Dad and Uncle Tony went to work, was to clean around the house, study for my upcoming exams and most importantly, I was to supervise our house help a boy named Ahmed. I didn't realise how important this was until a few days later.

Ahmed was about 23 at the time, he didn't speak English, came from a very poor family with whom he was no longer in touch, and this was the only job he had wanted to do.

His daily routine included boiling the bath water for Dad and Uncle Tony's morning baths, cooking their breakfast, washing their cars, making sure that there was enough water in the storage tanks and then, once they had left, he would have to clean up the whole house and later in the day, prepare dinner before they got back. Dinner was usually either fish or meat in a hot pepper soup with either rice or any range of Yoruba delicacies. A fresh pot of soup had to be cooked every day and any left overs from the previous night thrown out, even if he was making same kind of soup the following night.

One day, after Dad and Uncle Tony had left for work, I took Ahmed downstairs to get him to play some football; a lot of kids from the neighbourhood came round. We set up two goals in front of the house and picked teams. It was a regular occurrence, except for my inviting Ahmed along. We played for over two hours.

By the time we finally stopped, we realised that we were running very late to get all the house chores done before Dad and Uncle Tony got back. So we rushed upstairs and started cleaning the house. Ahmed also had to throw out the previous night's pot of soup and cook a fresh one but we didn't have enough time. So I suggested that we use the old soup and just add a little more to it, after all how were they to know that it wasn't a totally freshly cooked soup? So we took the short cut, the soup looked good, we rushed around and finished all the chores just before they got back.

Later on, dinner was served, I had even forgotten about our little charade with the soup. I was busy studying in my bedroom, while they ate in the living room, suddenly I heard Dad bark my name, I came out to see him and immediately Uncle Tony asked me if I had seen Ahmed cook a fresh pot of soup, I said yes I had, but they were not convinced and insisted to my astonishment that the soup tasted old! I just couldn't understand how they could tell, it tasted fine to me. After a lot of interrogation, we realised that we were not going to win this debate, so we conceded and told the truth.

They were both furious so Dad asked for Uncle Tony's whip. I stood there not believing that it was becoming a case for the whip but Uncle Tony came back with his horsewhip and passed it to Dad who asked Ahmed to stretch both arms out sideways with palms facing up and he began to whip him, each time Ahmed pulled his arms down, the count started all over again.

He cried and kept apologising and begging for mercy but eventually managed to keep his arms out for ten lashes on each palm. He continued to cry while Dad called me across and asked me to stretch my arms out. I was already used to being caned or flogged at this stage from school, so I was determined not to cry. I stood there arrogantly with my arms spread out and Dad proceeded to whip expecting some reaction from me, but I didn't flinch, to his annoyance, so he tried harder, I could see the fury in his eyes, but I refused to flinch.

Uncle Tony also noticed my arrogance, so he got up asked Dad to pass him the whip, he then started, by this time my palm had gone red, but I still stood there and took it with my determination intact, but Uncle Tony never lost a battle of wits, there was a good reason why he was feared by all the cousins. So he caught me unawares, rather than continue to lash out at my palm he caught me on my wrist, I felt the whip wrap around my wrist then he pulled it away, I screamed and pulled my arms down to have a look at my wrist, I still have a little scar from that whip on my wrist today.

For the rest of my holidays, I only spoke to Uncle Tony and Dad when I had to. I could not wait to get out of the house and back to school. I still played my football every day once they left for work, but Ahmed never played again, he occasionally came downstairs to watch.

Most of the half-term holidays were spent at Mary's family home in the village of Ikenne, about two miles from the school.

Dad felt that it was more convenient than him having to make the round trip of over 200 miles twice in the space of a week. Ironically, at her Ikenne home, I had no major problems with Mary, perhaps because she was pre-occupied or maybe because I was always out wandering around and getting to know the village.

Her family house was just two blocks away from one of the most famous politicians in Nigeria at the time. I had read about Chief Obafemi Awolowo in my history books, many Nigerians hoped he would one day take over as president of the country. Since its independence, Nigeria had only ever had one political leader, all the other heads of state were military leaders who had usually come to power by violently overthrowing the incumbent government.

Awolowo was more of a missionary, he was outspoken and his ideas were very public and made a lot of sense, for these reasons I was intrigued and therefore spent a lot of time outside his vast premises just trying to get a glimpse of the man, which I managed to do on a number of occasions.

Back at Mayflower, I was entering my final term before the GCE exams, my friendships with Biodun and Bukki continued to blossom, we remained close and studied together, I still played football but was yet to break into the first team. I had also decided not to spend any more time at Mary's school quarters; I was already fed up of my constant squabbling with Ade, it was an argument I was not going to win, so I refused to leave the school premises at the weekends.

Mary was furious about this and insisted that Bisi and I must come over to her quarters, but I was adamant in my refusal, the tide was also slowly turning in my favour, some of the other matrons no longer wanted to force me to go against my will in spite of the fact that they might get caught up in Mary's wrath.

I avoided Mary as often as I could and although Ade remained a constant nuisance to both Bisi and me, I didn't fight him as often as I used to.

The arguments carried on with Mary but I was determined not

to go back to her quarters and with Biodun's mum encouraging me to stand my ground, Bisi and I stayed at the school every weekend.

Eventually it all got out of control. Mary was clearly not happy at my defiance, especially now as Ade had been exposed and subsequently punished for wetting his bed. The following Saturday, Mary summoned me to report to the dispensary, I obliged and hurried over. When I got there, she was clearly not in a charitable mood; she accused me of getting Ade into trouble because the previous night I had got a matron to wake him up after he had wet his bed and his urine had soaked through his mattress and onto me below.

I tried to explain, but she was having none of it, instead she instructed me to get into a position used for punishment. Whilst balancing on my right leg, I had to bend over forward, touch the ground with just one finger, my left leg had to remain at least a foot off the ground and I had to stay in that position for anything up to half an hour or till she got bored.

The punishment was familiar; I had suffered it previously at Uncle Tony's. This time however, I was not keen on being made a scapegoat. I got into position but kept arguing with her, quite a few of my fellow pupils came near by including Bisi, Biodun and Bukki, some kids even pleaded with Mary insisting that all I had done was to let the other matrons know that Ade's urine was dripping down on me!

But she was in no mood to listen and I had to continue with my punishment. I must have been about ten minutes into it when Dad suddenly walked in to the dispensary on one of his irregular visits, no one was expecting him this time, not even Mary, he hadn't been able to get a message through in advance, as he had been working nearby and had decided to use the opportunity to stop by.

For the first time, he had seen with his own eyes, some of the things he had refused to believe, worst still for Mary, was that everyone present was willing to corroborate my story, even some of the matrons so once we had all been cleared from the dispensary area, a row broke out between Dad and Mary, it was escalated to some of the senior teachers and it was stipulated that Bisi and I no longer had to spend our weekends at Mary's quarters, instead, we were required to stay on the school campus at all times unless instructed by Dad.

It was also stipulated that Ade take the bunk below me with immediate effect as he clearly had a tendency to wet his bed.

Dad came back to talk to Bisi and me, he told us about what had happened and just asked us to be careful around Mary and Ade from now on. It was one of the best moments of my Mayflower days, I was so relieved, finally all the palaver would go away, I could concentrate on my forthcoming exams, I could go to bed without having to worry about being peed on, and best of all Bisi and I did not have to suffer anymore ignominy at Mary's quarters.

Biodun spent a lot of time with me telling me how happy she was that this affair was all over, she also warned me to steer well clear of Mary as often as I could, and that was my intention.

The rest of the day was perfect for me, I had a smile that no one could wipe off, but I behaved myself around all the matrons, it was clear that some of the matrons were not pleased, since they had been shown up for being biased.

That night, I had one of the most peaceful sleeps, Ade did wet the bed, and he had to get up in the middle of the night, but for once I didn't have to smell his urine all over me. The following morning he got caned for wetting his bed along with the other culprits while I savoured the moment. Then as usual, I got my bucket of water from under the bed and headed to the bathing area with all the other kids. Some of the matrons were there overseeing events as normal.

I peeled off my towel, stood there naked, and squeezed some toothpaste on to my toothbrush. As I started brushing Mary walked into the bathing area! I had never seen her in here before. The other matrons also seemed shocked but promptly made themselves look busy. Mary walked straight up to me; she asked me if I had enjoyed myself after the previous day's events? I took the toothbrush out of my mouth and responded by greeting her "good morning" then she said to me, the words that I will never forget.. "You are a green snake under the green grass, just like your father" and then she slapped me right across the face, sending me sprawling across the yard, and my toothbrush flying out of my hands.

I got up in shock, as the rest of the boys scurried away to the far corner of the bath yard, I was too stunned to feel the impact of her slap, so I didn't cry; I was more worried about having hurt myself as I flew across the rough and wet concrete ground from the impact. I stood up and looked around for my toothbrush, picked it up, not knowing what to do or expect next. So I went back towards my bucket, where Mary was still standing, I moved closer to try to rinse the dirt off my brush, I stood up still naked and before I could utter a word, she struck again, catching the raised arm I had used to protect my face, I reeled backwards again and this time I cried, the slap had really stung, and my pride had been slapped right out of me.

Amazingly, the other matrons who had always feared Mary suddenly stood up to her, they warned her not to touch me again, a loud argument broke out and there was mayhem all around the yard. The matrons ushered all the boys out of the yard and back to the hostel while I stood there with blood trickling from one corner of my mouth, I had stopped crying, wrapped a towel around myself and just stood there frozen as the matrons continued to ask Mary to leave the yard.

She eventually left the yard; the other matrons came over to me and helped me wash up my toothbrush. I had a couple of tiny grazes on my thigh, from skidding over the floor; they cleaned these as well and then took me back inside. At this point I was shivering; I put on some clothes and eventually managed to get myself together.

That morning, I didn't go to the dining hall for breakfast, I had lost my appetite, instead I found a quiet corner of the playground and sat there alone. This was becoming a usual habit of mine, I always wanted to spend some time on my own away from everyone and everything, it helped me look back on how we came to Nigeria and made me more determined to get on with my life and to not allow people to hurt me.

A lot of the boys were upset about the events of that morning, and spent time talking to me asking if I was OK, but the more they tried to console me, the more it made me cry. So I found myself another quiet spot and just sat there. Bisi came to sit with me for a while; we talked about the events of the day and spent a long while together. Bukki also came over to sit with me, but this time I was too upset, I kept picking up pebbles and throwing them, but I hardly spoke to her at all.

Later that afternoon, I went into one of the classrooms and sat in a private corner on my own, got one of the "Air Letter Cards" that Dad had bought me, and began to write a letter to Mum. This time I was really upset, I had written to her on more than three previous occasions with no response from her, so this time, I let her know how mad I was that she had not come to get us, and how I was growing up on my own now and did not really need her anymore. I didn't tell her about the events of that morning because there wasn't enough space on the card, but I did let her know that I was miserable on the day.

As usual, I got the sealed letter over to Mr Smith who kindly posted it for me. For the rest of the day, I continued to pick myself up, and with so much help from everyone around me, I was soon back on my feet smiling and running around again. One thing was for sure though; I was never going to forget that day.

Amazingly, I never discussed this incident with Dad, of course he knew all about it, but we never talked about it.

The rest of my time at Mayflower was less eventful, I ran into Mary once in a while at the dispensary in particular, I was a frequent visitor to the dispensary because as a kid, I had always suffered from eczema, but since living in Nigeria, and perhaps due to the heat, it had become more severe.

I used to have the occasional rash around the back of my neck, on my arms and the back of my legs; I now had a breakout of sores during the hottest periods of the year. So I was a regular at the dispensary for creams, bandages and plasters.

As a result of the bath yard incident, the school authorities put a stop to my conflicts with Mary; she had been warned that she could lose her job if there were any more incidents. She rarely spoke to me even when I came in for treatment and I avoided any contact with her.

There were still occasional fights with Ade at school, he was always looking to start a fight with me, but I was too big for him and quickly put a stop to these confrontations. Better still, he rarely slept at the hostel now, his mum kept taking him back to her quarters most nights.

∞

When the GCE results came back a few weeks later, I had passed with flying colours; I had a wide range of colleges to choose from. From the moment Bisi and I came to Mayflower, I had always dreamed of going to Mayflower Secondary School, the teachers were also keen for me to stay. It would have meant staying close to Bisi and a lot of the friends I had made that year; it would also have meant that I could have fulfilled my ambition of growing up over the years and confronting Mary in the future.

I came so close to choosing Mayflower, it was in my heart, but after Mary had slapped me in that bath yard incident, my mind was made up. I'd had enough of Mayflower, even though Bisi was going to be there for another year. So I chose a school more than 200 miles away.

The school I chose was Government College Ketu, it was just outside Lagos State, the then Capital city of Nigeria. It was actually near a small village called Epe, which was famous for only one thing, its plywood factory: "Epe Plywood" fondly called "Epe Firewood" because of its numerous fire breakouts.

I chose the Ketu College because it was a very new school, it was only four years old at the time when I joined and my first year there would also be the year that the college would be turning out its first graduates.

In spite of my experiences with Mary, I had enjoyed my time at Mayflower overall. It was hard to say a final goodbye; a lot of my fellow pupils had opted to stay on at Mayflower Senior School. That summer I said a final goodbye to Bukki, I didn't expect to see her again as her family were moving further up North. I also said my goodbyes to Biodun who had to re-sit one paper before she could start thinking about a college of her choice. I gave Mr Smith a hug and he wished me well, he reassured me that I had made the best decision; he was also leaving Mayflower and moving back home to Johannesburg.

I was really excited about moving on to secondary school, I couldn't wait to get started but there was still the six week holiday break to enjoy beforehand.

So once again, Bisi and I were split; she stayed with Aunt Lola, while I was at Uncle Tony's.

I still hadn't heard from Mum in a very long time but I was keen to tell her about my new school and all the continuing changes in my life. On average now, Mum only replied to about one in six letters from me, it was getting frustrating but it didn't deter me from writing to her. Sometimes the tone of my letters was of excitement, other times they bore my anger and frustrations at Mum for not coming to get us. Bisi didn't write that often because she hated the fact that Mum rarely replied.

I now knew how to get around Nigeria on my own by public transport. It was something that Dad was keen for me to learn, he had been telling me right from my final term at Mayflower that I would have to learn to travel to school on my own once Bisi and I started travelling to different schools in separate parts of the country.

Catching a public minibus, the bigger bus or even a taxi was a very daunting event.

Taxis were expensive and therefore a last resort for short trips, also a taxi driver could squeeze up to seven individual passengers into their car for different destinations on route. Two passengers in the front with the driver and five more on the back seat. As soon as one passenger had departed, they would be on the lookout for the next person they could find to squash in beside you. Size was irrelevant they just had to squeeze in even if it meant squatting one buttock on your lap. In the same way, it didn't matter if they stank; you just had to hold your nose.

The minibus was the most popular choice for the short trips, they were mainly Volkswagen vans, and were built to fit four average sized passengers in each row, but the minimum they actually sat was five, you could also sit two in the front cabin beside the driver, so naturally they squeezed in three!

The buses were actually designed to carry 22 passengers plus the driver but in fact carried a minimum of 33 passengers and sometimes as many as 40, including people hanging from the open doors. Worse still there was no order at the bus stops, as the bus approached the stop, you could see the conductor hanging on to the door and announcing the bus destination, then an almighty scramble would commence with everyone trying to get on to the bus at once, pushing, shoving and shouting. I used to stand back and watch in amazement whilst choosing to wait for the next bus, but I soon realised that it wasn't always the best idea to wait for the next bus in temperatures often reaching 45°C knowing full well that even the following bus could also cause a stampede.

Getting off the bus was another daunting experience, as all the buses where privately owned and therefore in constant competition with one another. Every driver wanted to be the first to each destination and be the first to pick up waiting passengers. It was a complete rat race, so most of the time, to disembark, the bus would slow down to jogging pace and you would then jump out of the bus run forward whilst leaning backwards just so you could keep your balance and not fall over.

The third means of transport, was exclusive to Lagos State the Capital City, they called it the "Molue" it was a bigger bus, not quite a coach but much larger than the minibus. It's clearly advertised maximum capacity was 100. With the sign saying "44 sitting and 56 standing" but reality was even much more striking than this. A Nigerian musician whose music I took an instant liking to, "Fela Kuti" mentioned the big bus in one of his songs picking on the fact that we all travelled with about 44 sitting and over 99 standing.

Fela could not stand the Nigerian government at all, and he used most of his songs to state his disgust at injustice and the shabby life the government were forcing us all to live. But I will come back to Fela later on.

I learned very quickly how to catch and to disembark from the minibus, without ever injuring myself and it quickly became my favourite choice of transport.

Once in a while I would fight my way onto the bus just like everyone else, but more often than not, I wouldn't wait at a crowded bus stop, instead I would walk on to the next, and if that was crowded too, I would carry on walking, sometimes I would continue like that till I walked the entire distance which could be up to three miles. On other occasions, I would get lucky and one of the buses would stop because it wasn't full, and pick me up before I even made it to the next stop.

So soon I knew how to get to Mayflower by bus and often went over to visit Bisi there, I sometimes went to Agege, our first home in Nigeria, to visit my cousins and Maami, and once in a while I ventured out even further to visit Tunde at his parents' house on the other side of Lagos, a town called "Suru-Lere" which translates as "patience has its virtues"

In Nigeria, Dad's first car was an MG "BGT" coupe, it was unique in the country so everyone knew his car, with the big black bumpers front and back. Inside, as long as you sat in the front, it was moderately comfortable, in the back, even as a kid, it was a very tight squeeze and a neck breaker, you had to sit with your neck tilted as the roof at the back was very low.

In the early days, I travelled with Dad to visit Bisi or my cousins, but I was keen to become independent, and Dad wanted me to learn my way about the country, so later on, even when we were heading for the same destination, I would sometimes find a reason to opt for public transport.

That holiday, I experienced some more whippings from Uncle Tony, for various offences, but now I rarely cried. I just took whatever punishment they cared to deal out. The one thing I still could not stand though was his sudden thump on my head with his knuckles. I hated it even more because he would call you closer and closer to him whilst questioning you, I knew what was coming, but I just never knew exactly when, so somewhere during my explanations or claims of innocence, there would be a sudden thud on my head, just above the forehead, it hurt but it was more annoying than the actual pain. He knew I was always disgusted, you could see it in my eyes and my reactions, but again, I refused to cry in front of him.

Days like those made me miss Mum more and more, so once I was left alone, I would lock myself up somewhere, weep a little, get bitter and then write to Mum.

CHAPTER FOUR

SECONDARY SCHOOL YEARS

In September 1978, four years after arriving in Nigeria, I was on my way to secondary school. As usual, I had a new mattress and a lot of provisions.

My list of essential provisions had expanded since primary school days. I still needed powdered milk, tins of fish, Ovaltine or Milo for chocolate drinks, bars of soap for washing, detergent for my clothes, Several packets of gari which was precooked cassava and could be quickly made up into a kind of porridge as a useful staple for a hungry student, I wasn't a big fan of gari but I could see its benefits. I also now had a kind of machete we called a cutlass, a hoe, a lantern, a torch and a new padlock to keep my provisions relatively safe.

I had three sets of my new school uniform, which were white shirts and shorts and white socks, I also had three pairs of the familiar khaki shirt and shorts for boarding school, all of my uniforms had my name written on the inside.

It was a long drive, I was nervous and excited at the same time.

When we finally approached the village of Ketu, I began to wonder if I had made the right choice of college, the village was very small, with just a few houses on one side of the road. The other side of the road was all rainforest, just like most of the route had been.

We drove up to the college security gate, Dad had a brief chat with the guard and he let us through, we turned right and headed towards the administration building. There were a lot of other parents and new students all registering. My college identification number was 645. I was the 645th student to have registered at the college in its four year history.

Once registration was completed, we drove from the admin building back past the gates and further on down to the boys dormitory. It was a huge building, and from what I could see, the whole school looked impressive. Dad said his goodbyes and reminded me that I was grown up now and therefore he wouldn't have to visit me that often, perhaps once a month or whenever he could, he also told me that I had another Uncle who lived nearby who would drop by to see me at some point.

I nervously waved goodbye to Dad then carried my suitcase into the hostel. One of the school prefects showed all the new students round the hostel, it was on two floors in a huge square with a large play area in the middle of the square, there were four communal bathrooms inside the building, much better than the old bath yard that I had got used to over the years.

All the new students had to start off with lower bunk beds and a senior on the top bunk, every student had a little bedside cupboard for storing away their provisions, you had to provide your own padlock to try to keep your provisions safe.

Later in the day, I went for a walk with some of the other new students to familiarise ourselves with the compound, the principal lived on the school compound, his residence was just to the right as we came out of the hostel's main entrance. Just ahead of us was the dining hall, it was much larger, but quite similar to the one at Mayflower, except of course, the chairs and benches were higher. We carried on past the girls' dormitory which was an identical building to ours, then came a whole lot of classrooms and science laboratories.

Further up the path, towards the administration block, was the main block of classrooms it was a vast four storey building with rows of classes. All the first year classes were on the ground floor and the fourth and fifth forms were on the top floor. In front of the class block was a big football pitch and playground, and there was another vast playground behind the block. Once again, the whole compound was full of grass and bushes and of course the customary clay paths and roads.

We walked on towards the administration building and to the left of it there were some more classrooms, behind these classrooms was a field with hundreds of rows of maize plants. All in all it was pretty impressive.

There were over 200 new students that year, so I didn't feel alone, but I missed Bisi and wondered how she was getting on at Mayflower. As usual, I found a quiet moment and updated my diary, then I wrote a letter to Mum giving her my new school address.

On Monday morning, the wake-up bell went off at around 5am and we were all told to go and have a wash, first we had to get some water, once again you had to do this at the stream, so a group of us followed some of the older students, it was a long walk through the usual narrow and eroded clay path, with twigs and bushes from either side whacking you in the face. It was about a two mile walk. I washed myself near the stream and carried a bucket back with me.

I put on my white school uniform for the first time, and felt really proud, by 7am, the breakfast bell rang and we all headed to the dining hall. An hour later it was time to head to the assembly hall. There were over 700 students packed into the hall, most of the senior students were sitting near the front, the rest of us were standing up behind them, it was quite noisy with so many excited voices all talking at once. Suddenly, it all went quiet, the teachers were seated on the stage and the principal had just walked in and barked out "good morning", we all shouted back "Good morning Sir" to him. He welcomed all the new students and went through a brief introduction of the school and staff, then he introduced us to the School Prefects, they were all final year students, there was a senior prefect who was in charge of all the other prefects. There were prefects for class, hostel, food, environment and many other areas. We were warned to obey these prefects 100% otherwise there would be serious repercussions.

Even as we talked, a few students were led up to the stage by one of the prefects, they had all made their way to the assembly hall five minutes after the bell had stopped ringing, so they were all late.

The principal invited them all to stand on one side of the stage, there were nine students in total including two first years. The most senior of the culprits was instructed to lay down prostrate on the stage floor in the "push-up's" position, he knew what to expect, one of the teachers got up and with one of the biggest canes I had ever seen, he dished out 20 lashes to the back and thighs, I stood there in awe! After his lashes he got up dusted himself down and stood at the other end of the stage, we could all make out the lash marks on the back of his thighs.

The next student jumped up screaming after a few lashes and took nearly three minutes to get back into position, the lash count had to start all over again from one. There were also a couple of girls to be flogged, they had to kneel down with their arms stretched out at either side, and they were caned on the palm of the hand and around the wrist, once again, if they got up or wasted time, the count would have to start all over again!

I was already petrified; I knew I was going to be a good boy!

∞

The one thing that was constant in my time in Nigeria and at all the schools that I went to was my ability to attract controversy and adversity. Government College Ketu or "GCK" as we fondly called it was to be no exception. The only difference was that I was growing very fast and I was learning to be independent.

Once again, I started off very well at school, I was quick to adapt to my chosen subjects, English language and literature were compulsory and no problem, maths was also compulsory. For the first two years, we all had to study general science as well as Bible and Islamic knowledge.

Although I had never been in any real fights since arriving in Nigeria, there had always been the occasional squabble especially with Ade, but in general, I had always managed to avoid any potential brawl. However it only took two weeks to find that kind of trouble at GCK.

Among the fresh students that year was a boy called Funsho Benson, he settled in a lot quicker than most of us because he had four older brothers in various years at the college, so he was quick to get cocky, knowing full well that he had his brothers for back-up.

I had always seen him and heard how he wanted to bully his fellow students, but in the first couple of weeks, our paths had never directly crossed. This all changed one evening in the dining hall. We were all still making friends, weighing up who to roll with and what group of people to avoid, and on top of that, there were still new students arriving at the school. That evening, I got my food and was heading towards a quiet table when Funsho bumped into me and demanded my food. I was quite surprised, because in those first weeks, I had been very quiet, I hadn't spoken to many people, Funsho and I were actually in the same class but I had never spoken to him.

The dining room went silent as it became clear that a confrontation was brewing, I ignored him, turned around and continued to head to my table, he then rushed round and slammed the aluminium dish of food out of my hand scattering my food all over the floor, I spun round in fury, but still quite aware that his brothers would jump in, so I calmly asked him what he thought he was doing, he then raised his fist towards me, and I thought, oh boy! This is going to be ugly… But before I could even think of what to do, someone had grabbed Funsho from behind, and got him in a head lock, he tried to fight his way out, throwing wild punches, but could not get out of the grip, I couldn't see who he was fighting, but I was amazed that none of his brothers had come to his aid. It was a normal thing in any walk of life in Nigeria for people to encourage fights, and whenever a fight broke out, everyone would form a circle around the fighters and watch; only very rarely would a Samaritan try to break it up.

So on this evening, most people in the dining hall, gathered round to watch and yelled encouragement, within seconds, Funsho had been pulled across the hall still in a head lock, and then as he threw another desperate punch, I noticed that he was fighting a girl, she maintained her lock on his head and then shoved him, head first, straight into the wall, where he collapsed for a few seconds in agony. Some of the school prefects stepped in to break up the fight and ordered all the students to get back to their dinner, Funsho and I were taken away to be questioned. I turned round to say thank you to the girl who had just made a mockery of Funsho's bad boy image, she was already smiling; it was Biodun!

She had chosen GCK over Mayflower Secondary School, her mum hadn't been keen initially, but had respected her decision.

So once again we were united, it was good to have someone I actually knew at the new school, Funsho, certainly never messed with her, while I knew that next time around, I would have to be quicker to stand up for myself.

Next day in class, everyone was talking about was how Biodun had saved me, and how tough she was, I didn't mind, she was my good friend and we had agreed between us, that we would look out for each other in future, should either of us be in trouble.

My best friend in school that first year was a boy called Ayo; we met one evening in class. Most of the students were out in the playground, but I was in class drawing pictures, I loved art, and used to draw all the superheroes from "Marvel Comics" Captain America was my favourite, but I also drew, "The Mighty Thor, Incredible Hulk and Daredevil".

I had finished my drawings and decided to go out to play, as I walked past Ayo's desk, I noticed that he was drawing too, I had to stop; he was actually drawing up his own comic story! I sat down beside him, while he explained what he was doing and within minutes, we were both drawing and bouncing ideas off each other.

We became instant friends; his parents lived in Lagos, on the same street as my Aunt Lola, just a few blocks up. We knew some of the same places in Lagos, we read the same comics and we both liked football. He was a Manchester United Fan; I found that strange at the time, as he had never been to England. But he knew all about the club and its players, his hero was George Best. I supported Liverpool, but we both just loved to talk football.

Ayo suggested that we make a comic together, he had already created his very own superhero called "The Tornado". I loved the idea, so at first I helped him with his comic, he was good at the drawings, but couldn't make up a story, so I planned the details of the story, told him what to draw at each stage and he did his part, then we took turns colouring in the comic and within a week, we had finished our very first comic.

We read it over and over again, it was 18 pages in total, and we were really proud, so we decided to show it to a few friends, which in turn generated more interest, and even some of the senior students liked it and suggested we make a sequel.

Once again, Ayo and I knuckled down, we drew out a story, this time, it finished with our hero in serious trouble and we marked it "To be continued" and so the interest in our comics continued.

I then went on to create my own superhero, I called him "The Red Lion" he wore a black mask and a special red suit with the picture of a lion's head on his chest. His special power was a devastating one inch punch and his weakness was when he was not in his super hero costume. The Red Lion was an instant hit. So our comic series continued throughout the first year. Ayo and I were so popular, people even paid us with provisions such as biscuits, tins of milk or sardines, just to borrow and read the comics at their own leisure.

Ayo was a much better footballer than I was, we played a lot of football with other first and second years, but the seniors spotted him and another boy called "Hilary Adikki" almost immediately. It was unusual at that time for any student below Year 4 or 5, to get into the school football team, partly because the juniors were usually too small and mainly because the seniors all wanted to be in the team themselves.

Ayo and Hilary were so good, that they had to make an exception despite their size, I was so envious; I really wanted to join them in the team.

The first match they played in was a big one, it was a National College Championships Match, and the first leg was at our school. The school grounds were packed full of students from both schools, I remember sitting on the balcony on one of the main class floors; it was packed as were the floors above and below.

The match kicked off and we already knew which seniors were good, they were always showing off and were all well respected on campus, but Ayo and Hilary looked very small compared to all the other players. We won the match 6-1 Hilary had been fantastic, he had all the skills and had run rings around boys nearly twice his size, but just to outshine him, Ayo, scored five of the goals!! What an amazing match that was.

For days afterwards, Ayo was a hero amongst us first years, we also thought that it might mean that we had made some new friends with some of the seniors, but that wasn't the case for long. For a couple of weeks some of the seniors would say hello to us, they knew me because of my British accent and our comics. But soon the match was in the past and I was getting myself in trouble with a group of seniors.

I had already been in a few fights in the first weeks at school, it was becoming a way of life for me, I was stubborn and on the one hand, some of the older students wanted to pick on me because I was quiet and seemed like a soft touch.

So I would get into fights with older students and if I lost the fight, I would keep looking for a re-match until I eventually fared better and sometimes came out better off.

The most memorable fight in my first year came up just before the mid-term holidays. We were in the playground playing 7-a-side football, with the losing team all walking off for a breather while a new team comes on to challenge the winners.

The winning team was usually the first to score two goals. A team full of seniors had just lost their match, and it was my team's turn to challenge the winners. As we walked onto the pitch, one of the seniors from the team that had just lost, came over to me and told me to sit my turn out because he was going to take my place. The guy who approached me was well known amongst us juniors because he was unusually small in size compared to most of his classmates, he was also very boisterous and liked to bully the juniors, perhaps because he was the same size as us.

I was already very stubborn and was not one to back down, so I declined, he wasn't impressed and told me to go and sit down, insisting that he was taking my place whether I liked it or not. I had already decided that I was not going to back down, but when his classmates started encouraging me to stand my ground, I began to think that maybe his fellow seniors hated his attitude as much as we did. For once, I thought that the seniors were on our side against one of them, so I took their advice and refused to leave the pitch. He shoved me hard in the chest, I got up and shoved him back, then he threw a punch, which I blocked and then I caught him with a couple of shots, which made him mad, so all hell broke out, we tussled for a few moments, I continued to rain punches on him till he started bleeding from the lip, eventually a few people stepped in to pull us apart.

Football was over for the day, no one else was allowed to play, and it also seemed that all the seniors had let me off even though I had fought one of them in the public playground. Most of my friends kept telling me to watch my back for the rest of the day, but all seemed Ok. We had dinner as usual, and soon the "lights out bell" rang which was the signal for us to go to sleep.

I was fast asleep when someone woke me, it was a prefect telling me to get out of bed. It must have been about 12am.

I climbed out of bed slowly, trying to keep my eyes open, I followed him out of the room and downstairs, we then went into the large room that most of the prefects shared. Waiting for me there was the senior I had beaten up earlier in the day and at least 12 of his fellow pupils including some of the school prefects. I immediately knew that I was in trouble.

"Like fighting seniors do you"? "So here's the lad who thinks he can beat up seniors" etc. the questions kept coming, while I tried to explain that some of them had encouraged me earlier to take him on.

"Well, you are about to learn a lesson, that you won't forget in a hurry" someone told me. They led me out to the middle of the boys' dormitory, we called it the "quadrangle" it was a large, muddy, grassy square area around which the dormitory was built, it usually served as an assembly point for any announcements the prefects needed to make to just the boys.

I followed one of the prefects into the quadrangle where he then told me to bend over, standing on just one leg, the other leg pointing away from me, was to remain airborne at all times. I had to touch the floor with just one finger, whilst keeping my other hand on my back. I then had to stay in that position till I was relieved. It was a common form of punishment, one that I had come across before but never to the extent that I was about to experience. I had to keep that position for over an hour and a half, and every time my other foot would touch the ground for balance as I got tired, someone would hit me on the head, or kick the offending foot.

Around 1.30am, they let me get up and take a five minute break, I had refused to cry or show that they could hurt me, they even asked how I felt and although it was clear that I was distressed, I just told them defiantly that I was OK.

After my five minute rest, it was time to resume punishment, they had a different proposition for me as well, this time I had to squat down, hold my ears and do frog jumps round and round the quadrangle, another form of punishment that I was already familiar with. It took on average about 50 leaps to complete one full circuit, by the time I had done three circuits, I was shattered but they would not let me stop, I plodded along, really feeling the pain this time, still they would not let me stop, I completed my sixth circuit before I was finally offered a two minute recovery period. This time when they asked me how I felt, I couldn't even talk!

Two minutes later, to my amazement, they sent me back for more frog jumps, I could barely get going now, and soon I was crying as they laughed at me, I continued hopping and crying, and the crying got louder with time. Eventually, I was crying so loud and now pleading for mercy, that I had pretty much woken everyone up. Some of the juniors who dared to get out of bed to have a look were soon sent packing back to bed, with a few harsh words or in some cases lashes for comfort.

Soon it was abundantly clear that I had no more energy, I couldn't even stand up properly for a few minutes, and so, after just over three hours of punishment, I was sent back to bed. A few hours later the "wake up bell" went off.

One thing the seniors were right about was the fact that I would never forget that night! It remains a vivid memory and even one which a lot of my old classmates remember me by to this day. No one had ever been punished to that extreme at the college before. I ached for days, I only spoke to seniors if I absolutely had to, but I still refused to let them break me.

Just to compound my misery and anger at the time, the seniors even had the last laugh for quite a while. I decided the following morning after speaking to a lot of my classmates and other older students, that I should report this incident to the school principal. It was an unprecedented incident, the seniors had abused their powers after all, and it was right to defy them and speak to the principal. I had never spoken to Mr Shittu the principal on a one to one basis, so it took me a while to gather up the courage to walk over to his premises. Some good friends accompanied me over, then waited outside while I knocked on his door and went in.

It was a Saturday morning and he looked like he had just been woken up, he invited me in and asked me what the problem was. I stood there and explained what had happened last night, he seemed shocked and annoyed by it all, and so he asked one of my friends outside to get the school head prefect over to his premises immediately.

The prefect arrived and Mr Shittu questioned him about the incident, he had not stayed in the dormitory that night so was not able to give a full account of the incident, next, the senior who actually led the punishment routine that night, a prefect called Raymond was summoned to the principal's quarters. He turned up and was questioned. He immediately responded by claiming that he was my older cousin and that my dad had authorised him to keep me in check at all times, he claimed that I had picked on a senior just because he was smaller than me and therefore he decided that he had to take action.

The principal's face changed, he looked at me in anger while I stood their astonished, "So why have you wasted my time young man? He is your brother as far I am concerned, and he has your father's blessing to discipline you as he deems fit". I tried to argue with the principal the fact that I did not even know this guy, but he had heard enough, he was clearly tired and wanted to get back to bed. So he showed me the door, with just a brief warning to Raymond advising him not to go to those extremes again.

I walked out in disbelief, Raymond flicked me behind the ear, telling me that I was in trouble and my friends who had been waiting for me which also included Biodun and Ayo, were stunned when I told them what had happened, some of them even knocked on the principal's door to explain that Raymond was no relation of mine, but once again the principal ushered them all away.

Over the next few days, Raymond and some of his classmates would constantly pick on me, they wanted me to hand over my provisions to them, fetch them water and so much more, as much as I could, I would remain stubborn, only doing the chores that seniors were genuinely allowed to request of juniors.

Soon I found myself getting into physical fights with Raymond or one of his colleagues on a fairly regular basis. One of the things about school in Nigeria, is that age was not an indication of level of academic education, for example, Festus was three years older than me when we met back at All Saints School, but we were classmates.

Some of the seniors at GCK were in their mid-twenties and so, were a lot larger than the average secondary school student, which meant that people like Raymond who I had to keep fighting were nearly twice my size! That wasn't enough to deter me, nor was the constant beating that I received, I just kept going back for more, and I refused to cave in. And so it went for the rest of that school term.

During the holidays that year, there was an attempted military coup; the Head of State, General Murtala Mohammed, was killed in an ambush. There was panic everywhere and the soldiers set up a curfew between the hours of 6pm and 6am. The soldiers had authority to shoot on sight, anyone who broke the curfew.

The leader of the coup, General Bukka Sukka Dimka, was captured and subsequently assassinated a few days later.

General Olusegun Obasanjo had been Murtala's deputy in the government so when Mohammed was assassinated Obasanjo replaced him as head of state. Obasanjo served until October 1, 1979, when he handed power to Shehu Shagari, a democratically elected civilian president, becoming the first leader in Nigerian history to surrender power willingly.

In late 1983, however, the military seized power again. Obasanjo, being in retirement, did not participate in that coup, and did not approve of it.

Bisi spent her holiday with Aunt Lola as usual, while I spent some of my time at Uncle Tony's. I decided that I needed to get bigger and stronger before going back to school in about three weeks' time. So I bought myself a "Bullworker" A body-building device that had been advertised in all the local papers, I also got a "Chest Expander" and a skipping rope, and I religiously worked out three times a day every single day, pushing myself further and further. I hid it from Dad and Uncle Tony initially, as I was not sure if they would have wanted to know how I managed to afford my new exercise equipment. The simple answer was that I rarely spent the pocket money Dad gave me at school; I always saved it because I was never sure if he would be coming to get me during school holidays, or if I would need to get home by public transport.

I still played football downstairs just like the old days, and our house-help Ahmed, always came down to watch. I was one of the best players in the neighbourhood and loved to show off my skills, especially as across the road from us, we had new neighbours, a girl named Rita, who became my very first girlfriend. Rita along with her younger sister and parents had moved in a few months earlier.

Rita was a year younger than me; she was very pretty, her parents had just moved back from England where she was born. Every time we played football outside, I would spot her on their balcony watching the game, and I always did my best to impress.

I was a little shy at the time, I really liked Rita but apart from a few quick hellos, I rarely spoke to her. She also did her best to show off; she would play her music so loud, that I could hear it from across the road, I would then step out on to our balcony, and she would be on her balcony dancing and singing away, she always looked good and she knew that she had sparked my interest. Her favourite album was a new one from "Boney M" and the tracks that she played over and over again included "Ma Baker, Plantation Boy" and especially "Have you ever seen the rain"

Most of the boys on the street fancied her and tried to chat her up, I was no exception, I liked her, but I was too shy to make a move.

Finally my luck changed, Ahmed was on his way back home from a shopping errand one day, as he walked past Rita's house, she stopped him and ran downstairs to talk to him, and he already knew that I liked her. Ahmed came rushing upstairs screaming for me, he was all excited, beaming from ear to ear, he still spoke very little English, most of which he had learned from me. So how he managed to communicate with Rita, I'll never know, but he kept yelling "She wan talk" "She wan talk." He explained that she had asked for my name and wanted to talk to me.

I was so excited; I went into my bedroom to clean myself up a little and then took a deep breath, before heading across the road. I turned up still wondering what on earth I was going to say to her. She had come back downstairs to wait for me, she also looked a little less confident now, which made things easier for me. We both said hello, then we sat there and talked for ages, we smiled and just kept talking.

We talked about England, our parents and school; she also told me how she liked to watch me play football, while I told her that she danced well. She wanted to grow up to be a lawyer just like her mum, while I still wanted to be a doctor.

I also told her about my trials and tribulations at school, which she found quite fascinating. We promised to write to each other when I went back to school.

Every day once her parents had gone out, and my dad and uncle had also left for work, I would meet Rita, we would study together for a short while then walk down the road hand in hand just talking.

I don't think I ever kissed her, at 10 or 11 years old I was far too naive and way too shy anyway. We had some good times, but we had to keep it all quiet, away from our parents. Her parents were very strict and I knew Dad would not approve either; he didn't like me playing football, spending time with girls or anything at all that would keep me away from studying.

Although Dad could no longer hurt me by whipping me, I was still very much afraid of him, he was very dominating and when he shouted at you, he could shake a room! Worse still was the fact that he never ever gave you an opportunity to argue your point across to him. I would try on various occasions especially when I knew what was going on, but conversations usually went like this "No Dad I was actually..." He'd chip in with a loud booming "YES" "but no Dad..." "YES" he'd interrupt even louder, "and the arguments always finished with "Get out of my sight" I really hated that the most, the confrontation was over, once again, I had lost the argument before I had even had a chance to make a point of any kind.

So there was absolutely no way that I was going to let him know about Rita, even when they finally suspected and asked me, I just ignored the questions entirely.

Rita made me promise to write to my mum more regularly, even if she never replied, she told me, "you can't change your mum; she's always going to be your mum"

She was so upset on the day before I had to go back to GCK. She was not a boarding student like me, so she was always home with her family in the evenings, we promised to stay in touch by writing to each other as often as possible.

I knew it was going to be a very busy term at college, it was the final term for the fifth formers, and they needed to study hard if they wanted to proceed on to university. For all other students it was also going to be a very busy time as we were all working towards promotion to the next school year.

The prefects were too busy now, to carry on with their extracurricular activities, so some students from the forth form were now elected as shadow prefects for the rest of the term.

A lot of us youngsters were willing to help the seniors where we could, like fetching them water from the stream, collecting their meals from the dining hall and so on; it gave the seniors more time to concentrate on their studies. Some of the seniors hardly slept at night, they would be over at the classroom blocks, studying straight through the night, sometimes falling asleep at their desk, then waking up to start all over again. Electricity power cuts were a regular occurrence in Nigeria, it happened as often as five or six times a week, so the seniors were prepared for that too, they would take their kerosene lanterns, candles and torch lights along with them.

For us first year students, there was no real pressure; it was unlikely that a first year student wouldn't make the next grade. So we studied a little, but for us it was more a case of finishing near the top of the class rather than the bottom.

In spite of his studies, Raymond still found time to resume his battles and arguments with me. As usual, I was not willing to back down any more than I had to.

One very early morning, some friends and I were on our way back from the stream, we had left the dormitory as soon as the "wake up" bell had rung that morning. It gave us time to have a wash by the stream, and then carry a spare bucket of water back to the hostel, which we would use for drinking and for the next day's bath.

We were running a little late, we needed to get back to the hostel quickly, get changed into our uniforms, have breakfast and get to the assembly on time in order to avoid the public spanking for lateness. As we approached the hostel, I could see three seniors waiting by the entrance, we headed towards them and then tried to squeeze past, one of them stopped us and asked one of us to give him his bucket of water, he duly obliged even though he was clearly upset. The other seniors then took buckets of water off some of my other friends. The rest of us felt really bad, because we knew how tough it was to carry a bucket of water on your head for over two miles, only to have it taken away from you.

As we continued through the hostel, Raymond appeared and tried to pull my bucket of water while I was still balancing it on my head, I held it tighter as I turned around to face him and asked what he was doing. He simply told me that he needed my bucket of water right away!

I refused, I told him that I had worked too hard to get that water and if he wanted half of it, I would let him have half, but he declined he wanted it all and would not let me put the bucket down. We argued for a while, but once it became clear that I was not going to keep my water, I calmly asked him if he definitely wanted my water so much that he would not let me keep any of it? He confirmed that he was confiscating the whole bucket. I looked at him and asked if he was sure, by this time, there were so many students around watching the confrontation. Raymond again told me that he was taking the whole bucket away from me, so I took a deep breath, and threw the whole bucket of water all over him!

People jumped back to avoid being splashed, I could hear some people laughing and others drawing deep breaths of shock. Raymond was in a rage and dived at me, knocking me sprawling over, but I was ready this time, I got up quickly as he charged at me again, he threw a few punches, but I had my arms up protecting my face, just as I had learned from watching all those Muhammad Ali fights.

He continued to throw punches, but none of them connected, I just kept my hands up and they took all the impact, I was a little scared and didn't know what else to do, so I just kept defending myself, then amongst the noise I could hear someone saying "hit him back Yemi, he's not hurting you" I heard the shout a few more times and realised that I wasn't hurt, so as Raymond attempted another punch, I side stepped him to get him off balance and threw a flurry of punches, at his head, face and belly, he wasn't expecting that, especially as he was so much bigger than me. He tried to hit me again, but each time, I was faster and soon he was on the floor. I was petrified, I stood there shaking, but I knew that for once, I had beaten Raymond up.

Raymond lay there in pain, while I stood over him still shaking, no one could believe what had just happened, I had beaten up a guy nearly twice my size, and he was in a lot of pain. I now felt really bad, so I leaned over to ask if he was alright, he nodded, so I offered my hand and helped him up, I started to apologise, but he told me not to worry. The crowd that had gathered dispersed quietly, Ayo and some other friends started telling me how proud they were, and they promised that should the seniors decide to punish me that night, that they would share in my punishment no matter what!

I went to bed that night and lay awake, waiting for someone to come and get me, but no one came. Soon it was morning, I had fallen asleep at some point, but I was still very tired, Ayo and I went down to the stream, talking about yesterday and our disbelief that the seniors had neither taken retribution nor even had a word with me of any sort, we still believed that they had a plan.

We returned to the hostel with a few other friends, and once again, I could see the seniors bullying and taking water off the juniors further ahead, as we approached them, it became clear that they would antagonise us, so Ayo & I decided to throw our water all over the ground, we were about 200 yards from them, so they could see us clearly throwing our hard earned water out, then we walked up to them carrying our empty buckets, so they decided to let us through without any trouble.

The whole day in class, I kept wondering what was going to happen, the longer nothing happened, the more nervous I became.

A few days later, Raymond sent a set of twins from two years above me to pick a fight with me, one of them kept trying to taunt me and eventually, rather foolishly, I yielded and got into a fight with him, I was immediately in control, but I was worried, I kept trying to look out for his twin brother, they always fought in two's, and I knew he would appear.

As expected, he did, from behind, knocking me over the head and straight to the ground, they both jumped on me and threw punches, within seconds, Ayo & Hilary joined in to help me but I was already bruised and battered.

Raymond saw me later that evening and started laughing, I swore at him, so he rushed at me, flew in with a Kung-Fu style kick, catching me in the ribs, I whacked my head against the wall, before I could get up, he was all over me kicking me in the ribs, once again, I got myself to my knees and fought him.

We continued like this day after day, sometimes I would gain the upper hand, but sooner or later, Raymond would retaliate harder and rougher. Things got so bad, that eventually Mr Shittu the principal, had to get involved, He sent an urgent S.O.S to Dad, summoning him to the school.

That weekend, Dad turned up to meet Mr Shittu, who told him that I seemed to have a death wish, he felt that I had a serious problem, and would get myself badly injured if I kept getting into brutal fights with people much bigger than me.

Dad asked me what was going on, and I tried to explain, but he was stern especially as he was in front of the principal too. Dad also knew one of the seniors, a guy named Bola, so he asked him if he could look out for me and to try to keep me away from Raymond. Raymond himself got a sharp warning from Mr Shittu who threatened him with expulsion from the school.

So things calmed down a lot between Raymond and me, he was worried about being expelled from school in his final year and I was happy enough to stay out of his way.

Early one evening, a senior whom I had never spoken to before called me over. I had always seen him in the dormitory but he was one of the more quiet seniors. His name was Kayode but everyone called him Kay. The only reason I even knew of him was because he always seemed to be in bed studying and the fact that he was quite handsome.

I had noticed him a few times before, but I had never actually spoken to him before this encounter. He told me that he wanted to speak to me about something that had come to his attention. At that point I didn't actually know his name, so when he asked me if I knew who he was, I just shrugged my shoulders and said "no". The moment he told me that his name was Kay, it all made sense to me, my heart skipped a beat and I thought I was in trouble, he could see it in my face, so he smiled, and told me to calm down. He told me that he was aware of my secret and that we could help each other.

My secret was a simple one. In the first term at school one of the female prefects had called me over one day and asked if I was Kay's brother, she told me that we looked identical, aside from the fact that I was clearly younger. She continued by telling me that she just wanted to say hello to me and she also gave me some money. So I gladly played along, I admitted to being Kay's brother in spite of not having a clue who he was at the time! In return, I got to know all the senior girls who fancied him; they all rewarded me for passing on their messages, gifts and names to Kay. Of course I never actually passed on any messages, and I kept all the gifts, which I shared with my friends. We all thought it was cool, all the senior girls liked us and everything seemed so easy until someone told Kay all about it.

Thankfully, Kay saw the funny side of it, he thought I had been sly but clever, I explained that I didn't know who or how to find Kay at the time, plus I had initially tried to explain to the girls that I wasn't his brother, but no one believed me, which was all true.

So now I was making friends with Kay, he liked me and my group of friends, so for the rest of the term, he helped keep me out of trouble, away from the likes of Raymond and in return, I delivered messages and other errands to any of the senior girls that he liked. I had to keep convincing them that I was now indeed Kay's brother. Once in a while my friends and I had to bring him back a spare bucket of water from the stream or collect his dinner on his behalf from the dining hall but that was all OK He asked politely and he looked out for us.

I think Kay enjoyed himself just as much as we did. He used to ask me to get names of not just girls in the fifth but also from the fourth Form. I'd come back with messages from all sorts of girls, for him. Ayo and I enjoyed this just as much, because we knew that we at least had a senior on our side for the rest of the year and we got to chat to girls' way above our league at the time.

I continued to write to Rita as promised, she was doing well at her school too, and she kept telling me how much she missed me, I missed her too, but I didn't really like spending my holidays at Uncle Tony's or the other various uncles and Aunts we had lived with over the last few years. I wanted a home for Bisi, Dad and me, just the three of us in our own home.

Rita understood my feelings; after all, I could travel to see her from wherever we lived, but all that seemed a pipe dream, Dad seemed to be happy the way we lived, he wasn't married so it seemed he was better off living with his brothers.

I occasionally heard back from Mum, but it was taking about three or four letters from me, just to get one response but I always looked out for my post in great anticipation that I might have a letter from abroad.

In my spare time, I also found a penfriend in the UK and joined a writing club my main motivation was simply the fact that they were all based in the UK.

Soon it was time for the year-end exams, the 5th formers were taking their exams and we rarely saw them now. Ayo & I always offered to help Kay with water and anything else, he had been pretty good to us in return and we knew that we were going to miss him the following year. On the other hand, we were also quite looking forward to moving into the 2nd form; we would no longer be first years and we would have a whole year's experience behind us.

Dad came to pick me up at the end of term, he had Bisi with him. She had now gained a place at an all-girls Federal College in Ogun State. It was just about 40 miles from Mayflower School. I don't know if she was more excited about her appointment or the fact that she was finally leaving Mayflower. But she was clearly ecstatic.

The graduating seniors had said their final goodbyes earlier in the day, I actually felt sad as we wished them well. Most of them had gained places at top universities, but a few, including Raymond, would have to re-sit their papers.

I finished top of the entire first form, and picked up some individual awards for being top overall and for finishing top in various subjects. I was proud and I was now looking forward to the holidays.

I said goodbye to Ayo, who was still waiting for his parents to turn up, I also promised to meet up with him during the holidays.

I sat in the front and Bisi in the back, we were both excited as we hadn't seen each other in over three months, so we had a lot to talk about. Dad was talkative too, he had finally found a house, we were going to have a place of our own, it wasn't going to be ready for us to move in to for a few months yet, but it was still great news.

We went to Aunt Lola's first to drop Bisi off; I would be staying with Dad at Uncle Tony's again. I liked Aunt Lola's house, it was a massive duplex in one of the plush parts of Lagos called Ilu-Peju. She lived there with her husband who we called Dr Olaoye and their three children Yomi, Bukki & Funmi.

Aunt Lola also had a son from her first marriage, Akin, he was about six years older than me, but I knew him very well from meeting him a few times in England. He actually lived in Dallas, but had flown over to see his mum in England from time to time. I liked Akin a lot, and always looked forward to his visits back then.

CHAPTER FIVE

SCHOOL HOLIDAYS

Over the next couple of years things took on a certain pattern: my school holidays were always spent at Uncle Tony's, and there were a lot of chores expected of us. They still had a resident house-help but I did all the ironing. Between Dad, Uncle Tony and any other Uncles who stayed over I could have up to 30 pairs of shirts and trousers to iron on a Sunday, and they all had to be done perfectly, especially Dad's. He was very fussy about the quality of his shirts; the collar had to be folded perfectly on the crease and pressed down properly, all the sleeves had to have one perfect crease line, and the same applied for his trousers, he would make me iron them over and over again, yelling at me till I got it right. Sometimes, he would give up, and take the iron off me, then show me how it should be done.

I was quite determined to prove that I could do anything I wanted to, so I soon got the hang of professional ironing, and my reward was for Dad to tell all his friends not to iron their own clothes, because Yemi could do a much better job and so my weekend laundry pile grew and grew.

I also had to wash Uncle Tony's and Dad's cars every single morning. The roads in Nigeria were all dusty red clay, therefore cars were filthy by the evening, so every morning around 5am my first chore was to get a few buckets of water and wash the cars thoroughly.

Uncle Tony had three or four cars back then, he was a

mechanical engineer and owned his own company with two partners he had met back in England. They called their company "Holloway Motors" and they were a specialist and authorised Mercedes Benz dealer and service centre. So Uncle Tony loved his cars and always had some of the best, which was cool. He had a couple of Merc's and a Honda Prelude and Dad had his little MG BGT Rover. If I had to wash cars every single morning, they might as well be ones that fascinated me.

The best part about washing the cars was that I got to start them up every day as well, to warm up the engines, so I always looked forward to that part. You had to be responsible for them to even give you their car keys, let alone allow you to turn over the engine.

Another thing Dad wanted Bisi and me to learn at an early age, was how to cook. Bisi had been taking lessons from Aunt Lola and soon Dad would have me in the kitchen, showing me how to cook all the different Nigerian delicacies.

The soups had to be cooked to perfection, Dad loved any kind of meat, but he mainly taught me how to cook, chicken, beef, cow foot and fish. Most Nigerians like their food very spicy, so you had to get the right amount of peppers and just enough tomatoes and onions to complement the sauce.

If I had to cook a sauce for the evening, I would go out to the local market earlier in the day to buy red peppers, onions, tomatoes and whatever meat we were having. Going to the market was a real chore, they always seemed to be located in the busiest and muddiest places; they were noisy, with every trader calling out at the top of their voice to attract your attention; there could be a row of up to 20 traders in one section all selling the same items, most people had their favourite stockist and always went straight to them, I always looked for the cleanest stall…and that was quite a challenge!

Once you had decided who you wanted to deal with, the next thing was to haggle for a mutually acceptable price. You haggled over everything and anything. I often used to pay the immediate asking price because I was too scared to haggle for a better one, but

Dad knew that I wasn't getting the best value for the money he was giving me, so occasionally he would go to the market with me on a Saturday. Most of the meat traders knew him so he'd introduce me as his son and then leave me to haggle a deal. , Because he was around, the traders would be a bit more willing to listen, so for example, if a trader's asking price for a large portion of meat was 30 Naira, I would haggle it down to about 22 Naira and be really proud of myself, then Dad would get involved, with a cheeky smile and stubborn determination, the trader would eventually give in, accepting 6 Naira! As for me I would stand there with my jaw still dropping half embarrassed and half in awe, I would feel so sorry for the trader, it was as if someone had just snatched his dinner from his tight grasp.

Dad always told me to stop feeling sorry for them, "they make enough money off people like you who don't haggle", but I couldn't help it, I was always a lot more lenient, I did haggle, but I always had a price target in mind, and as long as I got to within my target, the deal was done for me.

Back at GCK things were also changing, we were no longer the first year students and although we didn't have any special privileges in years two and three, we at least knew the college inside out and the seniors knew us too.

I still got into fights, I was still stubborn and would not allow anyone to try to take my rights away from me, but I also started standing up for juniors and other pupils who wouldn't, or couldn't, stand up for themselves.

My problems with seniors continued unabated even when I got to year three. I got so riled, and couldn't wait to become a senior, I had it in my mind that I was going to be tough on all juniors, like the seniors had been on me. That was the usual way things happened, it was a vicious cycle and when you became a senior you just felt the need to get some payback.

One of the most memorable things in year 3 was being re-united with my old friends Festus and Augustine. They turned up at GCK in the start of the school year 1980/81. Their parents were best friends and had both decided to move them from their previous school to GCK. They were joining as year 2 students while Festus also had his younger brother Edward, who I had never met before joining the first year.

It was great to meet up with the boys again, Augustine had grown really tall since I'd last seen him back at All Saints, he was also muscular, a very agile goalkeeper, long distance runner, hurdler and high jumper, but even more interesting for me, his favourite hobby was drawing comic characters.

I immediately introduced them both to Ayo; it seemed as if we had started off a business partnership, three artists and Festus who did all the editing. Augustine was by far the best artist, his drawings were so accurate, and he had no problems drawing male or female, whilst any female I drew was fairly muscular.

By the early 80's, Nigeria, which has a lot of natural resources and is still one of the world's largest oil producers, was riddled with corruption.

The military dictatorship had given way to an elected parliament headed by the president, Shagari, but a slump in oil prices and accusations of electoral fraud as well as religious tensions plagued the new civilian government.

∞

By 1981 in the Middle of Shagari's time in power, you didn't need to be an adult to know that Nigeria as a democracy was on a rapid downwards spiral; corruption was so rife, even at school. You no longer relied on academic ability to get into the best colleges or universities; it was just a case of who you knew and the size of the bribe you were willing to pay.

It was the same everywhere, the police were corrupt, and they had road blocks on just about every heavily populated urban road and motorway. You had to pull over once they flagged you down, otherwise the vehicle would be shot at on sight irrespective of any passengers on board. They didn't really want to check for documents or anything else, their popular opening question was "Wetin you bring?" the pigeon English for "What have you got for me?" You could sit there and show them your best documents if you wanted, but the sooner you gave them some money, the sooner you were on your way to the next road block.

The State Governors were looking after their own families and immediate associates, government projects were only won by people who knew people, who probably also knew people! This once-rich country was being blatantly squeezed dry by the very people who had been democratically elected into power to make the nation a better country.

Shagari was eventually deposed on December 31, 1983 in a bloodless military coup, led by Maj.-Gen. Muhammad Buhari a former military governor of Borno State and federal commissioner for petroleum during 1976-78. This coup was regarded with relief at the time by many Nigerians.

By the end of June 1979, Bisi and I were really excited, we had heard Dad going on and on about the fact that he had found a place for us to live, so by the time the holidays came around, we couldn't wait to find out if we were really going to have a place of our own. Just the thought of our very own home got me so excited, no more having to go to Uncle Tony's in the school holidays.

Dad picked Bisi up from her school first then drove up to Ketu to get me, Bisi and I were so happy to see each other; it had been three months since we set off to our separate schools for another term. We had a lot to talk about, not least the fact that we were actually going to spend a holiday together in our own home for the first time since we left England nearly six years previously.

I inspected Dad's new jeep. He had got rid of the tiny claustrophobic MG for a much larger, more spacious Nissan Patrol Jeep, it was yellow with partly leather seats, he was really proud of it and I liked it too but kept thinking how difficult it would be to wash.

We headed off to a little village called Iju; it was just five miles on from Ifako where Bisi and I had once gone to school. Iju was in Lagos state, all buses turned around at the final stop in Iju which seemed to be where the roads ended. It was only famous for providing water for most of Lagos State through the one major company in the village 'Iju Water Works'

The main roads to Iju were in very bad repair; they had pot-holes which filled up with water from the rain, some of the holes where so deep you had to be careful not to get your vehicle stuck in them. The best line of action was to follow the path and actions of the vehicle in front, unless of course it was a lorry.

As we entered the main village, the roads narrowed with gutters on either side, the gutters were the only way of letting dirty water and other waste run from houses and businesses to a sewage source. There were planks of wood laid across the ditch at strategic points so people could walk over the gutter to the nearest shop or flat.

We turned just before we reached the village centre and drove on down a very dusty track leaving a trail of red clay smoke in our wake, we could already see that there weren't many houses down here and most of them were unfinished but nevertheless occupied. One final turn down a rough bumpy and worn clay road and Dad pulled up. "Here we are, welcome home." Bisi and I jumped out all excited, it was an unfinished building consisting of two flats side by side. In between them was a dusty stairway leading to the roof where there was a foundation to build two more flats above us, but that project had not started yet. There was a porch surrounded by white railing and a gate in front of each flat, we walked up to the flat on our left, the one on the right belonged to the landlord and his family, so we were his very first tenants.

Dad led us through our little white gate and slotted his key into the main glass door lock and then we were straight into the living room, it was a big room, but the only furniture in it was a large empty barrel with a huge circular piece of wood planted on it for a makeshift table, it was surrounded by three large building bricks for sitting round the table. This was the only form of furniture in the living room.

My bedroom was behind the door at the back of the living room; it was a big room and had a single bed with one of my old mattresses from school on it. Bisi and Dad's bedrooms where to the right as you entered the living room. There was a door which led to a small hall, to the left was Dad's double bedroom, to the right was Bisi's room, just a little smaller than mine, with her single bed and old mattress, and in between their rooms were two more doors, one for the shower and the other for the toilet.

One bonus, in spite of the sparse furniture, in our new house was that we actually had tap water. We could use a shower, flush the toilet and cook with clean water. It made me appreciate how lucky we were.

We walked back into the bare living room, past my room and onto the large area which Dad said would be the dining area, to the left of the dining area as we approached it was the kitchen, it had a few storage cupboards, a kerosene stove and a small fridge, it was a long narrow room which had a door at the end leading out to the back of the flat. The back was just a narrow walkway fenced off by an eight foot wall to deter would-be burglars.

Bisi and I were so excited about having our own home, it was hard to be concerned that night about how barren the flat was, as if to make the point the power cut out. We were left in darkness for a while till someone found the kerosene lanterns and matches we lit a couple of the lanterns and continued to look around the house.

Dad told us he was going out to get some dinner for us, we said bye as he locked us in the flat and drove off. We chose a brick each and sat down at our roughly assembled table, looking at our large shadows cast against the walls behind us from the lantern on the table.

That night we all had dinner together taking care not to tip the table over by leaning on it. I remember having a good night's sleep and being keen to get up and outside to have a proper look around in daylight.

I was up by 7am, and got a bucket of water and some soap which I carried outside and started washing Dad's jeep. I climbed up on to the roof to wash it, it had to be clean otherwise Dad would pick out any dirt spots and I might have to wash it all over again. I polished the inside and then gave the car its customary warm up.

I then went out for a walk on an errand to find a local shop so that I could buy bread and eggs. It turned out to be a longer walk than I had hoped, the nearest shop I could find was all the way back in the main village.

A few days later Dad arrived home with one of his work pickup trucks a Peugeot 404, he had built some wardrobes at work, there was one each for Bisi and me and a double one for his room, this was our first real furniture for the house. We also had some entertainment: Bisi and I had found an old portable radio/cassette player with twin speakers so we could listen to music. We loved that radio player; we would sit in Bisi's room for hour after hour recording music from the radio onto cassettes whilst trying to cut out the constant DJ interruptions. We would also plug a microphone into the stereo and record our own songs so loud that the neighbours often heard us.

That summer holiday, the only furniture in our flat was our beds and wardrobes, one radio/cassette player and our modified table and brick seats, but Bisi and I were happy, we didn't care, at last we had our own home.

The week before we went back to school, we had been out all day with Dad at a party; we had seen some of my cousins including Femi and Tunde and had a good day. We headed home around 11pm; everyone was tired and ready for bed. Dad pulled up, we got out of the jeep and walked into our flat. Dad went for a shower while I said goodnight to Bisi. I then went to my room to get changed into some shorts, I opened my wardrobe and couldn't see any of my clothes, and then Bisi came running in screaming about the back door having been forced open. A few seconds later Dad checked his wardrobe to find all his clothes missing too. We had just been burgled and I could not believe it. We hardly had anything in the house and they had still bothered to break in and steal our clothes. Thankfully, they found our portable radio too shabby for their liking and at least left that for us.

Back at school, I was now a year 3 student and I had chosen to study physics, chemistry, biology, mathematics, English, geography and agriculture. My goal was still to study medicine, and if that didn't work out, then I wanted to do something in engineering.

It was just my luck and the luck of all the senior students that we no longer had a chemistry lecturer and GCK could not find a permanent one no matter how hard they tried. We sometimes were lucky to get part-time teachers, but they had to focus more on the senior classes and they charged the school heavy wages for their services.

I was still finishing top of year 3 overall, and my only weak subject was mathematics, I was petrified of the maths teacher, Mr Abiodun, he was the one teacher in the entire school you most definitely did not want to get on the wrong side of. His caning was lethal, he had the most perfect use of a cane that I ever saw in Nigeria, and it was punishment from him that made Dad's caning so mediocre to me.

If Mr Abiodun called you up in class to explain the previous day's formula you had to be on the ball, otherwise you were guaranteed strokes on the palm. I sat at the back of the class as I was the class prefect, and I used to try to hide down in my chair whenever he was looking to call someone up, he caught me off guard on many occasions and no matter how often I felt the impact of his ten strokes on my palm, I never cried, but I definitely never got used to them. On every single impact, I could feel and hear the impact of the stick on the bones in my hand, he actually once caught me firm on the thumb of my right hand, dislocating my thumb!

This also meant that for the rest of my school years in Nigeria, I had to make sure that no teacher ever caught my thumb again during caning. Of course I couldn't always avoid it, and so there were many times when I would have to carry my swollen thumb around for days.

Some students formed study groups where anyone who wanted to study and learn together could meet and share knowledge, I joined the chemistry and physics study groups, we had people from years 3, 4 and even 5 in the groups, all with varying depths of knowledge and we all took turns explaining theories, making formulae, and reading our text books. I joined the chemistry group because I knew I needed chemistry if I wanted to study medicine, and the physics class because of my fascination for the subject, I was renowned for my love of physics, I had read so many books and my knowledge at year 3 was very good. I also had the bonus of studying with one of Dad's colleagues during the holidays. His name was "Sunday" and he seemed to know everything and anything there was to know about Physics.

Dad rarely visited me now, for one he was really busy but also it was getting expensive to get around and I was very independent. But whenever he did come round, the only thing I wanted from him was pocket money, he would always ask me how much I had left over from his last visit and even if I had nothing left I would always make up that I was doing just about OK. Years later he found out that whenever he gave me my pocket money, I would either take a trip over to Bisi's college to give her some more money or I would send her some.

There are two incidents that will always live with me from Year 3; the first one was Dad's impromptu visits. He had been summoned by the principle to visit as I was probably the least visited student at GCK, so he brought an Uncle whom I had never met before along. Uncle Muda lived in Epe, a village just five miles from Ketu, so since Dad couldn't visit and could rarely pick me up for mid-term holidays; he wanted to introduce Uncle Muda as my guardian.

∞

On this day, I was called up to the principal's office and was shocked to see Dad there as I wasn't expecting him, they explained why he was there and all seemed to be going quite well, apart from Dad's continuous insistence that Uncle Muda had to keep me in check and severely discipline me if I was in the wrong, then as if to emphasise the point, he looked at me, pointing out the dirty uniform I had on, it was filthy, more grey than the white colour it used to be, he also asked if I brushed my teeth regularly as they were dirty and again he was right, I didn't brush as often as I should have, so he called me a "disgrace", asked for a cane and commenced to lash out strokes at me, all over my back and thighs, I had never seen him so angry before, even the principal had to calm him down.

For once he had made me cry, not just because of the caning, and not even because of the fact that he had embarrassed me in front of my new Uncle as well as the principle, but mainly because he had chosen to do this out of the principal's office and instead near the car park where just about any student nearby could see what was happening.

Looking back, I did learn my lesson, for the rest of my time at GCK I took the ultimate pride in my appearance, I knew that I had been too dirty, so I convinced Dad to get me some new school uniforms, and I washed them every day, I kept them perfectly white, and the same applied to my teeth and my general appearance.

The second incident was very different, I had been carrying an injury to the side of my left calf muscle for a while; I didn't know how I got the injury. It just seemed to have appeared! I had this very hard lumpy line along the calf muscle and when I touched it, the pain was bad. I had been to the College clinic a few times and they tried various treatments, from soothing it with ice, to massaging it with warm water but the swelling never went away.

A few nights later, I remember being in so much agony in bed, so I touched my thigh, where I could feel the pain, and realised that the hard lumpy line along my calf muscle had now extended all the way up my thigh, anyone who touched my leg could feel it immediately, I could barely walk. A couple of nights later the pain was unbearable so a senior student got me out of bed and took me over to the principal to explain the problem. The principal immediately insisted that I must go home the following morning. He knew that I didn't want to, I hated showing Dad that I had a problem which I couldn't deal with myself, but on this occasion I knew that he was right.

The following morning, Ayo, Festus and Augustine had helped me pack a bag, I knew I didn't have enough pocket money left to get me back home, but I hoped that I could still make it back somehow.

As it turned out, I was right in guessing that I didn't have enough money to get me all the way home. I just about had enough to get me to the outskirts of Lagos. I got off the last bus, and then started considering my options; the best bet was to take the 4-6 mile walk to Aunt Lola's house, in Ikeja. I knew she would be leaving for work by 5pm that evening, so I had to be quick, and just to make matters worse, it was raining.

I could barely stand on my badly swollen left leg, and here I was, trying to walk a few miles very briskly in the rain! I remember walking for what seemed like an eternity, I was restricted by my bad leg, but was determined to get to Ikeja in time.

As the rain got heavier, I had to keep wiping beads of rain away from my face and eyes just so that I could see ahead of me. I still remember Aunt Lola's surprise as she turned around and saw me limping towards her in the rain. To my relief I was just in time, she was standing by her car just about to set out for work.

Aunt Lola drove me over to Dad's, he was just as shocked as she had been to see me, he wanted to inspect my injured leg and within seconds, he was sure that he knew the cause as well as the cure for my injury. I said my thanks and waved goodbye to Aunt Lola.

I asked Dad what he thought was wrong with my leg, "You've been playing football and got yourself injured haven't you"? "No…" I responded, and before I could even finish that single word, Dad was yelling back… "YES".

I was quite used to Dad's method of arguing with us: his simple rule was that he was always right and no one was allowed to try to tell him otherwise. He would growl over you "YES" and it didn't matter how hard you tried to argue, you could not get a word in.

I had to back down and let him win, I kept muttering under my breath, I haven't been playing football, but I could hear Dad barking away " I pay this huge school fees for you to get an education and all you do is play football".

He told me that what I needed was a warm towel over my leg to help the bruising, so for the next couple of days, he would boil some water three times a day, dip a towel in, and then massage my leg. I had to go to work with him and sit around all day.

He worked at a company called Leo's Construction where he was the very well respected site manager; he was a very good architect. Dad's ambition had always been to run his own construction company in Nigeria, Leo's was a big company and was deemed as Dad's last step towards setting up his own business.

I would sit in his portakabin office on site, I took a few books with me so I could keep up with my studies. The most exciting parts of my day was looking forward to lunch and closing times.

One of Dad's best friends at the time was a man called Morbise, he was Dad's right-hand man at Leo's; he was a really funny man, always full of jokes. He had a deep slurry and growly kind of voice and seemed to know every joke in the book. He got on very well with Dad despite being about ten years younger, Dad was renowned for his quick fire jokes so he and Morbise were a good double act and they shared the same interest in construction as well as the ambition to run their own company.

Morbise was a breath of fresh air for me too, he walked into Dad's office and introduced himself to me, he asked me what book

I was reading and I showed him my "junior Physics" by Isaac Newton. His eyes lit up immediately, "wow physics! That's my favourite subject" he exclaimed, in my mind, I thought "here we go again" "someone else trying to cheer me up by wasting some of my time" Morbise sat down and showed me an easier way to calculate Velocity, distance and speed, within a few minutes he had my complete attention, it didn't take long for me to realise that this guy was a genius, after all I loved physics.

He asked me about my leg too and later suggested to Dad that the hot towel treatment on my leg was wrong, that I needed ice cubes run over it instead. Over the next few days, everyone had an opinion about the right treatment, one day it was warm water, the next it was ice cold, in the meantime, the swelling got worse, and soon a boil formed up on the side of my calf muscle.

On my fourth day at Leo's construction my injured leg took a turn for the worse. We arrived at work that morning, I settled down in Dad's office while he went out onto the site as usual. Within minutes, the boil that had formed on the side of my calf had started to weep. The pain was sudden and excruciating. I remember clutching my leg in shock and crying, I couldn't move to get help as the pain got worse. It seemed like an eternity as I continued to cry in agony when, as luck would have it, one of the foremen on site saw me crying. He was quick to alert Dad who came running in with Morbise, they could see that my injury was a lot worse than any of them had feared. They hustled me into one of Leo's Peugeot 404 Pickup vans, Dad drove while Morbise sat beside me in the front; we also had another worker sitting in the goods compartment.

Dad sped out through the gates and we jolted from left to right over the bumpy red clay road from the site. We soon joined the main road, where Dad put his foot down some more, within seconds we spotted flashing blue lights and Dad had to slow down for a police patrol man on his bike. I was not in the mood for this; I was in too much agony. He started to signal for us to pull over, as he moved up alongside us.

While we were driving, I had calmed down a little, I was trying to be brave but as soon as I saw the policeman wave us over, I decided to cry again, to show what sort of agony I was in and to leave him in no doubt as to why we were speeding. After Dad explained what was wrong, he told Dad to follow him as he gave us a police escort to the local hospital. Even in my pain, my relief was very clear as I managed a wry smile.

We pulled into hospital; Morbise thanked the patrolman offering him a 10 naira handshake, the policeman pocketed the cash and rode away. We rushed into the emergency unit where, within seconds my injury had been diagnosed, the treatment was to lance the boil.

I was led into a small room with Dad, Morbise and the foreman who had come along with us, I sat down in an upright office chair and watched a huge nurse rush around the room collecting a small aluminium pan, a pair of jagged edged scissors, some bandages and lots of tissues.

She asked everyone to hold me down while I sat. Dad was holding my right arm, Morbise my left, the foreman held down my right leg whilst the nurse balanced her huge frame on my left shin, just above my foot. Without further warning, she began to use the scissors to pry open the boil and the puss began to seep out faster, I couldn't believe the pain I was in, I struggled very hard to get free, determined to throw them all off, but I couldn't.

She then placed the pan directly under my leg and began to open up the wound a bit more, she pushed the scissors inside the wound until suddenly it began to bleed, I looked down, exhausted but still full of fight as little chunks of dark clotted blood poured out of my leg. A few seconds later, she paused, got off my leg and got another pan to place under the wound; I took a deep breath and calmed down a little. I could tell that I was over the worst of the pain, I'd been surprised by the treatment, but I now had a few seconds to pull myself together. Dad and Morbise let go of me as they looked at the state of my wound, I peered down too and could see a big hole in my calf, about two inches in radius, I could see deep inside my leg, the flesh and blood made me feel sick. The nurse asked me if I was OK and then asked everyone to get me ready for the last part.

Everyone held me down once more, the nurse sat on my bad leg again and began to clean out the rest of the clotted blood from inside my leg, and she then dressed the wound and gave Dad some pain killers for me.

Over the next couple of weeks, we had to return to hospital a few more times for treatment on the wound, the first couple of times involved a soaked piece of bandage being pulled out of my calf. It had been stuffed into the wound to soak up any more bad blood and it was painful to pull out as the flesh around the wound had started to heal.

Three weeks after the impromptu operation I was ready to go back to school. Dad saw me off to the interstate taxi park; I waved goodbye and was soon on my way.

The rumours about the future of the school continued right through the year, we kept hearing that there would no longer be boarding facilities next term. In 1981, the oil boom was over and now the buzz word in Nigeria was "austerity" we all learned the meaning and consequences very quickly. Everyone was affected; Nigeria had begun a steep decline from being one of the richest nations in Africa to just another very poor nation.

∞

Lagos, once the proud capital city of Nigeria was now suffering the effects of austerity just like the rest of the country. The once famous colleges were now a poor shadow of their old selves, many had closed down, businesses suffered in the same way, money was getting hard to come by, crime and corruption seemed the way forward for most.

Parents were finding it hard to afford the high school fees, and more and more students had to withdraw from schools all over the nation and look for jobs so that they could help to support their parents and families.

∞

By late 1981, the rumours were already rife that Government College Ketu, just like a lot of other colleges especially in Southern Nigeria, was on the brink of going bust. The College was struggling to raise funds, Government education budgets were being cut, GCK could no longer attract the best teachers, and the only good news was that it managed to keep most of the teachers who were already there.

It came as no surprise when in August 1982 we got a letter telling us that Government College Ketu had closed down its boarding facilities. Dad had already been weighing up the options, there weren't many schools left with boarding options and those that remained were very expensive. He also had to consider the quality of education at other colleges compared to GCK. In the end it was decided that I would move into Uncle Muda's flat in Epe and attend GCK from there.

I didn't know Uncle Muda well at the time, I had met him on a couple of occasions. He was my dad's cousin. His mum and Dad's mum were sisters. Uncle Muda was from Ibadan, the capital of Oyo State, which is the largest city in both Nigeria and Africa (larger than both Lagos and Cairo in geographical size). It is located in south-western Nigeria, 78 miles inland from Lagos and is a busy transit point between the coastal region and the areas to the north. Its total population was over 2.5 Million with over 1.3 million of them in central Ibadan.

Ibadan had been the centre of administration for the old Western Region of Nigeria since the days of British colonial rule, and parts of the city's ancient defensive walls still stand to this day. The principal inhabitants of the city are the Yoruba people.

Most natives of Ibadan had tribal markings on both cheeks; they were three straight lines down the jaw side sitting above three more parallel lines. Tribal markings were originally used to distinguish members of particular communities, but they were widely adopted as a kind of beautification. Of the over 250 ethnic groups in Nigeria, only a few forbid the practice.

Uncle Muda also had these tribal markings on both sides of his face, they were the first thing I noticed about him, he had a big friendly smile and spoke just enough English for me to feel comfortable with him.

It was yet another person to live with and I was initially unhappy about it. Ever since we had come to Nigeria, I had spent home time at Agege, Uncle Tony's, with Femi's dad in Ibadan, sometimes with aunt Lola, I had even spent the occasional day at Tunde's parents in Lagos. We were repeatedly uprooted and now, I was going to start living with Uncle Muda.

As it turned out, Uncle Muda was fun to be around, he had never travelled abroad in his life and had no ambitions to either but he was quick to treat me like a European as often as he could. He always spoke to me in English even though he knew I could now get by in Yoruba, and he left me to come in and out in the evenings as I wished, as long as I wasn't too late.

His apartment in Epe was a typical communal residence in the rural areas, as you approached the 2-storey block, you could see a "goods" shop on the left and a tailor's shop on the right, the tailor himself was sat outside of his shop in front of his sewing machine listening to some loud traditional music. There was a balcony above the shops which kept the tailor out of the direct glare of the burning sun.

You had to walk between the shops to the main entrance which led to a long communal hall way, on either side, there were six doors, each leading to a family's little rented one room bed-sit home.

Uncle Muda had the most expensive room of the ground floor

which was a double room: a small living room which led to another room, the bedroom.

All the other rooms on the ground floor were single rooms, so entire families had their living and bed rooms rolled into one, most of them didn't bother with TV, a radio was good enough and took up far less space in their little homes.

As I walked on through the hall exploring my new home, I said hello to other tenants I passed. Directly in front of me at the end of the hall were two little kerosene stoves, there was a woman cooking some traditional soup and you could pick up a whiff of the tasty aroma right through the hall. This little area was the communal kitchen. If both stoves were in use, you would have to wait your turn.

To the right of the kitchen was the communal toilet, three little cubicles each built with a floor of concrete for permanence and a small hole in the middle of the floor which was covered with a square piece of wood.

With this type of pit latrine, the pit is periodically emptied, usually by a pump mounted on a large truck which also carries a tank for storage. The waste is transported by road to a sewage treatment facility, or to be composted elsewhere.

No one bothered with toilet roll; it was cheaper to use old newspapers, which you softened by rustling in your hands. The other method was to pour water directly over your bum, wash with your left hand and then wash your hands afterwards.

Outside the back of the hall was a flight of stairs leading to similar communal homes and a similar lay out on the first floor.

By most of the standards around us, Uncle Muda lived in relative luxury, he had a double room, in which he had a small sofa, an old record player system, a "14" inch television and even room for a small coffee table in his front room. He had a double bed in the bedroom.

He did offer me a share of his double bed, but I chose to sleep on the sofa. My favourite thing in the flat was the record player, Uncle Muda had a lot of traditional Yoruba music, I had heard some of it before and never really enjoyed any of it, he also had one album by Fela Ransome Kuti called "Zombie" which was sung in pidgin English.

The A-Side of the album had the half hour long title track "Zombie" and the B-side had a half hour long track called "Mister Follow Follow"

I listened to the A-side and thoroughly enjoyed Fela's style of music which he called Afrobeat, essentially a fusion of jazz, funk and Traditional African Chant. It is characterized by having African style percussion, vocals, and musical structure, along with jazzy, funky horn sections. The "endless groove" is also used, in which a base rhythm of drums, muted guitar, and bass guitar are repeated throughout the song. This is a common technique in African and African-influenced musical styles, and can be seen in funk and hip-hop.

Fela's songs were almost always over ten minutes in length, some reaching the twenty or even thirty minute marks. This was one of many reasons that his music never reached a substantial degree of popularity outside of Africa. His songs were mostly sung in Pidgin English, although he also performed a few songs in the Yoruba language. Fela mainly played the saxophone and the keyboards but he also played the trumpet, horn, and guitar, he also did the occasional drum solo.

The lyrics of Zombie were very short but referred to the Nigerian military soldier, describing how they have no mind of their own but only do things to a leader's orders and move around like Zombies.

Fela was a rebel, often arrested and beaten up by police and various incumbent governments; He wrote about all the same things that I felt about Nigeria at the time. He wrote my kind of music and his rebellious ways suited me just fine.

The American Black Power movement influenced Fela's political views. He was also a supporter of Pan-Africanism and socialism (although in a 1982 documentary he can clearly be seen rejecting both capitalism and socialism in favour of a third way that he described as Africanism), and called for a united, democratic African republic. Fela also changed his middle name to "Anikulapo" (meaning "he who carries death in his pouch"), stating that his original middle name of Ransome was a slave name.

He was a fierce supporter of human rights, and many of his songs are direct attacks against dictatorships, specifically the militaristic governments of Nigeria in the 1970s and 1980s. Most of his songs referred to the level of corruption, injustice and dictatorship regimes in Nigeria, he even called leaders out by their names in his records, calling them international thieves, VIP's (Vagabonds in Power) and much more.

He was also a social commentator, and criticized his fellow Africans (especially the upper class) for betraying traditional African culture. The African culture he believed in also included having many wives (polygamy) and the Kalakuta Republic was formed in part as a polygamist colony.

I went on to buy many Fela albums in my time in Nigeria and he never ceased to impress me. Aunt Lola's house in Ikeja was just 5km from Fela's house. I walked by his house many times and saw him on a few occasions, I always felt like going up to say hello and tell him about how I came to be in Nigeria, but his entourage looked mean and I never actually plucked up the courage to visit.

Uncle Muda loved to boast about the fact that he had his nephew from The U.K. living with him, he was very good to me, but loved to show in public that he was teaching me how to live as a Nigerian, if I learned to cook a meal he would be up and down the hall screaming so that everyone knew that Yemi had just cooked eba, or a stew for the first time.

I got on well with most of the residents, I liked sitting down outside beside the tailor in the evenings as he sewed his garments. I always told him how my mum was also a really good tailor and dress designer back in England. I made sure I stayed out of trouble and greeted the local elders with the appropriate level of respect to.

One person who fascinated me was a skinny lady called "Mama Abiodun". In Nigeria a lot of parents were never referred to by their names instead they were labelled according to their first child, so my dad was also called "Baba Yemi" sometimes "Baba Bisi" because he was more often seen with her than me.

Mama Abiodun's little boy was about three years old at the time, the first time I came across her, I was sitting outside talking to the tailor one evening, whilst watching one of the tenants fetch a tub of water from the public taps, suddenly I saw the skinny lady screaming at the top of her voice in Yoruba "she was at the tap first" she exclaimed, within seconds it had become a scrap, Mama Abiodun was throwing left and right hooks, the other woman was pulling her hair, the scrap went on for a few more seconds, by this time they had ripped each other's clothes to bits. Mama Abiodun won the fight, seconds later; she brushed past me into her room trying to cover her naked body.

I just couldn't believe it! She was one wild woman, the tailor told me never to cross her, and he explained to me that this was an everyday occurrence. Apparently, once she got to the taps, she wasn't willing to wait in case the water tanks ran out. So she would pick a fight with the nearest victim.

Over the year I spent in Epe I saw her fight and beat many women, but she always had to run back indoors half naked. I thought she was mad. On a few occasions I did try to see if she would pick on me by going to the taps around her favourite times; she saw me there but never said a word.

I met her husband Baba Abiodun a few times; I would never have guessed he was her man. He was quiet, very polite and very hard working. The first time we got talking, he was interested in my science studies and invited me into their little room, I was a bit wary, but liked him. I walked in to their room, a large bed dominated most of the room, Abiodun's little cot was against one of the walls, they had a small sofa up against the opposite wall. I sat down and watched his wife stomp around the house.

He asked me to show him what we had studied at college that day and within seconds he had shown me so many easy formulas in both maths and physics; he was even more brilliant than Morbise!

I continued to go round to their place regularly and became the top student at physics and maths in college thanks to Baba Abiodun. Unfortunately, I stopped calling round one day when after Mama Abiodun had stormed in from yet another successful bout outdoors, he decided to stand up and tell her she had to stop embarrassing them. She glared at him and started yelling, he responded and then she slapped him right across the face and sent him flying across the bed and over by the cot on the floor. I stood there in amazement, I could still hear the slap ringing in my ears, I was furious, I wanted to jump at her, but I looked at Baba Abiodun, he was rubbing his jaw, he sat there for a while, then got up and never said a word.

I left their room still angry and spoiling for a fight, I tried harder over the next few days to antagonise her, I even jumped the water queue ahead of her, but she never took the bait. Her husband left her a few months later.

CHAPTER SIX

A SENIOR AT LAST

The first term of the school year 81/82 was an important one for me. I was now a fourth former and therefore a senior, there were many advantages to being a senior, obviously respect was a main factor, there was also less labour, less punishment and if you worked hard, you were also likely to be elected as a shadow prefect by the third term at which point the incumbent prefects need more time to focus on studying for the West African Examinations Council's (WAEC) GCEs.

I had gone through a lot of punishment in my years as a junior, I had been into many fights with seniors, I had seen my provisions or food taken off me on many occasions, I had slaved to one particular senior at some point, fetched water from the streams for seniors, cut grass till I had blisters all over my hands and been a guinea pig for many a seniors newly invented punishment. I was also frog marched around the boys dormitory all night which was my worst experience, but there had been many others inflicted on all juniors, there was a lot of bullying too.

I had made up my mind that once I got to year 5, I would take my turn bullying the freshmen and women and all other juniors, I kept telling myself, as did others, that payback would be so sweet. A lot of my classmates in year 4 couldn't wait to start strutting around in their new found power circle.

As it turned out, I couldn't do unto others as had been done to me, I saw all the new kids, and remembering how I had felt as a freshman realised how they must be feeling. I felt sorry for them. Most of the new kids were locals now as there was no longer any boarding facilities.

I kept my head down and rather than take my turn at pushing the younger kids around, as I had always planned to right from my first days at GCK, I actually looked out for them as much as I could. I took one or two of them under my wing and protected as well as advised them.

I continued to work hard at studies as well in the first term, the travelling from Epe to Ketu and back didn't really bother me much.

The mid-term holidays were spent again with Uncle Tony, Ade was there as well, we still argued, but without his mum about we didn't get into any fights. I had also started working out a lot more, I had bought a lot of "Mr Atlas" books to learn how he developed his body, I started boxing, I bought a bull worker, a chest expander, wrist grips, ankle weights, skipping ropes and much more, all from the pocket money I saved every term.

Bisi and I had also occasionally been in fights, as close as we were, we still had moments. I remember our very last physical fight very well. I had always been the stronger, our fights only lasted about 30 seconds, then Bisi would run off crying her heart out, I would look at her feeling all sorry, so I would walk over try to cuddle her and apologise, she always rebuffed my apologies until someone saw her crying and I got into trouble. This happened on all but one occasion, our last fight. On this occasion, as usual I went over to Bisi to apologise, I felt so sorry for her watching her, with her back to me, still crying from over half an hour ago. There was no adult in sight so she hadn't stopped crying, I put my arm around her and before I could say sorry, I felt a thud against my head, I went sprawling across the hall and realised she had just thumped me with an iron. The roles were reversed, I was the one crying now and Bisi was the one who got into trouble, much more trouble than I had been in.

By the time we returned to school after the holidays, I hadn't studied at all, I had played football, been out to see friends and spend time with Bisi. Now back in Epe, I was fairly popular so I spent a lot of time going to see Uncle Muda at his office in Epe Plywood or just out in town shopping. I was getting on OK in day to day lessons at school and was rarely late and never absent.

I was now the School shadow punctuality prefect, which meant I had to make sure that other students were early otherwise punished for being late to assembly.

My physics was better than ever, maths was still good, but we no longer had a chemistry teacher. Some of my classmates paid for private lessons but I studied on my own. I still spent a lot of time at school drawing comic books too.

By the time our final promotion exams came around in June 1982, I was having the best freedom I had enjoyed since being in Nigeria, the only thing that bothered me was that Mum still rarely wrote and I was getting fed up of begging her to communicate. The tone of my letters to her had changed too. I wanted her to know I was growing up and since she didn't want me, I didn't need a mommy either.

I sat my promotion exams and began to realise that I perhaps should have studied a bit more. When it was all over, I still felt quite confident, after all, I had always been within the top three in class right through my school life.

It came as a massive shock and let down to me, let alone Dad, when we got the exam report and I had failed. I had failed in maths, biology, chemistry and literature; I got only an average score in English language and geography and had actually passed only in physics and agriculture.

I had to repeat year 4. I could not believe it, how would I face my classmates who would now be my seniors? Bisi would also be in year 4, so we had caught up with each other again. Worse still, how do I remove the thunder in Dad's eyes? He was livid, worse than I had ever seen him, he asked me to show him my report sheet again, I picked it up from the floor where he had thrown it and walked back over to his armchair, he snatched it out of my hands again, "Look, you can't even pass English" he yelled and threw it away again.

"Bring that back to me" he yelled and he went over the whole process again this time complaining about another subject. This went on for what seemed an eternity.

The whole summer holiday seemed an eternity, I had to keep my head down, I was disappointed in myself, and I didn't need Dad to rub my nose in it at every opportunity. He had a new name for me which also hurt; he called me "olodo" which means dunce or roughly translated means scorer of zero's in class.

Anytime I did something wrong, said the wrong thing, or watched too much TV he'd be there to call me olodo. Uncle Tony also joined in telling me how my cousin Akin rarely watched TV and how he was always studying.

As a result of having to repeat my class, Uncle Tony also took the opportunity to seize the new portable cassette/Radio player I had just bought. I had saved up for it and it ended up in his bedroom.

Dad told me that I could no longer stay at Uncle Muda's and paid for me to stay at a mini dormitory set up by one of the maths teachers at GCK. Mr Folusho was one of the most feared teachers at GCK, no one was better with a cane, he whipped with such ease and flair that only the toughest would not cry after an encounter with him. He and his wife had set up a small dormitory for boys and girls on their premises which were just three miles from GCK.

I can't say I was looking forward to going back to college in September 1983, but it was still a huge relief to get away from home. There was nothing to look forward to at college, I didn't really like Mr Folusho by any means, how would I face my old classmates let alone my new classmates, I felt so ashamed.

Dad dropped me at the Folusho's dormitory; he spent some time with the teacher and was soon on his way after leaving me some pocket money.

Mrs Folusho was very welcoming and reassuring, this was their first time of running a project like this and they wanted it to work. Quite a few parents had tried to get their kids into the dormitory but they could only take 20 boys and 16 girls.

That evening Mr and Mrs Folusho showed us all around the compound, the girls' hostel was part of the main building, not far from the Folusho's living area. It was a very large room, big enough for eight double bunk beds. They had a poultry farm across the path opposite the main building; it housed about 100 battery caged hens. The boys' hostel was separated from the main building, just a further 200 yards away, it was a lot larger than the girls' hostel and had 10 double bunks.

Mr Folusho laid down the rules, leaving the premises for anything but college or authorised purposes was strictly forbidden, we had to wake up by 5am Monday to Friday and "lights out time" was 7:30pm. There was a compulsory study hour every evening where you could work on your own, as a team or help other students with their studies, this was carried out in the main play area between the boys and girls hostel. We also had housekeeping duties, the girls had to sweep around the whole compound every day and keep it clean, and we all had turns cooking for the entire group including the Folusho's. Cooking duties were done in groups of four, two people to wash the food, prepare and cook it; the other two did all the dishwashing afterwards.

Some of the boys had to cut the grass regularly while some of the more responsible ones were chosen to look after the poultry. I was one of only two poultry boys.

The poultry was something new and exciting for me for a while, duties included picking and counting all the laid eggs on a daily basis, looking for sick or dead hens and cleaning the cages as well as getting under the cages to scrape up all the hen droppings with a shovel.

As you went under the cages you just prayed the hens wouldn't do any of their droppings on you, it stank as you shovelled up too, but every evening the poultry farm looked good as new.

The sick hens were quickly killed and cooked for dinner; this put me off chicken for many years to come.

As the number of chickens increased, Mr Folusho decided to build a bigger better poultry shed so he bought bricks and cement and then chose four boys to help build the new chicken shed. I was one of the four, I learned how to mix cement, sand and water for the building, and how to make more building blocks, we dug the foundations and a few weeks later we had built a very good new chicken shed.

The girls were a quiet group, they usually did their errands and then stayed in their hostel gossiping. As for the boys, there was a good mix in age and seniority but we all got along very well. There was Godspower who was the tallest amongst us, he was quiet and a 3rd year student at the time, we also had Tobi, and his younger brother Funsho.

Tobi was new to GCK but he was a fifth former, he had transferred to GCK because his former college had closed down. He was born in England but came to Nigeria as a 3-year-old with his family, he loved the Jackson five especially Michael and his favourite word was "Beachcomber".

My worries about returning to college to repeat class were pretty much unfounded, I had told myself that I was in this situation due to my own faults, I kept reminding myself that I had to put up with the ignominy it brings as this will always remind me never to let it happen to me again.

When I did return, my old classmates who were now my seniors were shocked that I had to repeat class, there were a few others who were repeating with me, but most of them had been expecting it. Everyone was sympathetic towards me, I admitted that I hadn't studied hard enough; that I had grown too cocky and had forgotten what I was at college for.

I was nominated the class prefect for year 4, a duty which I tried to decline. I had a quiet time at college that term, I studied more than ever, I remember virtually reading my physics book from front to back which put me nearly one year ahead of my class.

One evening just before the promotion exams of 1984, an incident occurred that has stayed in my mind ever since. Everything seemed as usual on this night, my poultry duties had been done, we had all burned the candles at both ends studying for the forthcoming exams and we had since had dinner and gone to bed.

Suddenly, around 3am Mr Folusho walked into the boys' hostel and switched on the lights, he asked us all to get out of bed and come outside to the play area. We were all baffled as we stretched and asked each other what was going on. Mr Folusho was not in a good mood, he bawled at us to get a move on, so we put some clothes on and stepped outside, where Mrs Folusho and the girls were waiting.

He told us that he had been into our hostel and had tried to touch everyone on the chest to see if he could determine who had just been to disturb the girls in their hostel. It turned out that one of us had got up in the middle of the night, sneaked over to the girls' windows, ripped open the mosquito net that covered the window and with the aid of a stick tried to undress one of the girls who had then jumped out of bed screaming. Most of us boy's never heard a thing as our dormitory was not in the main building. It was clear that one of us was the culprit especially as our main door was still ajar when Mr Folusho sneaked in to check on us.

Mr Folusho asked us who the culprit was and threatened to punish all of us if no one owned up. The description from the girls was that they had seen a silhouette of a tall boy that seemed to match Godspower's description; even Mr Folusho had inkling that it could have been Godspower when he touched us all on the chest but he couldn't prove it.

He asked his wife to bring all his canes out and told us all that the punishment will be 50 lashes each. We knew he was bluffing, he was just trying to scare someone to own up or if anyone else knew and was trying to cover to let the beans out. He gave us our last warning as we all stood their shivering. "Right then, who's first" he bawled, I was still sure he was bluffing, it was Funsho who stepped forward.

Mr Folusho got up from his chair, put his glasses on and looked through his canes, he must have had at least 20 there, he found the one he needed, rubbed his hand up and down the cane, then asked Funsho to turn around, as he turned, the first whack hit his back, Funsho stumbled and ran forward. "OK, the count starts again Funsho, you broke my rhythm" Mr Folusho told him.

I stood there in disbelief as I watched Funsho take a total of 51 lashes on his back, his shirt had been torn open by the cane and I could already see his skin peeling and bleeding as he cried out loud.

"Who is next?" at this point I knew we were all in for it, so I stepped forward...

I had always done my best to stay on Mr Folusho's good side at school, his reputation as the most feared teacher with a cane was no joke. I remember he once dislocated my thumb while flogging me on my hands in class for not completing my homework.

Now I had just witnessed him dish out 51 lashes to someone's back with immense ease and accuracy. I stood there trembling a little, I really did not know what to expect. I had endured my fair share of the cane and whips in my time in Nigeria, but nothing like what I was about to experience now. I was annoyed inside, but I kept reminding myself to be brave, as I had done many times before both at school and home. I also kept telling myself that no matter how bad this was, I had to stay on my spot, so as not to have a repeat count.

The first lash hit my back, I yelled and ran forward out of the spot, and my eyes filled up. "get back here now, before I count to 10" he shouted, I took some deep breaths, he must have got to about 6 when I reluctantly returned to the spot to start my 50 lashes all over again.

This time I knew it was for real, I stood there and took stroke after stroke, yelping occasionally, jumping occasionally but making sure I stayed within the caning circle.

After what seemed more than an eternity, I heard one of the girls calling out '49, 50, that's it sir' I wanted to pass out, my back stung and hurt at the same time, I was livid, I stepped out of the circle Mr Folusho had drawn in the dusty ground and glared at one of the girls, I couldn't hold my tears back any longer, I think it was a mixture of having just had the worst whipping of my life for something I hadn't done, and the fact that I could hear one or two of the girls giggling that set me off. I started to cry, and then I saw one of the giggling girls and rushed at her calling her names.

Mr Folusho threatened to give me another 50 lashes, at this point I didn't really care, and I told him so. I asked if it was fair for the girls to be laughing as we got whipped bearing in mind that most of us had to be innocent. I told him I could take anything else he wanted to throw at me; I had no intention to be quiet or good now. My pride had already been whipped out of me; I couldn't care less for any threats he was going to throw at me.

One of the more quiet girls called Kemi then stood up and told the other girls that I was right; she told them not to laugh; after all there were some innocent boys amongst us.

We were not allowed to leave the play area even after the whippings, we had to stay and watch our fellow pupils get flogged too.

This was the worst single night of my life in Nigeria, I had scars and sores all over my back, but it was my pride that hurt the most. Next day at school, I was extremely quiet at class and out on the playgrounds, most students had heard what had happened the previous night and tried to be good to us.

I remained a lot more quiet than usual for several days after the flogging incident, I remember time after time, I would walk alone into the nearest bush, and start thinking about that night, how innocent myself and a lot of my friends were and yet how severely we had been punished for something we didn't do. I felt hatred at the way my life was going, I felt resentment at Mr Folusho for what we had done and at Godspower because everyone was still sure that he was the culprit.

I settled down one evening soon after and wrote a long letter to Mum telling her about the incident at Mr Folusho's, I told her how mad I was at her for not making any effort as far as I could see to try and find us let alone come and take us back to England. A lot had changed in my life since 1973, I knew I didn't need a mother anymore, in fact I had never really known what it felt like to have a mum with whom you shared a loving connection, instead in my mind, all she had become to me was my biological mum and that really hurt the most.

Kemi stayed a good friend to me, initially, like the other boys, I did not want to talk to any of the girls. We had all decided to stay away from the girls. As time went on, I realised that it wasn't their fault that we got caned, it shouldn't have happened but it still wasn't their fault. Kemi had come outside to the play area and sat with me on a few occasions trying to cheer me up; she would even offer me some of her food at dinner. Eventually she said something that I couldn't stop myself from laughing at, and the ice was broken.

She told me how the girls had been adamant that Godspower was the culprit of that night and how she wished the boys would gang up on him, I then told her that none of the boys spoke to him anymore. I soon convinced most of the other boys to talk to the girls again, but of course there were some who were still too mad.

Kemi became the closest to a girlfriend that I ever had at GCK. We were almost inseparable, she was a year 3 student, so a year below me, but we realised we got on well together. I helped her with some of her lessons and we studied together on the Folusho compounds.

By the time we got to mid-term that year, it was clear that everyone just needed to go away for the week and re-group themselves. Even Mr Folusho needed the break; he had decided to go away with his family. I had to go to Epe for my short break, because Dad was away, he had been offered a new job by the United Nations as a diplomatic architect and constructions advisor. It meant that he had to travel around Nigeria as well as to parts of Asia including India, Bhutan and Burma. He was going to be busy during our short break.

Uncle Muda had moved back to Ibadan, where he had found work and could now live at his own home with his wives and kids.

I missed him and wanted to see him, but this mid-term he had arranged for me to stay at his old flat in Epe with his friend Mr Peters who now lived there. Mr Peters was really nice, he was good to talk to, but I didn't see him much as he was always out overnight with one woman or another.

When we returned to the Folusho's a week later, everyone seemed to be in a better mood. Mr Folusho invited us all round a campfire in the play area where we all discussed our short breaks. The only student missing was Godspower who had moved to a different hostel.

We resumed our duties as usual, but Mr Folusho was keen to keep a good bond and spirit at the premises now. So every evening he would invite us all to squeeze into his family living room where we discussed social and economic matters together, we also took turns in choosing and providing the music that we would all listen to each night. Of course Tobi's choice was always The Jacksons or Michael Jackson. Most people had some soul or rare groove tracks; I hated most of the music from the 70's and early 80's maybe because it all came along in a period of my life where I wasn't happy.

My choice of music was from Jimmy Cliff. Jimmy Cliff was by far my favourite artist, I liked Bob Marley, Michael Jackson, Billy Ocean and of course Fela but Jimmy Cliff's fundamental reggae style was tops for me. Most of the students at the site found my choice odd and laughed at me, but Mr Folusho told them not to pre-judge, he asked them to listen to the music and the words. We listened to "Suffering in the land," "Vietnam" and the track I related to the most, "Time Will Tell".

The song focused on the story of a man recalling the question he asked his dad when he was just a six year old boy. He wanted to know what the future holds for him. His dad's response was simple "time alone will tell". Now as a grown man he finally understood what his dad had told him so many years earlier.

As it turned out, Jimmy Cliff was one of Mr Folusho's favourite artists too. From that evening on, I had established a bond with Mr Folusho, I suddenly felt more comfortable around him and we discussed new albums from Jimmy as soon as we could get hold of them. Of course for me it was more than just lyrics, I had grown up on Jimmy Cliff, my mum listened to him quite a lot when we were in England and this was my mother's roots showing in me.

In June 83, I was more prepared for the exam than I had ever been. I also had a huge advantage over most of my year 4 classmates in that I had studied at the same class level the previous year and had sat the exams before. I also had the benefit of experience behind me. I had failed once before and I wasn't going to let that happen again.

When the exams were all over two weeks later, I felt good within myself, I was sure I had done enough to pass, I felt happier to discuss the papers with my classmates than I had felt the previous year. The results arrived and I had been promoted to year 5. I had passed every paper very well apart from chemistry where I scored about average. I finished top of year 4 which was my goal, bearing in mind my year of experience. I was very proud and relived that I had made it to the final year at secondary school.

Dad still played his usual tricks; he wasn't impressed with my scores for one reason or the other. I had only scored 94% in English, so he would throw my report sheet across the room only for me to have to retrieve it for him. At least this time I saw him showing off my results to his friends.

That summer the three of us were at our new family home in Iju. Living at home in Iju was a huge experience and a defining moment for the sort of character that I grew up to become. There were lots of positives, and many negatives too, along the way.

We bought our first television a 14 inch colour TV which we were so proud of. It needed an electricity stabilizer to keep it in good condition due to the constant power losses. In Iju, you were guaranteed at least two power cuts a day and most evenings we only had half power at best which wasn't enough to switch on the TV.

Soon we had a three-seater sofa and two armchairs that Dad had made at work, then came the dining table and chairs, it was almost sad to throw out the old bricks we had been using.

Whenever Dad went out at the weekends, Bisi and I would get two empty milk tins and place them at either side of the centre of the table, we then balanced a plank of wood on top of them, we would get two small square pieces of ply wood and we would have ourselves a game of table tennis. We did this just about every weekend as soon as Dad had left and made sure we were all packed and cleaned up before he got back. There was one morning however; where we had got into our regular routine as soon as Dad left for the market. The plank was up and we had started the first game, just five minutes into it, Dad walked back in through the front door. I couldn't tell you who was more shocked. Bisi and I stood there as if frozen; Dad could not believe his eyes. He had come back because he forgot his wallet and caught us right in the middle of our secret game. Fortunately, he was in a good mood and he loved table tennis but that was the end of our hobby.

Bisi and I learned to cook properly. I could cook all sorts of traditional meals and stews from scratch. Dad was a very good cook; he was enjoying his bachelor life and loved to show everyone that he was an excellent cook who could cope very well on his own.

He loved a wide variety of meat; his favourites included beef, especially cow's foot, and other speciality beef cuts, he also loved goat, chicken, giant African snails, most varieties of fish and various bush-meat delicacies. I don't think there was many kinds of meat that he wouldn't eat, I once asked him if there was any meat he hadn't tried, he told me how great snake meat tasted but I just thought "no thanks". Bisi took after him as far as meat went. Even though she was very fussy generally about food, she liked some of the same meats as Dad apart from snake and snails. As for me I was a lot more reluctant to try most meats, right from when I had arrived in Nigeria I had decided that I would rather concentrate on the other parts of the meal than the meats. I limited myself to beef and fish in particular, although I liked fried giant African snails too. Initially I loved chicken but a few years later, after having worked on the Folusho's poultry farm, I had been put off chicken and didn't touch it again for years.

To learn to cook in Nigeria you had to know everything, you had to learn how to wash rice properly before cooking, how to pick pods and insects out of black-eyed beans before cooking, how to pick the right kind of cooking leaves, you needed to learn how to know the correct quantities of fresh tomatoes, little red chillies, large red peppers and onions which you needed to grind together to get the base for your stew, it shouldn't be so fiery that you couldn't taste anything else nor should it taste only of tomatoes; it had to perfectly right.

You also had to learn the basics of some of the meats used. If you went to the butcher's stalls in the markets, you needed to know all the types of meat required. In a single sitting at a traditional Yoruba meal, most adults could have five or more different varieties of meat with their food. In my case living with Dad meant that I also had to learn how to kill, pluck and cook hens. I didn't like this at all but I knew it was the way of life and ever since I had been in Nigeria I had always tried to prove that I could do anything that I wanted to do.

So after watching Dad a few times, I had learned how to get the hen out of its cage making sure it didn't escape because if it got away, you would have a daunting chase on your hands trying to retrieve a hen. Local boxers used to have hen catching as part of their training, they could have you running round the blocks bending from side to side and diving into the dirt whilst missing

123

them. So I had learned my lessons and always made sure that I lifted their wings up properly and lifted them out of the cage clasping both wings together in one hand. They would make a lot of noise but if you held tight they couldn't get away.

Before attempting to pick the hen out of its cage it was always best to have a sharp knife and bowl of water ready. Most people believed that it was cruel to let any animal see the knife it was going to be slaughtered with, so I always made sure mine was out of sight.

Lifting the fowl by its wings I would take it over to the small outdoor tap at the back of the house, then lay it down on its side placing its wings under my left foot, I then had to stretch out its legs and step on them with my right foot. Then I would bend down, place my left hand just under the hens head at the top of its neck taking care to make sure that I had covered its eyes and had its head tilted back then I had to get my knife and cut its throat taking care to make sure that I cut clean on the first attempt whilst not cutting its head right off. If the head was cut right off, blood would splutter everywhere, the dying hen will give an almighty struggle and with the spray of blood you would be forced to let go and I have actually seen people caught up in this scenario having to leave the headless fowl to run around till it died. Talk about chasing a headless chicken!

Once dead, the slaughter area is cleaned and all blood washed away. The fowl is then dipped into a pot of very hot water; this makes it easier to pluck its feathers.

Although I have never slaughtered a goat or cow, I have seen it done many times and had to help on a lot of occasions. With both these animals, the belief of keeping the knife out of their sight remains the same. In their case, as they are much larger animals, more space is required. A hole about a foot deep is usually dug in the ground to contain the blood flow. Three of the animals legs are tied together leaving just one hind leg free. Once it has been laid on its side, its ears are placed over its eyes while helpers hold the legs down to reduce the struggle. Usually Muslims say a very short

Young Mum &
Dad, London 1966

Bisi, Ricarda & Yemi 1972

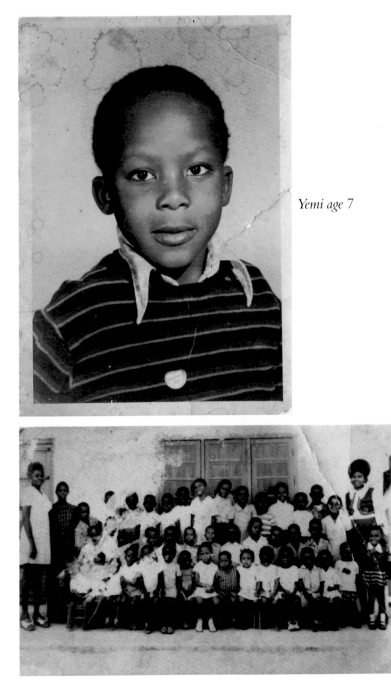

Yemi age 7

All Saints Primary School, 9th June 1974

Yemi, Bisi, 1977

Damian & Yemi, Nov 2000

Dad, Yemi & Uncle Muda 2004

2004 Dad with Uncles Joe & Tony

Dad's house

Yemi, Gani & Dad 2004

Dad in the UK 2010. Dad greets Uncle Charles

2010 Yemi and Dad at football in Bedfordshire

2010 Dad in the UK.
Left to right: Antonia, Yemi, Oliver, Dad, Shaya & Bisi

Mum busy at work 2013

Yemi, Uncle Derrick, Shaya, Mum & Step-Dad Feb 2013

Yemi and Jonathan Banjo

prayer before they slaughter the animal. Once the blood is all drained, the hole is filled in and the process of removing its hide begins. This is done by cutting a small slit about a couple of inches long in one of the hind legs, a long thin stick is then inserted down the slit and forced down the leg till it reaches the stomach area. The stick is then removed and someone blows into the slit as if blowing up a balloon with their mouth continuously until the animal is swollen pretty much like a balloon. The fur is then washed with warm soapy water and a few people with razors start to shave off the fur. I have done this many times.

Even now, I still find writing about things like this rather gruesome, it was also a factor as to why I was never the biggest fan of meat but it is part of life in many countries around the world.

I had to run every errand at home which I didn't mind too much. If we needed anything from the shops whatever time it was, I had to take the long walk up to the village centre. It came as a great relief when one day, I took the longer route from home and having only gone about 600 yards, I discovered that there was a local supermarket just about to open up. This was great news; it meant we could finally shop for everyday accessories locally.

On the day of first business I popped along to see if the store was any good, to my delight, it was reasonably big and had most of the amenities we would usually buy. The store was managed daily by the owner's two young sons Deji and Remi. Their dad owned the entire block, and they lived above the store. Deji was about my age while Remi was a couple of years younger. From the first time we met, we got on very well and all became good friends.

Whenever I was at home in Iju, I would go up to the shop at least twice a day and spend hours there just chatting about music, films, football and anything else that came to mind. They had a good business, they were the only local shop and they stocked good quality products, so they were always busy. Their parents had seen me in the store a few times and as long as I didn't disrupt their workflow, they didn't mind my presence. Quite the contrary was the case as I used to help them with deliveries and other work at the store.

I also made one other friend that holiday, a guy called Jide, he lived about half a kilometre from our home, he was a couple of years older than me and rented his own single room bed-sit in a block of single room flats similar to the one I lived in at Epe. He had just finished college, his dad lived in the same block but there was a lot of friction between father and son so his dad rented Jide his own room in the block.

He came to the store one day while I was there and overheard our conversation about music, he joined in and we immediately had mutual respect for one another. Jide invited me round to his place a few days later. I walked in to his tiny room, it was just about the size of my bedroom at home, but I was immediately impressed. In his small bed-sit he had managed to cram in a double bed, a study table, one armchair and a 15 inch colour TV but his pride and joy was his mini hi-fi system, it was a top of the range Sony and it sure stood out in his room. He had a good collection of tapes too. His favourite artist was Teddy Pendergrass.

Jide and I became really good friends and I spent a lot of time at his place. Dad knew that I had made a new friend but it took me a while to invite Jide round to ours, mainly because I didn't want him to see our tiny TV and our old faithful portable stereo. When he finally came round, he was just impressed at the size of our place and the fact that I had my own bedroom.

After a while, I grew less and less keen to go anywhere with Dad in his jeep especially in the evenings. He was a lady's man, I don't know if it was his looks or maybe he came across as rich, whatever it was, it worked for him. One evening Dad and I were on our way back from visiting Bisi at Aunt Lola's. Even though we now had our own home, Bisi still spent a lot of her holiday time at Aunt Lola's, Dad's reasoning was that it would help Bisi to live with a woman who would understand all her needs better.

I still had to spend parts of my holidays either at Uncle Tony's or at Uncle Duro's, Femi's dad. I was very reluctant; I couldn't understand why we still had to spend holidays at other people's houses especially since no one else ever had to spend their holidays at our place. Ade was always at his mum's in Ikenne, Femi always stayed at his dad's, so did Tunde, but we had to keep going round to everyone else's. I found it very frustrating and Dad knew. Besides, if I really wanted to see Femi, Tunde or any other cousin or Uncle, I could get to them by public transport quite easily.

As we made our way home that evening, I had a lot on my mind when Dad suddenly slammed on his brakes, he paused for a moment looking into his rear mirror and then he then started to reverse backwards. A few seconds later he we came to a halt again. "Get into the back" he told me, I didn't understand what was going on, but I opened the door, stepped out and lifted the front seat up as I squeezed my way into the back. Just as I settled into the back seat a lady came up to the passenger window, Dad spoke to her in Yoruba and a few seconds later she was in the car and coming back home with us.

This was soon a regular occurrence; I had seen some of the ladies before Dad had even stopped. By the time he had pulled over I was hopping out of the front seat and in to the back. Some of the women he picked up barely noticed me in the car.

Each morning that Dad had one of his visitors, he would get up around 5am to give them a quick lift back into town then he would come back home to get ready for work.

I decided to avoid travelling with him wherever possible. I decided that I hated having to jump in the back every time he wanted to pick up a woman, most of whom were not even polite enough to say hello to me. It turned out that we were sometimes going to the same place but I would leave home earlier and sometimes head back home before him.

I was also a very light sleeper back in those days. You only had to whisper my name, switch on a light or make just about any movement and I would wake up. This was quite handy for Dad as quite often he would come back home from a party in the early hours of the morning absolutely drunk. Somehow he could drive the jeep all the way back home and park it. Then he would pull himself out of the jeep, sometimes with the keys, other times without it. He would make his way down the alley round the side of the block to the back and over to my bedroom window where he would then whisper my name "Yemi" I woke up and made my way to the back of the house and then I would have to help him walk back around and into the house. I would undress him, take him into the shower if he had been sick and then put him in bed. It always amazed me that the same now helpless man had driven all the way home.

My final year at GCK soon arrived. The school year of 1983/84 was the one I had looked forward to ever since I came to GCK in September 1978. I remembered how I had always admired those seniors in their final year, how good it had been to see them visiting the school after they had graduated. Of course I wanted to be a prefect, I was looking forward to seeing the fresh students joining and most of all, there was no senior year above me, no more general labour for me at school. It felt good.

I was back at the Folusho's for one final year. They had fewer students than we had the previous year. Some had pulled out because the boarding fees were expensive and others just didn't want to repeat class.

As usual, I was back on poultry duty, I no longer ate chicken and I rarely ate any form of egg either. I had bought myself a new personal stereo to replace the one Uncle Tony seized from me previously, I also had a new collection of Jimmy Cliff albums alongside some Bob Marley and a few other artists.

I had studied hard during the holidays, especially on maths and physics; I was determined to be ahead of the class at the start of the term. Once back on the Folusho premises I continued to study regularly with Kemi. It was good to see that she was back too. We were still very close and were in many people's eyes officially boyfriend and girlfriend, although back then I was far too shy to ask her out right how she felt.

At college I was nominated the year 5 class prefect, which meant during class hours I was in charge of making sure that all students especially year 5 students and all the school prefects attended their respective classes and were well behaved in that period. It meant I was the last one in to each class as I had to check around the campus that everyone else was in class.

As prefects we were in charge of handing out and supervising general labour duties to the juniors which was mainly grass cutting duties on the campus just like I had done in the previous four years. It was now my turn to be lord of the manor and I was going to enjoy it. In the end however, my class repeating year had taught me to be more humble, I wanted to respect my classmates as well as the juniors. I was determined to help and encourage them rather than push them around unnecessarily. I remembered how I felt when I was a freshman. They had enough seniors ready to bully them anyway.

So if a junior wanted to talk to me, I was there and willing to listen and help. A boy called Hakeem came to me constantly; he wanted help with his studies and in return kept offering to run errands for me. I would send him on one or two errands occasionally but I was determined to do my own work for myself as much as possible.

Hakeem felt protected under my wing, if any senior wanted to bully him or punish him for being wrong, I intervened where necessary whilst making sure not to give him too much preferential treatment.

Soon after I met another year one student, a young girl called Nike, she was very pretty, all the senior boys seemed to like her; she was well dressed and very polite. I saw her doing her grass cutting duties and really struggling. One of the seniors had given the girls the same size plot as the boys because there was a lot of work to be done. Some year 5 students including me decided to help some of the young boys and girls with the grass cutting after all we were bigger, stronger and had a lot more experience.

It was during one of these sessions that I met Nike. I liked her, but I had always known that I was never going to try to date a student in their first couple of years at college; I didn't feel it was a well advised move. I went over to Nike and could see she was really struggling, so I offered to help her. I took her cutlass and did a lot of work for her; I left her with just a bit more to finish off while I went to the next student and started helping them. Later that day, I was on my way to catch the bus back to the Folusho's when Nike came running up to me calling out "Senior Yemi, Senior Yemi" I turned round and said hello.

She had come round to thank me for my work earlier, she really appreciated that a senior would consider helping the juniors and she told me that she wanted to be like that when she became a senior. It all made me feel good. I liked her politeness and the fact that she took time out to thank me. I told her that if she ever needed my help not to hesitate to come to me.

Next day, Nike came to find me at college, she had a bowl of rice and stew with her which her mum had cooked and asked her to give me. She was a local girl from Ketu village, her parents owned a small hut, her dad was a local butcher and she had three younger brothers who didn't go to school. Nike was the one her parents wanted to push to get a good education.

I couldn't believe that she or her mum would go through this much trouble, so that evening I walked with her up the road from college into the village to meet her mum, I thanked her for her kindness and spent a few minutes in their hut before I caught a bus back to the hostel.

Thereafter, Nike became my official "school daughter" in my final year at GCK. Having a school son or daughter was a regular thing at most schools in Nigeria, seniors saw it as a way of helping a younger kid, who would in return run errands for them. In my case with Nike, it was more a case of genuine admiration for each other. I looked after her, helped her with her studies and made sure she performed well in class. The other seniors knew she was my school daughter and never attempted to bully her.

In June 1984 I sat my West African Examinations Council (WAEC) O/Levels. I had prepared well; we still had no chemistry teacher so that was my weakest subject. Apart from chemistry, I felt good and quietly confident. After each paper, a few of us would get into groups to discuss the questions and answers, I would go into the groups but I didn't really want to know if I had got any questions wrong. I knew in my mind that I had struggled in the chemistry paper, apart from that I didn't want to come across as overconfident.

The holidays came round and it was time for the 5th formers to say their final goodbyes to GCK. There was the possibility of some of us returning the next year, but only if we hadn't passed the final exams. I said my goodbyes to all my teachers and friends and I promised Nike I would stay in touch to monitor how she progressed. Soon it was time to say goodbye to the Folusho's for the final time and all my fellow pupils at the hostel. All in all, I had learned a lot at the hostel, but the whippings from the previous year remained fresh on my mind.

Mr Folusho and his wife had decided not to carry on with the hostel next term; it had been too much of a burden for their family even though the money was good. I said goodbye and thanked them for their hospitality over the couple of years I had spent there.

When Dad picked me up from the hostel, I said goodbye to Kemi, we swapped addresses and promised to see each other during the holidays. We did meet up once or twice but our relationship never resumed and we soon lost contact.

I was so excited to see Bisi. I took one last look at GCK as we drove past it and I looked back on how great the college had been in 1978 and how bleak the future looked for the almost derelict college now, just six years later. I was a little sad to leave six years of memories behind but very pleased to see the back of GCK.

A few weeks later the West African Examinations Council or WAEC as it was better known, produced its exam results. I had failed chemistry but passed all other subjects very well. Now I could relax and think about A/Levels.

CHAPTER SEVEN

SURPRISE HOLIDAY

There was a major surprise for us that summer holiday, we had no idea that Dad had been planning this, but in August 1984 Dad told us that Bisi and I were going away on holiday to England to stay with Mum, 11 years since we had last seen her.

To this day, I still don't know how Mum and Dad communicated and agreed to this. Looking back, I don't think it was a comfortable decision for either of them, Dad's brothers and sisters had warned him that if he let us go, he might never see us again for one. Another factor was how could he even afford to send us away on holiday? Work wasn't exactly great at the time. For Mum there was the fact that she had since re-married, she still lived in the same old flat at Norland house but with her husband.

Bisi and I were also very confused, we hadn't seen Mum in over 11 years, last time I saw her I was not even 8, now here I was an 18 year old boy, I had never really known my mum, at school I used to tell my friends that I sometimes felt that I didn't have a mum or dad. I had always admired those who had close-knit families but could never imagine myself in a family like that. I had no idea how I was going to get on with Mum. What would I say, what could we buy her? I had no idea.

Dad had left us with no notice either, just like when we first came to Nigeria. It was just a matter of telling us that we were going to London to see Mum at the weekend. He told us that he had booked us on a four week holiday.

Even on the eve of us flying out, I remember Uncle Muda coming round and pleading with Dad not to let us go to England yet. His argument was that we simply won't come back. "Florence will hide their passports away, she will never put them on a plane back to Nigeria" he went on and on in Yoruba, I don't think he realised how much Yoruba I actually understood at the time. Also he had never even met nor spoken to my mum in his life! So how he knew what she would or would not do baffled me.

In the time we lived at Iju I realised that although Bisi and I had brought nothing with us from England when we left abruptly in 1973, Dad had actually taken all his main belongings with him. He had a briefcase which I had seen him stuff with letters from England in the past; he always hid it in his bedroom and made sure that it was securely locked. I was always curious to find out what actually happened between Mum and Dad, why Dad had felt that his only option was to smuggle us out of the UK and away from our mum and home without warning.

It didn't matter who we asked, if I wrote to Mum to ask, she would respond saying "ask your dad", if we asked Dad, he would tell us to ask Mum. I asked my uncles and aunts in Nigeria, and they all claimed not to know what went wrong "Lekan and Florence were really close, they never quarrelled" that was the usual answer I would get. Yet we knew that some of the Uncles, in particular the oldest two Uncle Joe from Agege and Uncle Duro, Femi's dad had played a pivotal role in Dad's decision to take us.

None of this did anything to dampen my curiosity so I took it upon myself to find out as much as I could. Whenever I was home alone, I would go into Dad's room and rummage through his drawers trying to find any memories or clues; once in a while I would find an old photo which only increased my determination to investigate. Soon I started concentrating on cracking the number code on his brief case lock. I put the case very close to my ear and turned each digit knob till I heard a slight click. In no time at all I had managed to crack it, I opened up the case whenever I had the opportunity and read letter after letter. They were mainly letters from Mum and Dad blaming one another, there were a few photos, our passports and some other documents but I couldn't find anything that gave me peace of mind or any answers.

The night before our flight to England I just couldn't sleep, thoughts and worries about Mum and what awaited us in England were swirling in my head. Dad had really caught us by surprise, I was more nervous than excited, yet I knew I wanted to see my old home once again, I knew I wanted to see my old toys, my school, my friends and much more. I was sure I wanted to see Mum too, but I was worried, I didn't know what to say to her, would she even recognise me? I had so many things on my mind.

The following morning, Dad and Uncle Muda drove us to Murtala Mohammed International airport in Lagos, Bisi and I were both unusually quiet that morning. Dad gave me our passports then he shook my hand, he then gave Bisi a big hug calling her his "only daughter" as he always did. He seemed confident that we would come back in four weeks, but he knew that this could also be the last time he saw us.

We made our way through customs now feeling a bit more excited, at last we could see that we were really going to England and we would soon be with Mum once again. We hadn't been on a plane since we came to Nigeria and we were very nervous. We waved goodbye to Dad and Uncle Muda at the departure gates and made our way into the lounge.

By the time we landed at Heathrow airport, I was more nervous than I ever thought I would be, I still didn't know how I would react nor what I would say when we finally saw Mum. Would she have a placard with our names on it at arrivals or would she really instantly recognise us.

I had written so many bad things to her in the recent months, I kept telling her how I didn't need her anymore, how I was a man now, and so much more. I also didn't really know how it felt to have a mum anymore. Once I realised that I had lost my mum, I became determined never to let any woman come close to trying to be a motherly figure to me.

Bisi was extremely close to Aunt Lola, so much so that she actually called her "Mummy" out of respect. A lot of young people called motherly figures "Mummy" in Nigeria even when they weren't their real mums; it was just another way of showing respect. Aunt Lola actually asked me one day why I insisted on calling her "Aunty" she wanted me to call her "Mummy" like Bisi did and although I knew she wasn't trying to replace my mum, I told her that I could never call anyone else "Mummy".

Aunt Lola wasn't best pleased by my reaction and for a while she tried to keep me away from visiting her. Years later she understood my feelings better and although she still never liked the fact that I insisted on calling her aunty, she took me back under her very caring umbrella.

As Bisi and I walked through to the arrivals lounge, I was convinced that Mum would need to hold a placard of some sort with our names written on it just to be sure. I knew she might recognise Bisi, but could she possibly recognise me too? I barely had time to think about what I would say to her or how I would greet her before we saw her. She hadn't changed a bit, she was as beautiful as I had always remembered her, she didn't look any older, she still had her huge smile and she looked exactly as I remember her from so many years ago.

We all recognised each other instantly, we walked over to Mum and as she hugged us as she burst into tears and pulled us closer, she sobbed for quite a while, I just continued to hold her.

Mum had come to the airport that day with her closest friend Aunt Winnie, partly because she didn't believe that Dad would really put us on a plane and fly us out, so Aunt Winnie was there to comfort her in case of any disappointment, she was also there to help Mum in case we really did turn up. So as we all stood there and continued to console one another, Aunt Winnie was busy explaining to anyone in the arrivals lounge near us who would listen about how Mum had lost her kids for nearly 12 years and what an emotional reunion it was. Aunt Winnie was just as relieved as Mum that we had really turned up.

Mum soon composed herself, we all had so many questions for one another, I wanted to know if she still lived at Norland House, was my old school still there? How about my old friend upstairs Beverly Brown, were Uncle Sam and Aunt Mary the older couple who used to babysit for us still alive, I had so many burning questions but I knew we had a whole month together and I wanted to take in the sights as we left Heathrow and I wanted to see how much I still remembered.

It was a very peculiar feeling, one I still struggle to fully describe, I was excited, I had waited very impatiently for this day from the moment I set foot in Nigeria nearly 12 years earlier, I had always wanted to see my mum again, to see her smile and to hear her call my name again. I wanted to feel like her son again and I wanted to see the life that had been taken away from us restored. But there was also a downside, I had written a lot of nasty things to Mum, she rarely wrote to us, I had forgotten what it even felt like to have a mum. I remember that I had written to tell her once that she was only my biological mum and how I was now a grown man who didn't need a mother any longer. So our first meeting was mixed with genuine excitement and a genuine amount of wariness.

Bisi was very quiet, she was very opinionated now and the fact that she had spent even less of her life with Mum than I had was clear. She was very excited to see Mum no doubt, but she knew Dad much better, he had been like a father and half a mother to her, so for Bisi the reunion must have been harder.

As Mum drove us home, we talked generally about life but steered away from the difficult subjects. Once we got to Shepherds Bush, the memories began to flood back. I knew where we were, I began to tell Mum the way home, I pointed out where my old school used to be, and all the places I used to play at. I was so excited

I had to beg Mum to drive up further around the block so I could take it all in. The memories kept flowing back. Then I saw the old Kentucky Fried Chicken restaurant that Bisi and I used to love going to and I started to cry. Fortunately it was dark, so I kept wiping my tears away as quickly as they flowed. I kept pointing out places to Mum almost as if to convince her beyond any reasonable doubt that it really was me, her long lost son.

Finally we drove back to Norland House, you couldn't miss the three tower blocks on Queensdale Crescent; they were each 22 storeys high and stood out in Shepherds Bush like a sore thumb. The buildings looked pretty much as I recalled them, but the surroundings had changed. There was a security gate that blocked the playground entrance now, there were security cameras around the premises and you needed a key fob to get through the communal door and towards the lifts, the days when kids could play in the park without a parent having to worry were over.

Once inside the communal hall, I raced ahead of Mum, Bisi and Aunt Winnie, I had already pressed the button to call for the lift. Once in the lift, just as Mum was about to ask me, I was already pressing the 15th floor button; we looked at each other and laughed. We got to the 15th floor and I was first out, I immediately turned right and headed towards number 119. The door seemed further away and much smaller than I remembered. Mum started to unlock the door but someone opened it from the inside and let us all in. We put our luggage down in the passage and Mum told us to take a seat in the living room.

The man who had opened the door to let us in was Owen, he was Mum's husband, they had met a few years after we went missing and they married in 1979. They had one son between them, Damian who was four years old when we met him.

In the little correspondence we had managed in the previous 11 years, Mum had neglected to mention that she was married or the fact that we had a little brother. It was not really an issue as it turned out, for one, I knew Mum and Dad were both old enough to do as they pleased but more significantly, Bisi and I loved Damian from the moment we set eyes on him.

He was an adorable little kid; he was initially shy and probably just as confused as we were. He kept popping into the living room to look at us or say hello then he would run into the kitchen to hug Mums leg. Sometimes Mum would have to call him away from staring at us. There was something about him that reminded me of how I once was when I was about his age.

I could see Mum's absolute pride and joy in Damian, he made her smile every time and he loved his mum. It pleased me how Mum would say from time to time how much Damian looked like I did when I was his age or whenever he was naughty she would tell him how his brother Yemi was such a good boy. I couldn't really remember if I was a good boy or not, but I guess I can't have been that bad as even to this day Mum still tells me what a good boy I was.

Owen was quick to try to make us feel comfortable, I liked him pretty much instantly but just like I didn't need another mum, I definitely didn't need another dad. Still I had the utmost respect for him. Like Mum, he was also Jamaican and had lived in England since he was a teenager. He had a family from his previous marriage but I knew nothing about them. He was about 6ft two inches tall, close to 15 stone and had a deep growling voice and an infectious laughter. His favourite word was "innit" and he loved to watch cricket. "the West Indies is gonna beat England innit?" you would hear him growl in his Jamaican accent from time to time.

I had never realised when I was a kid how strong Mum's Jamaican accent was, now she sometimes seemed like a different person but when she laughed, she had the happiest and sweetest laugh and I would have known that laughter anywhere.

The first day was a little awkward for everyone; we all had a lot of questions and we had to get to know each other a little better. I got up and washed early that morning, Damian was also up, he had come into the living room and switched the TV on to channel 3 just as Thames Television was starting for the day. As the Thames TV intro music came on Damian would hum at the top of his voice to the short tune, he did this every single time that little jingle came on and Bisi and I loved his enthusiasm.

That day we talked a lot about our education in Nigeria and some aspects of our life but Bisi and I could also see that Mum was not too interested in much about Nigeria and certainly not anything to do with Dad. Not once in any of our discussions did Mum talk about the day we left and what she did when she realised we were missing. The one thing I began to sense as the days went by was that Mum seemed to be blaming Bisi and me, maybe subconsciously, for going with Dad to Nigeria, at least that's how I felt and she did nothing to make me feel that I could have been wrong.

That morning Mum cooked up a lavish breakfast so we could all sit and dine as a family. We all sat at the table and Mum started to dish out some scrambled eggs onto Bisi's plate, Bisi and I both stopped her reminding her that Bisi didn't like eggs. In fact Bisi to the best of my memory had never liked eggs in her life but of course Mum had forgotten. A few moments later she asked me if I wanted baked beans again I had to remind her that I didn't like baked beans.

Bisi and I could both see the hurt in Mum's eyes. Naturally Mum could still remember more about me than she could Bisi, I say naturally since she had known me till I was nearly eight years old while Bisi had only just turned five when we left, also I was her first boy, at this stage I used to think I was her first child. (Years later I learned that Mum actually had two daughters before she met Dad).

So Mum remembered that I didn't like sugar, cakes and not too many sweet things she also remembered very clearly that I didn't eat fish, she was busy telling Owen how I couldn't eat fish as I had an allergic reaction which would cause my lips to swell. She was so proud that she remembered this that I felt so uneasy when I had to tell her that I had outgrown that particular allergy and now ate more fish than any other meat!

Bisi hated so many kinds of food you could write a book on what she didn't eat. Aside from eggs, she didn't like any other beans except baked beans, she hated most cereals, pasta, bacon, grapefruit, and the list went on so by the end of our fourth day, Mum had run out of patience and one day angrily asked us both to cook our own meals in future. I remember asking her why and her response was simple. "You don't like anything I cook". I was hurt and surprised she would react like that especially as I felt that I had told her over and over how much I loved and remembered her cooking and since the only food I didn't like was baked beans. I was angry and Bisi was even angrier so we started to cook our own meals from that day.

Mum still did the same old job she used to do when I was a kid. She was a self-employed clothes designer; she tailored hundreds of dresses at home for the likes of Marks & Spencer, Paul Smith and House of Fraser. I used to spend hours around her Singer sewing machine watching in awe as she tailored a lady's dress or a man's shirt and even now as an older boy I loved sitting next to her watching her sew and she still liked that.

She met Owen through work, he was also self-employed, he had a small truck which he used to collect completed dresses from tailors like Mum and deliver them to the high street stores in the West End of London.

While Bisi would stay at home with Damian and Mum, I went out every day with Owen to work. It was good for both of us as we got to know each other better; I saw it as an opportunity to be out and about while it meant that Owen could work faster since he had a helping hand. I enjoyed those days.

Each morning we went down to his little green Ford truck with bundles of finished clothes on their hangers from Mum, then we would do his usual rounds collecting more clothes. Once the rounds were done we would stop at a cafe for breakfast, and then head into the West End to make our deliveries and later collections. This took most of the day; sometimes we would stop for lunch if we were doing OK for time. We mainly talked about football, Owen wanted to talk cricket too but I didn't understand the game at the time. Owen paid me a little pocket money after each day's work.

Sometimes when we got home Mum would have cooked dinner for everyone but there were also times when Bisi and I had to then cook our own dinner.

In spite of our growing differences and disputes over food, there were some moments that made Mum proud, I loved grapefruits, Mum used to sprinkle a little salt on the fruit and then eat it when I was a kid, now I loved grapefruit so much and ate them just like Mum did with a pinch of salt, one of Mum's favourite musicians was Jimmy Cliff so once again we could talk about things we both enjoyed.

Mum was also amazed at the depth of my retention for things that happened when I was just a kid, for example I could even remember the colour of the hat I wore on my 3rd birthday and how I never ate cake, even at my own birthday parties. I also reminded her how I once won a lot of money from one of the slot machines at Madam Tussaurd's by putting a United States 5 cent coin in the slot when I had run out of pennies. I remember the machine just kept pouring out winnings it didn't seem to like my 5 cent coin at all which was great news. Mum whooped with joy as she collected all the money and then told me she would save it for me. I must have been about six at the time, but I remembered that moment so vividly Mum was surprised.

The relationship between Mum and Bisi was a bit frostier than mine with Mum, looking back, perhaps it could have been because they knew each other even less and Bisi was always less willing to forgive and forget as quickly as I was. For whatever reasons the relationship between the three of us started out promisingly but soon began to go downhill and there seemed nothing any of us could do to make it any better.

In the end I think the whole idea of us travelling to the UK to see Mum was planned and agreed in a rush without any thorough consideration. Nobody ever asked if we wanted to go or how we would feel, Mum should have written to invite us long before Dad decided to send us back to her, Mum should have told us about Damian and Owen so didn't come as a shock. I really wanted it to work. Although I had been mad at Mum for her poor communication and the fact that she never came to get us, and despite convincing myself that I didn't need a mother, I still wanted it to work.

I was back where I belonged, where I had been fighting and dreaming to come back to since that day in September 1973. Yet when Bisi and I sat down to talk, unbelievably, we both decided that we actually wanted to go back to Nigeria at the end of our month's holiday. I did not miss Nigeria for a second, but at that moment in time, I knew that I didn't belong at Norland House anymore; it was never going to be home to me again. Mum also needed more time in my opinion to decide how we would fit in to her life and to accept that her little kids had gone forever.

Even St James Norland School was no more, it had burnt down in a fire years ago and they had lost all their records. The school had been rebuilt but it was no longer known as St. James. All my dreams of going back to the school to ask them what happened the day after they realised that we had gone missing was now just a fantasy. There was so much I wanted to know but there was no-one to ask and nowhere to find that information.

Bisi and I both felt that we had to go back to Nigeria if we were given the choice but we knew it was in Mum's hands, after all, she had our passports.

For the next few days we did our best to see if we could make things work, Bisi and I loved playing with Damian, he was such a lovely boy and always had a smile on his face. I loved going downstairs to the park to play with him, I loved the thought of having a little brother and this was something I could see that Mum was really proud about. She wanted Damian and me to get along and we did. Bisi was no different; she had so much time for Damian.

143

A couple of days before our scheduled flight back to Nigeria neither Bisi nor I felt any more positive about staying any longer in England but we knew that if Mum didn't give us our passports back we would have to stay. We didn't know how to tell Mum that we needed our passports back; we couldn't even build up the courage to tell her that we wanted to go back to Nigeria. It would be the last straw for Mum I thought, she might never talk to us again, and she seemed to blame us for going with Dad to Nigeria in the first place, now we would be betraying her all over again. So it came as a surprise to us both when Mum asked if we had started packing our suitcases and if we needed to buy anything to take back with us.

I can't remember if I was more relieved that she had asked us, which meant she couldn't blame us, or If I was more disappointed that she didn't even ask if we would like to stay for even a day longer. It was a strange, awkward and tough last couple of days.

I was sad to be leaving Mum again, I could see that she was a little sad too, but it seemed to be the best situation for us all. She had a new family now, I loved Damian and liked Owen, but I was never going to call him "Dad" just as I was never going to call any other woman "Mum". There was not enough space in the flat for five of us to live in there too long and there was still friction between us and Mum.

Once again we were at Heathrow airport leaving England for Nigeria. At least this time we had our suitcases and we knew what we were doing and where we were going. We hugged Mum goodbye and promised to keep writing, she promised to try to write back more often and soon we were on our way back to Nigeria after just one month with Mum.

Dad was really glad to see us again, "my only daughter" he kept saying as he hugged Bisi; I just shook his hand. We talked all the way back home about England and all the old memories. Dad was certainly a little surprised that we chose to come back, I was sad to be back and I tried to make it clear that we came back because we had no choice, but Dad was not listening to that. As far as he was concerned, we needed him more than we needed our Mum.

I agreed, but in my mind, I knew that had Mum sat down and asked me just once what I really wanted, had she ever tried to explain what went wrong between her and Dad, I would have felt differently, had she refused to give us our passports back, I would have asked Bisi to stay. But it never happened so we were back with Dad who did want us back.

Coming back to Nigeria was definitely the lesser of two evils, as soon as we were back and settled down in Nigeria, I was back to my antics, I wanted to get away. I still didn't feel like I belonged in Nigeria. Some of the things I did at the time were just on instinct but looking back now, I can see why I behaved the way I did and it amazes me how the mind works, even one so young.

CHAPTER EIGHT

A' LEVELS

The Yoruba's love a good party, it didn't matter what the occasion was, an adult's birthday, kid's birthday, christening, funeral, wedding or anything else. If you were going to celebrate and throw a party, you did it in style! Months before the big day, the women would make a contribution towards buying a roll of material from which they would all have their dresses made for the party. The kind of meat slaughtered for the party was usually a good indication of the size of the event, with chickens being a small party, goats being a reasonable sized one and a cow or two meant a huge party.

The hosts would arrange for their local roads to be closed off to cars at the start of the party, if you were rich you would also pay a popular recording artist to perform live music, otherwise a DJ would do. You had to have at least two professional photographers and probably a video camera rolling as well. There was no such thing as a guest list, there was no need, everyone probably knew before you did that you were going to throw a party. Once you did invite one person, they told everyone they knew and soon the word had spread faster than any number of phone calls could ever do.

An average party would have at least 100 guests and you didn't even have to know the host. If you were lucky enough to mingle and no one spotted that you were a party crasher then you could eat and drink to your heart's content.

There would be a wide variety of food and enough women

running around to make sure absolutely everyone was full to the brim.

The family photographs were one of the most important moments of any party; it was the same in my family, that's how in later years you knew who had thrown the bigger or most memorable parties. The more genuine family members you had in one shot the greater the pedigree of your party and that's where one of my antics should have been more obvious to those adults around me.

At the time, I didn't know why I was doing it, but I had done so pretty much from the day I set foot in Nigeria and it was now part of my way. The build-up to a family shoot was always a lot of work, you had to get everyone to the same spot at the same time, in my dad's family which consisted of 10 siblings with numerous cousins, uncles, aunts and families of their own; it was a tough but necessary affair.

I never wanted to be part of the happy extended family, so I had a simple yet effective ploy, I always had plenty of advance warning that we were preparing for a big photo shoot, quite often I would volunteer to take the photo, since I was well respected as the gadgets guru, it always seemed logical to everyone that I should operate the camera especially as most of them didn't know how to switch it on. So I took the pictures and no one ever realised how easy it was for me not to appear in a family shot.

On the occasions when we had a professional photographer, I either still got away with offering to take an additional snap for a family member or I would pick that moment to go out on an errand that had been requested of me earlier.

While we had been away in England, Dad had been researching furiously for the best college for me to study for my A' Levels, there were a few obvious choices like some of the big Lagos colleges or even Mayflower which looked the most likely, however somewhere along the line a friend of Dad's told him about a new College far away in a town called Ilesha. Apparently it was privately owned and the rumour was that the college employed some top University lecturers on a part time basis. The level of education was meant to be second to none. It sounded good on paper. On the one hand I was pleased that it was far away from home, but I had never been to Ilesha before so that made me a little nervous.

It seemed like an opportunity too good not to at least investigate, so Dad and Uncle Tony decided to take a trip up to Ilesha to meet the college proprietor.

On their return from "Obokun College for GCE and Advanced Level Courses" as it was aptly named, Dad was beaming from ear to ear. "This college is fantastic, it's a new college, it's unique because they employ university lecturers" he told me, he was sure that it had to be one of the very best colleges for me. I was convinced too, I mean how could you fault a college that employed university lecturers? It was privately owned and they liked the proprietor very much and had already promised him that they had made up their mind to choose Obokun GCE as my next college.

I was pretty much fed up of the thought of yet another college in Nigeria, pretty much every school and college I had ever attended in Nigeria had been full of promise only to leave me hugely disappointed in the end. I felt sceptical towards Dad's enthusiasm for my new college; still it was hard to argue against the prospect of university lecturers and so on.

The good news for me, as it turned out, was that Bisi would also attend the same college, unfortunately, she had to re-sit her final year and re-take her O/Level exams. It was good news because it was the first time in over 10 years that Bisi and I would be at the same college again and get to see more of each other.

After a very long and rather quiet drive, we arrived at Obokun GCE; it was a late Saturday evening in September 1984. Dad dropped us off at the college, gave us our pocket money and soon we were waving goodbye to him.

This was registration and induction day for all the new students. I looked around as we headed up to the registration hall;

my first impressions of the new college were not great. The buildings were nowhere near as good as the old ones at GCK, it was a fairly small campus, to the left of me was a row of four classrooms all on one floor, ahead of us there were two more classrooms, a laboratory and a small library. On my right side as we passed through the main gates was the proprietors' office, the staff meeting room and the registration hall.

You could see the long queues leading to the registration hall; some people seemed to know each other perhaps they had been to the same secondary schools; while there were also a lot of nervous faces too. Bisi and I got in queue, we had our forms filled out and ready. The queue was slow moving, after about half an hour of slow progress I could overhear the registrar telling a girl that she needed to go back out and fill out a new form because she had made a mistake, she would then have to re-join the queue at the end which she wasn't pleased about, the more she tried to make her case the clearer it became that she was never going to win, so reluctantly she walked away from the registrar to go and fill out a new form.

I kept looking across to see who had been sent to the back of the queue, the first thing I saw was her legs, I just kept staring; I remember thinking wow, what beautiful legs. I looked up as she walked past me and she was so beautiful, never in my time in Nigeria had I been so attracted to any girl. By the time she came back with her completed form, we were near the front of the queue, for some reason, I asked her if she wanted to jump in ahead of me, she was very grateful, I could feel her frustrations and was just pleased to help.

After registering, Bisi and I headed towards the dormitories but I could not get the girl from the queue out of my head. I asked Bisi if she had noticed how pretty the girl was, Bisi just wasn't interested but I was not about to give up.

Bisi headed to the right towards the female dormitory I told her I would see her later at the Freshman's welcome party, I also asked her if she could find out my mystery girl's name at the very least.

The boys' hostel was about a 15 minute walk from the college campus, a narrow dusty path had been cut through the thick bushes it was just wide enough to fit one vehicle at a time. As I approached the dormitory, I noticed that the bushes were also getting thicker.

As usual, the hostel was a long narrow room with lots of small windows all fitted with mosquito nets and a row of double bunk beds on either side along the windows.

I picked out a top bunk and placed my mattress on it. Then I made my bed, set up my mosquito net and started to unpack my suitcase.

Unlike all the other schools and colleges I had ever attended in Nigeria, I started as a senior student at Obokun GCE. I was there on a two year term to study A/Level physics, chemistry and biology exams which was commonly called "PhyChemBio" on campus. I took A/Level chemistry in spite of it being my weakest subject.

Being a senior student from the outset meant that I had no worries of having to get into fights with senior students as I had done at GCK, it also meant that no one was going to kick me out of a top bunk bed.

By the time I had finished unpacking and securely padlocked away my most precious provisions in my little cupboard, I was ready to walk round the room, say hello to some of my new classmates and investigate the rest of the hostel grounds.

It turned out that I knew one or two of the boys from my time at GCK which was great, I also made friends with a set of twins called "Taiwo" and "Kehinde" these names were quite common among the Yoruba for twins. Taiwo refers to the first of the twins who came out to get a taste of life, while Kehinde means "Last one out".

I remember over hearing them talking about the English football league. Taiwo was an avid Manchester United fan and although I supported Queens Park Rangers as a kid, Liverpool Football Club was my favourite team and I had fallen in love with Liverpool F.C. after watching Kenny Dalglish play for them.

We were quite unaware of the intense rivalry between these two clubs and their supporters, the twins had never been to England, but that was Taiwo's dream. We would talk football nearly every night, with lots of other boys either joining in to listen or to pass on their own points of view. We also had a little transistor radio which we used to listen to football commentary on Saturdays.

My best friend at Obokun however was a boy called Charles; he was quiet, really polite and loved to lie in bed listening to Ray Parker Jnr. He knew many of the Parker Jnr. song lyrics word for word, I would listen to a lot of the songs with him and he turned me into a Ray Parker fan for life.

Charles was also an A-Level student and a freshman at Obokun; he was there to study law and economics. We took a walk around the hostel building on our first day there together and soon found the toilet which was about 500 yards from the actual hostel there was a very thin narrow path that led to the shabby aluminium built toilet. It looked like it had been built by someone in a hurry; you could rock the whole shanty building back and forth with very little effort. The toilet had eight cubicles, basically eight individual round holes in the ground, it was yet another pit latrine; I remember thinking that I would almost hug a normal toilet if I ever saw one again.

The bush all around the pit latrine was chest high at least and we knew there would be dozens of snakes around there.

I remember vividly one night a few weeks later I couldn't resist the urge to wake up and go out to the toilet any longer. I crept out of bed trying not to wake anyone in the dormitory, armed with my flashlight I headed out into the dark, the stars were out and it was a warm night. I pointed my torch in the direction of the toilet; 500 yards might as well have been 500 miles. I took a deep breath, said a little prayer and headed towards the path as fast as I could walk through the bushes.

You had to watch where you stepped, not only for the sake of trying not to step on a snake or scorpion which would obviously anger them, but also you didn't want to step in someone else's poo.

At night some students were too scared to take the horror walk to the toilet, so they improvised, they would discretely lay a couple of newspaper pages on the ground outside, not too far from the lights of the hostel, they would squat over the paper hoping that no one else could see or hear them. Once done, they would throw a "shot putt" which was the common slang for rolling up the paper and its contents and throwing them as far into the bushes as you could.

There was always a lot of poo to watch out for on the paths that lead to the toilet. I made my way into the latrine and checked for a reasonably clean pit which was also a rarity. I found an ideal one, pulled my shorts and pants down and squatted. A few minutes later with all sorts of thoughts going through my mind, my instinct had told me to look up at the shabby aluminium roof above my head, so I turned my flash light up towards the roof and there, wrapped around one of the planks that supported the roof, was a deadly poisonous green mamba. I was terrified; I shone my light away from the snake and took a sly glance around other parts of the roof where I spotted a couple more snakes looking comfortable. Immediately, I realised I didn't need the toilet anymore, I cleaned up slowly, stood up as quietly and carefully as I could. I was petrified as I took my first slow steps towards the exit.

I got out as fast as I could, yet it seemed like forever as I didn't want to disturb any of the snakes, as soon as I was out, I ran, I didn't care what I might step on, I needed to smash the 500 yard record back to the relative safety of the hostel.

That was the last time I ever went to the latrines on my own at night. From there on in, my options where clear to me. If I could not get anyone else to go with me in the dark, then it had to be the "shot putts" or hold it in until the morning.

I call the hostel relative safety as I also remember clearly coming back in to the hostel one afternoon for a siesta, the student who slept at the bottom of Charles' bunk was lucky to have picked up his pillow to fluff it up before lying down. Because under his pillow was a large python coiled up. He yelped and leapt backwards. None of us would touch that python as it was fairly big so we called out for help.

An elderly member of staff moved us all away from around the bed and managed to trap the snake into a big bag just as another snake poked its head out from under the bed spread. From that day onwards we always checked our beds thoroughly before getting in them.

In all my time in Nigeria, I was lucky never to have been bitten by a snake or stung by a scorpion. I knew a few people who weren't so lucky. I even remember one boy back at Mayflower being bitten on his buttocks while he sat in the grass.

It was time for the freshman's' party. I was looking forward to seeing my mystery girl from earlier in the day and I hoped that I wouldn't be too shy to ask her for a dance.

I still didn't know what to make of the college as we walked down the dark dusty lane back to the main campus. Of all the schools I had been to in Nigeria it was definitely in the most remote area; there was absolutely nothing else around within a mile of the college. My first impression of the college premises was that it was built cheaply but it looked well equipped. Only time would tell if Dad and Uncle Tony had made the right choice.

We walked into the large hall which had been made up of adjoining classrooms, some people were already dancing, the music was blaring and there were tables of food all around. Charles and I had a brief look round, I was looking for Bisi and my mystery girl, Charles was even shyer than me, he was looking for a quiet place to sit.

Bisi found us first, she had already made some friends and was looking quite happy; before I could ask… she whispered, "Her name is Yemi" it took a few seconds for the penny to drop. Wow, my mystery girl's name is Yemi too! What a coincidence I thought, I told myself that I really must get to know her now. Even when I did eventually spot her I was too shy, but both Charles and Bisi encouraged me to go over to her so eventually I did.

I can't remember what my first words were, whatever they were, she agreed to dance with me, she was so much more confident than me and she made every effort to put me at ease. After a few dances we sat down and talked for what seemed an age. Her full name was OyeYemi of course mine is AdeYemi but we both called ourselves Yemi. Her parents moved from England back to Nigeria just after she was born, she didn't remember England at all, but to me she was the most perfect companion to relate to.

Yemi had two brothers her older Brother was 10 years older than her and she, in turn, was 10 years older than her younger brother. She had such a gorgeous smile, I loved her eyes and it didn't take me long at all to ask if she would be my girlfriend and she was happy to say yes. From that day on we were pretty much inseparable. A lot of guys fancied her and tried to split us up, but to no avail. On campus we were the best known couple and people called us "Yemi squared"

Yemi was at Obokun on an A-Level course, she had come to study law and economics. She wanted to be a lawyer; her older brother was a trainee doctor.

She was my first real girlfriend, I was young and very naïve in love, but in Yemi I found a true soul mate. We helped each other settle into the new college and I think we would both have found it a lot more difficult without each other.

As Dad had already told us, Obokun hired University lecturers to work part time on the campus, so the quality of lessons was unquestionably high, we had a reasonably good science lab too and a class of just over 20 science students.

Although it was hard to fault Dad's choice, I never really liked the college, I hated its location, and it was the shabbiest of all the schools I had been to in Nigeria, it had the smallest playground and there was no football pitch at all.

In spite of all this, the first year pretty much whizzed by

without too many controversies. Yemi and I studied together quite often which was strange considering we were on entirely different courses. I loved reading her law and economics books, she took interest mainly in my lab-related lessons.

Bisi and I saw Dad less than ever before. He was working for the United Nations as a senior architect and advisor, he was travelling out of Nigeria to parts of Asia including Indonesia, and Bhutan and as Bisi and I were quite grown up, he didn't feel he needed to visit fortnightly like he had done in the past. Instead he now visited at most once a month.

Academically I had a good first year, I took it very seriously and was always amongst the top students in class. I passed my exams with flying colours and looked forward to my final year at the college. Yemi had also done well and got her promotion. We exchanged home addresses and I promised to come out and visit her during the term holidays. Bisi had passed her O-level exams and was going to move on to a different college. Before all that though, it was time to get away for a well-earned holiday at the end of July 1985.

1985 was time of changes in Nigeria; I was beginning to understand the word. "Austerity" and its implications, everywhere you went you heard it. Things were getting worse. The collapse of world oil prices and the sharp decline in output brought the precarious nature of the country's economic and financial position sharply into focus.

Corruption was rife in the government, there weren't many jobs and if you did find a job, you had to hope that your employer could afford to pay your wages. Food and other daily necessities had become very dear everywhere.

The officials were at it too, everyone seemed to want their share of dictatorship and corruption. The worsening economic and financial conditions along with the alleged widespread corruption led to the 1984 military coup which saw General Mohamadu Buhari oust President Shagari.

Nigeria's foreign debt had risen from around US $9 Billion in the early 1980s to over US $19Billion by 1985 and it was still rising.

Buhari had come in with a bucket-load of promises for reform, and how he was going to make Nigeria the pride of Africa again. Generally it was seen as a positive step for the country. He sought to reinforce the 1982 austerity measures by further tightening financial policies and introducing more administrative controls. The government also implemented draconian expenditure cuts and substantial tax increases. It dismissed close to 10,000 civil servants (almost five percent of the civil service). The expenditure cuts were successful in the short run, but as it turned out, his government fared little better than its predecessor.

Just before the completion of my 12th year in Nigeria, I witnessed yet another military coup. On the 27th of August 1985 there was a bloodless military coup that relied on mid-level officers who Major General Ibrahim Badamasi Babangida had silently and strategically positioned over the years.

He was a member of the Supreme Military Council under the Murtala Muhammad, Obasanjo, and Buhari regimes and had been involved in the 1975 and 1984 coups.

IBB, as he was popularly known, became Nigeria's first "military president" Babangida, promptly declared himself President and Commander in Chief of the Armed Forces and the ruling Supreme Military Council (an indication of his lust for power). He also set 1990 as the official deadline for a return to democracy and promised to bring an end to the human rights abuses perpetuated by the previous government.

Babangida was the 6th head of state since Bisi and I had been in Nigeria and only one, Shehu Shagari, had been democratically elected. All the others, General Yakubu Gowan, General Murtala Muhammad, General Olusegun Obasanjo, General Muhammadu Buhari and Major General Ibrahim Babangida had all become Head of State on the back of military coups. IBB was Nigeria's 6th military ruler and almost certainly the most powerful.

Military coups were always tense times for the public as well as for the personnel of the government that had just been overthrown. For us it meant curfew restrictions. From 6pm to 6am no one was allowed to leave their house or premises, Military and security forces patrolled the streets and set up checkpoints in neighbourhoods and streets. If you were found breaking these very strict curfews with no acceptable reason then you were in big trouble. If you were lucky, you would just spend two or three nights in jail, but in most cases you would have been, slapped, kicked and whipped by the military police before the mercy of a grotty prison cell.

For friends and family of the overthrown government, it was a definite time to panic, the incumbents had to know that you did not pose any kind of threat to them, so there was always a good chance of having their houses raided, they could end up in jail for very long periods without trial and even death could be on the cards.

As he strategically spread his political tentacles, IBB's first call was to release most of those jailed by his predecessor Buhari, including my favourite Nigerian music star, Fela Kuti who had been jailed in 1984 by the then incumbent military government on a dubious charge of currency smuggling. It was clear he had been jailed for his outspoken criticism of Buhari's government. His case was taken up by several human-rights groups and after 20 months he was finally released by IBB.

Nonetheless, Babangida went on to become a brutal dictator hated by millions

What all this meant for the average person was depression, no jobs, no money, no food etc. Life for Bisi and I hadn't changed too much in spite of all this after all we had never had much to start off with.

It was good to be back home. The following morning Jide popped round to see if I was back from college, we caught up on old times, he was now working as a part time mechanic and still didn't get on well with his dad. Jide and I would spend hours listening to music, watching movies and talking about our different experiences in living with our respective dads.

Dad was keen to know how we would summarise our first year at Obokun, Bisi was relieved not to be going back and I still couldn't entirely convince him that the college was more hype than reality.

I was determined never to have to repeat an exam again, so I studied diligently, as often as I could throughout the holidays but there were also a lot of other things I wanted to do, like visit some of my cousins, see some old friends, visit Bisi at Aunt Lola's and most of all I couldn't wait to see Yemi.

In those days we didn't have telephones at home and you couldn't rely on the national postage system so Yemi had told me that during the holidays she tended to be in most mornings looking after her younger brother, she told me to try coming over to her house any day I wanted, and that if she wasn't in she wouldn't be too far away.

So one morning after Dad had left for work I decided to try my luck, I was really excited and was hoping that she would be in. I bought a box of her favourite sweets and a t-shirt I knew she liked from my local market and then walked the half mile or so from home to the local bus stop.

I squeezed on to the first minibus headed from Iju to Agege, as usual the conductor was a young boy, probably 14 years old, he didn't have a seat on the now packed bus so he would hold on to a roof rack with one hand and then hang his head out the door swinging one leg and hand out of the speeding bus yelling "Agege" "Agege" at anyone walking trying to get more fare onto his full bus. He would then peer inside the bus and call out the names of the upcoming bus stops to see if any of his passengers wanted to disembark. The conductor also had to squeeze into the bus at some point to collect his fares from passengers who had recently boarded; there was no walking space on the minibuses so he had to lean his now sweaty body over other sweating passengers to reach over for my money. I handed him a note and then had to wait a few minutes till he had enough change to hand back to me.

Finally about half an hour and 16 stops later we arrived at the final destination in Agege. Agege bus stop was a busy one, it took up a long stretch of the very busy main road and there was a long queue of minibuses patiently waiting for their turn to load up. I could hear the conductor and driver of the loading minibus calling out "Iju" "Iju waterworks" "Iju" as they tried to attract passengers the other waiting drivers and conductors would be in a small group around some of the buses chatting.

The main road in Agege was not only busy with buses, it also had a market right beside the buses, so once you got off a bus, you would walk over the planks that bridged the smelly gutters and you were in the market. It was full of women selling anything from cooked snacks like "Puff Puff" and "Akara" (ground black-eyed beans mixed with chillies then fried in oil) there were the usual rice, beans and meat bukateria, there were fish markets, meat markets with flies buzzing all over them and stray dogs eating any waste meat they found on the ground, there were cloth shops and sweet shops. Then there were the little boys and girls who sold ice water in clear plastic bags, shoving them in your face before you could even climb out of the bus.

As busy as Agege was, it was nothing compared to Lagos which was the capital city at the time. I didn't travel to the heart of Lagos very often; I couldn't stand that mad rat race. To get to Yemi from Agege I had to get a Lagos-bound bus but I was only going to Ikeja a city I liked, and had lived in once before with my Uncle Tony, on the outskirts of Lagos.

The bus ride from Agege to Ikeja was a lot smoother as we were now travelling over better tarmac roads, I could smell the barley from the Guinness factory as we approached the busy industrial part of Ikeja. I loved that smell, I knew Aunt Lola worked at Guinness but I had never visited her there. A few more yards up from the Guinness factory and I shouted out "O Wa" in response to the conductors shout announcing "Ikeja roundabout bus stop". I didn't usually respond unless I had to, usually I would wait to see if anyone else was also stopping where I wanted to get off and let them respond. "O Wa" this simply meant yes there is someone who needs to get off here.

Having fought my way through a herd of passengers trying to rush on to the bus while I was disembarking, I then brushed my way past all the mobile sales people shoving their various goods in my face, I managed to get a bag of ice cold water from one of the little girls and soon I was walking past Uncle Tony's old house following the directions I had from Yemi. Her house was only about 800 yards from where we used to live.

I tried not to run those 800 yards in my excitement. Soon I was at the house, my heart was beating so fast, it had only been about 10 days since we waved bye to each other at college but I realised how much I had missed her and I hoped she felt the same. I knocked on the door and Yemi answered, she looked as beautiful as ever even though she was dressed so much more casually than she ever had been at college. Her smile was broad and cute and I just stood at the door for a second or so, shy and grinning, before she showed me in.

Soon we were both relaxed, we talked for ages about my life or what I remembered of it in England and about her parents living in England. We found it ironic that we had once both lived in Ikeja within 800 yards of each other but had never met. I also met her little brother Niyi, he was cute and had a lovely smile like his sister.

I was pleased that my visit had gone so well, Yemi even encouraged me to write to Mum again, so we sat down together and drafted a letter which she offered to post. I would visit Yemi and Niyi three more times that holiday, before we went back to college. About five hours later I decided it was time to go so that I could to beat the Lagos rush hour, known as the "Go-Slow".

The holidays were over and I was once again on my way back to college. It was a bright afternoon in September 1985, I had woken Dad up earlier to tell him I was packed and ready to go; of course all I needed from him was my travel fare, pocket money and term fees. He gave me the envelope with my fees and then a roll of naira bills for my travel and pocket money.

I thanked him, said goodbye and picked up my trusty old suitcase full of clothes and provisions as well as all my books. I then set out on my walk from home to Iju bus station, I had found out that it was only slightly more expensive for me to do the last leg of my journey by taxi rather than bus, the whole trip was about 300 miles and my total journey time over three busses was usually about five hours, I could save myself one and a half hours by paying a little extra and taking two buses and a taxi. The disadvantage of taking the taxi was that it left me with less pocket money for the term.

Still this was my preferred method of transport now. First the bus to Agege, which now meant that both me and my suitcase had to squeeze into one seat without barging other passengers with my case, so I would always wait for a bus that wasn't too busy and sit at the back, as Agege was the last stop I could be last off the bus. Then I would catch the 2nd bus to Ikeja from where I had a choice of bus or taxi to Ilesha.

All around me was the usual commotion, people selling everything, people begging for money and bus and taxi drivers screaming out their destinations, trying to attract potential passengers. I waited patiently and just kept telling any driver or conductor who asked me that I wasn't travelling yet. I always looked for a healthy looking taxi; the journey from Ikeja to Ilesha was still the best part of 260 miles so I wanted a clean taxi, one that didn't look like it would fall apart, one that looked like it could go fast and one with a driver who looked remotely smart. I also wanted to choose the front seat and I also had to be sure that they would carry no more than one passenger in the front seat.

Most of the taxis were Peugeot 504 Estates, which sat seven passengers comfortably but some rogue drivers would still try to squeeze 10 passengers in. I chose a nice 504, put my luggage in the boot and claimed the front seat. I knew it could be more than an hour's wait before the taxi was full and ready to go. Fortunately, half an hour later, six other passengers had joined us, the driver asked for his money so I gave him my 80.00 naira as did the other passengers. I whispered a little prayer in my mind knowing how scary the taxi rides where and soon we were on our way.

The boring part of the drive was always getting out of Ikeja and out of the Lagos principality, this was the rat race, vehicles blasting their horns, cars taking short cuts to avoid traffic by using the wrong side of the road, commuters fighting their way onto the congested buses, boys and girls with ice water, peanuts, sweets and various other commodities and then the red clay dust blowing into the car as you hit a part of non-tarmac road. It would take about half hour to get out of the city and onto the Lagos-Ibadan Expressway. This remains one of the busiest motor-ways in Nigeria with thousands of vehicles using it daily; it was also one of the most accident prone.

It was notorious for Lorries jack-knifing, for high speed accidents that nearly always resulted in fatalities as well as for hit and runs of poor villagers trying to cross this busy motorway.

Once in the open air of the expressway our taxi reached just over 85 miles an hour, a woman kept imploring the driver to slow down a little.. "Oga sir, make you slow down please sir, we are not in a hurry" but he would only acknowledge and just keep his foot stuck to the gas. I could hear the old man in the seat behind me snoring and further back there was another man who kept nodding off with his head on another passenger's shoulders.

I liked to go by taxi because of the time I could save but I was still nervous of the speeds and recklessness of their drivers. Dad didn't really like me taking the taxi either but he knew I was old enough to make my own choice between saving some of my pocket money or taking a five hour trip in a bus, sandwiched between other passengers.

Now that we were on the open road I let my mind wander away from the nervousness of the journey to review the long summer holiday that had just come to an end. Seeing Yemi a few times was definitely my highlight. On my last visit, we had discussed travelling back to college together but she told me that her parents always insisted on dropping her back. As we had no other means of communication aside from visiting or writing we agreed that we would look for each other once back on site.

I had visited Bisi and Aunt Lola a few times as well; I liked spending time with my cousins Yomi, Funmi and Bukki there. Yomi was the oldest of the three but still a lot younger than me, they were all lovely kids. Bisi was just relieved not to be going back to Obokun GCE.

Then there was Dad's new girlfriend. The story goes that he had gone to the University of Lagos campus to meet up with a girl he had picked up once before, on his way to the ladies hostel, he bumped into my cousin Tunde who was shocked to see his Uncle on campus. They told each other that they were visiting students on the campus and headed pretty much towards the same dormitory house before with relief they realised that at least they weren't there to see the same person. Tunde always remembered this story.

Her name was Mowunmi or Wunmi for short. I had met her a few times during the holidays; she would come over to the house regularly on a Friday and stay over till Sunday. She seemed o.k. I never tried to get too close and I wouldn't let her get too close to me, I wasn't used to having a Mum and no one else will ever fill that vacancy.

Anyway, I had seen so many girlfriends come and go, some stayed over some left in the middle of the night and a few lasted a bit longer. The only difference between Wunmi and any of Dad's previous girlfriends was that she was younger than any of them and she was a university student. I think she was only six years older than me which would have made her about 25 at the time.

Actually, there was one other difference; she had outlasted them all with the old man. I can't recall Dad having kept any of his other relationships for over a month at the very best. Yet he had met her long before my holidays and here they were still going strong more than four months on! Dad had even introduced her to his brothers and sisters and other members of the family. That was a major step because if the women in the family liked her they would keep Dad under pressure to start thinking about marrying her. She went with him as his partner to all parties and other meetings; it seemed as if the old man was settling down.

I had no reservations about Dad settling down again, after all this was now our 12th year in Nigeria, 12 whole years since Dad had last seen Mum. How time had flown!

I even remember asking Dad one day if he planned to marry again, he told Bisi and me that we were the most important people in his life and that he could not see himself settling down again. He asked us if we had any reservations and we both assured him that if he met someone who made him happy we would be happy for him. I always knew I would be happy to support Dad if he needed my endorsement as far as relationships go, I had decided that I didn't want him or my mum to give me any advice on my relationships as they had let me down. So I wasn't going to stand in the way of his happiness.

The one thing I made clear was that there was absolutely no danger of me ever calling another woman "Mum" I didn't want anyone to think that my mind would change with time and as long as they knew and understood that, I would respect them fully and treat them like family.

In the few times I had met Wunmi, I found her quiet, she was pretty and I was able to talk to her without many reservations. I just wondered if Dad would really settle down and get married.

CHAPTER NINE

THE CONFRONTATION WITH DAD

Suddenly I woke up! I must have dozed off briefly deep in my thoughts, but the taxi coming to a sudden stop woke me up. "Oga, wey your particulars" I heard the armed policeman ask our driver, I saw the driver put his arm with his clenched fist out of his window and pass some crumpled notes to the officer, a couple of quick smiles as if they were best of friends and they let us through. For the next few miles a few people talked to the driver about these corrupt policemen, he told us that he had only crumpled a couple of 1.00 naira notes together to fool the officers, he told us how much he hated them and how evil they could be should you fail to bribe them. Before he could even finish his story we were at the next police barricade.

We made one stop at a village market near Ibadan for a toilet break and an opportunity to buy some cheap food or stretch your legs. As soon as the car came to a halt there were people everywhere shoving their products through the car windows and at our faces, ice water, peanuts, fried fish, fried meat, chewing sticks, bread, palm wine, bottles of cola, roasted corn on the cob and much more it was a melee. Once upon a time I would have wound my window up before we stopped, but now it just seemed so rude to me to completely ignore all these people who had waited calmly for the next car to come along. They were just trying to make a living. So I bought some ice water and had a long debate with a few other people about why I wasn't buying things I didn't need from them.

It was close to 5pm when we finally arrived in Ilesha and I was keen to get to the campus just for the sake of getting out of the car. A couple of the original passengers had already disembarked and we had picked up one other along the way. ..." Ilesha is a town about 120 kilometres north-east of Ibadan with a population of about 100,000 at the time, on that Sunday evening I could barely see anyone. Soon we were on the shabby road that led to the college and my excitement grew.

I carried my suitcase and bags and walked along the narrow route towards the boys' dormitory, it was about a 10 minute walk from the main road to the dormitory and once in a while I would have to squeeze near the bushes to let a car go by as another parent dropped their son to the hostel.

It was good to see the old friends from last year especially Charles who had been dropped back a day earlier by his dad. I liked to come back on the Sunday before we went back to class, but some students were dropped on the Saturday. I had also heard sadly that the twins Taiwo and Kehinde wouldn't be coming back. As Taiwo had fallen ill and passed away. That was devastating news to all of us who knew him.

Soon my bed was made. I took the top bunk and Charles the bottom bed, he didn't like sleeping at the top which was fine by me. I relaxed on my bed for a while and just reminisced with Charles and a few other boys. Sometime later a new A' Level student called Lekan (my dad's namesake) came over and asked if I was Yemi, and then he handed me a note. It was from Yemi; she had arrived and sent a message to let me know that she was on the college campus in the law classroom waiting for me. Charles and I walked up to the campus together, we had to go there to pay our school fees which had gone up nearly 60% for the new term in spite of the crushing economy at the time. Charles was also on his way to meet up with his girlfriend.

It was great to see Yemi as usual, she was chatting with some of her friends; we hugged and then walked over to the admin offices together to pay our fees. We spent the rest of the evening talking generally and dancing at the annual freshman's' welcome party which had also been toned down this year.

On the first Monday, the college proprietor addressed the assembly, he welcomed all the new students and boasted about how this was the best college in the country. There was a warning for students who hadn't yet paid their fees to get it sorted quickly. Then the school prefects for 1985/1986 were announced. I was the new Laboratory Prefect which meant I had access to the lab keys; I was responsible for making sure we had all the equipment we needed. If any snakes were killed on the premises I could preserve them using formaldehyde and on a personal note it meant I could study in the lab with friends.

Things were going to plan at college, I kept to my principles from GCK now that I was a prefect again; I wasn't too pushy on the juniors and made friends with a few of them. I was now good friends with the new guy Lekan; he was a nice, tall and quiet lad. Another friend from the previous year was a guy called Daniel, he was from Eastern Nigeria in Benin not far from where Festus and Augustine where from.

We were in all the same classes so we became revision buddies. This year however, he was still waiting to pay his school fees and felt under pressure. His dad had recently lost his job and had now fallen ill, he was suffering from pneumonia. Daniel kept telling me how he had worked all through the holidays to raise some money for his final year, he had saved a portion of the fees needed and had tried to pay it into the school, but they had turned him down flat, they wanted the whole fees or nothing. I felt so sorry for him; he was a very bright student who had been clearly overlooked at the last minute for a prefect's role because of his issues with the fees. He was allowed to stay and study until after Christmas by which time he had to pay the balance.

The Christmas holidays soon came and then flew by and a few

weeks later in January 1986 I had travelled back to college by taxi again. Daniel was back too, his dad had died from pneumonia, he was still so sad, he told me how his dad had suffered and how he kept begging his children for forgiveness because he hadn't been able to send them all to school. He wanted Daniel as his oldest to fulfil his legacy. Daniel had worked through Christmas and now had more than two thirds of his fees, but still the college refused his payment point blank and gave him just two weeks to pay up in full.

Yemi and I, like all the other 2nd year A/Level students, were really busy now, we spent hours every evening studying most nights, then when it came to about 10pm the few of us boys who were studying would walk the girls back to their hostel before heading to ours, flashlight in hand.

We had fewer of the part time lecturers from the universities than we had had the previous year. Sometimes classes were held by students who just worked together to help one another. I also had a group of buddies about 10 of us including Daniel and Yemi who would all use the Lab for studying. We would stay there revising for our respective courses for hours after college had closed. We had kerosene lanterns and some had candles in case of the regular power cuts from the famous N.E.P.A (National Electric Power Authority). Then we also had flashlights to guide us back to our hostels in the dark. We would study till about 10pm, some would fall asleep over their books, others would say their goodnights and leave earlier.

On some nights, I would ask Daniel to look after the lab for me while I walked Yemi back to the hostel especially if none of her buddies where there. We worked so hard that final year especially as we were constantly short of lecturers. We were determined that our parents' money should not go to waste.

Just after my 20th birthday in February I got a letter from Dad telling me that he and Wunmi were planning to marry in March. He said it would be great if I could travel down to Iju to celebrate with them and that he would pick Bisi up from The Federal College of Arts where she was. He left it open to me because he wasn't sure whether I would want to go, he knew that I hated parties.

As usual I discussed it with Yemi, right from the outset I had made up my mind not to go but I wanted to know what she thought of me and my decision. Thankfully she understood, she supported me and told me she didn't know how to live without her parents. I can't remember why exactly I was intent on not going to the wedding but I think it would have been difficult for me to travel there and back, added to the fact that I didn't know Wunmi very well. I was pleased for Dad, but for me it brought back too many battered memories. So I wished him good luck and sent my apologies.

I later heard that the wedding had been a big affair and had gone down very well with the family. I was pleased for Dad and his new wife.

Just two months before my final exams, all hell broke loose at Obokun GCE! It was a Saturday afternoon in April 1986; I had seen Yemi in the morning and was now back at the dormitory, I had come back to hand-wash my clothes and I was also planning on having an afternoon nap. Charles and I had been listening to Ray Parker Jnr. and Michael Jackson's Thriller and Off the Wall albums for hours on our Sony cassette Walkman's. Now Charles was fast asleep and I had eventually nodded off too when I was suddenly awoken by Daniel's sobbing. He was packing his provisions into a bag, his bed was parallel to ours so I could see and hear him clearly.

"What's up Dan" I asked him, "I have been suspended from college the proprietor has told me to leave the campus until I can pay the fees in full" he told me and my heart sunk. I knew how much Daniel had suffered that term, we were struggling for lecturers, he had seen his dad lose his job, Daniel had worked throughout the summer and Christmas holidays then his dad had died, Daniel had to get into a university and hope for a scholarship, he knew he would have to be the father figure for his brother and sister in the near future and now, in spite of all his efforts he had been suspended.

I walked with Daniel over to the college campus because I thought I could help him, I had helped and advised a few of my classmates with all sorts of issues, some of the lecturers would always listen to me when I approached them and time after time we got a positive outcome.

This time however none of the lecturers could help me, this situation was out of their hands they told me that I would have to speak to the proprietor Dr Folorunsho as this was his decision.

I didn't like Dr Folorunsho at all, I had only been into his sprawling office once in my two years at the college and he was the man Uncle Tony had introduced to Dad as a friend which was how Bisi and I subsequently ended up at the college. His Office was definitely the best room on the whole campus; it was amazing that you could find so much luxury on our campus. Dr Folorunsho's favourite sentence whenever he addressed the college assembly was…"your fathers are all mellonaires" Even he knew the exorbitant amounts of money that he was charging and it was clear to him that if our parents could afford his fees then they must all be millionaires or "mellonaires" as he pronounced it.

With no other choice I decided to go and speak to Dr Folorunsho, I was probably the only student on the entire campus that felt brave enough to stand up to him, I had tried to approach him a couple of times before but never made it past his pit-bull of a secretary.

This time even as I walked up to her, she already knew why I might be there, "The Dr. is busy" she told me, I had heard that before, but this time I told her that I would sit down and wait. Daniel was not even allowed onto the campus, he was waiting for me outside by the gate. I waited and waited and about 45 minutes later a lady came out of his office, so I got up but the secretary rushed in to see him first then came out to tell me that he was far too busy today, I was sure that he had told her to get rid of me.

I told her that I wanted to wait for the proprietor, so I went over to the gate and told Daniel the situation and we decided that it was best he waited for me at the hostel.

I went back in and sat in reception for over two hours and still the proprietor would not come out of his office nor was I allowed in. I had decided that he would have to see me at some point even if it was when he had to go home and so I waited; suddenly I lost my patience after another young college girl had walked into reception straight past me and his secretary and into his office. I waited till she came back out of his office, then I got up, the receptionist warned me again "the Dr. has not got time for you" but this time I shot straight past her and into his office "Sir, I am sorry to come in like this…" I started to explain but Dr Folorunsho barked at me "Get out of my office now" I had no choice; I had to go back out in to reception.

I decided to wait outside of his office block so I didn't have to carry on listening to Dr Folorunsho's receptionist kissing her teeth and moaning to everyone about me.

Just after 6pm he emerged from his office, he was leaving for the day, I got up off the concrete step I had been sitting on and asked him if I could have a very quick word with him regarding Daniel, he told me again that he didn't care about anyone's family issues, he wanted his fees paid and that's the bottom line.

I did my best to explain that Daniel had lost his dad, that he had worked all holiday to try and make up all the money, that Daniel would pay the balance as soon as possible and how Daniel really needed this opportunity. "Look young man, I don't want to hear any more of this nonsense" he told me "Your fathers are all mellonaires maybe one of you can pay for him." At that point he had had enough of me, but I was fed up of him too, so I told him that the school fees were exorbitant and did not reflect the poor standard of education and facilities that the college had to offer. I told him he was cheating our parents by telling them lies and painting a very different picture to them about the college.

He was now livid, he growled at me telling me once again how he didn't care to listen to any soppy stories about our parents or their trials and tribulations at which point I looked him straight in the eye and said, "Well Sir, you are a thief. You are stealing from and cheating our parents, you have no lecturers here, if my dad does not know the truth, I do and I will make sure he finds out"

"That's it you are dismissed" "Get this boy out of my school now he is dismissed". Well he caught me by surprise, I couldn't believe it, but by now I was just as mad as he was and kept telling him that he was a "thief". Dr Folorunsho called for security to escort me off the college campus, he wanted them to see that I packed my stuff from the dormitory and handed in the lab key, he wanted me off the college premises immediately.

I walked back to the hostel with a security man behind me, and I started to wonder how on earth I was going to explain to Dad that I had been dismissed, not even suspended from college. Daniel had already been escorted off the premises too.

By the time I had packed all of my things into a suitcase and said goodbye to Charles and a few friends and then made my way back towards the college gate for my taxi, word had travelled around the campus. Everyone knew what had happened and the reaction was overwhelming for me. Nearly everyone I knew was inside the college campus and they were all protesting about my dismissal from the college, even some of our lecturers were upset about my situation. There were more than 100 people chanting outside the proprietors' office calling for Dr Folorunsho to come out but he wouldn't. The security guards closed the gates when they saw me. They had been instructed not to let me back in and in spite of the pleas of some of our lecturers, there was no turning back.

Yemi came outside the gates with a few of her friends to talk to me, she was so calm, she looked upset but she didn't want it to show. Instead she came straight over to me and we hugged and promised to stay in touch, she told me that she would do anything she could to help me with my studies and we both hoped that in a day or two that this would all calm down and common sense would prevail.

I said goodbye once again to Yemi and a lot of my classmates. I could still hear the protests on the campus as I turned away and walked on towards the taxi garage in Ilesha.

I was deep in thought throughout my three and a half hour taxi drive from Ilesha to Ikeja, I was grateful that the taxi didn't have to wait till it was full, which meant I didn't have to wait too long before we were on the road.

All the way back I kept thinking about my imminent meeting with Dad, I knew he would explode into one of his rages, he was bound to be mad at me this time.

I didn't think he would get his horse whip out, he rarely saw the need to use his horse whip on me nowadays, he still kept his beloved koboko just above the main door at home in Iju. The word "koboko" was originally used by the Hausas and Fulani of Northern Nigeria to describe a horse whip or a highly dreaded whip made of cow skin or horse tail and used by military officials in disciplining the unruly.

Dad knew that I could still take any whippings from him without too much fuss, so now his whip only came out if I had been really bad.

I had never really stood up to my dad, he had always been domineering and I could never argue with him, but this time for the first time in my life, my mind was made up. If Dad was going to shout at me then I was going to argue with him and I was not going to back down anymore. I was mad at him for not listening to me all the times I had tried to tell him what a joke that college was. I was in a foul mood after my confrontation with Dr Folorunsho and there was no way this time that I was going to let Dad belittle me again.

Soon we were in Ikeja. Two bus rides later and I was at Iju bus stop, I took my suitcase and walked down that familiar long dusty road home. Things hadn't changed much since I had last been in Iju four months ago apart from a few new buildings. As I approached home I also noticed that our landlord had now completed his block of four flats, he had built a flat above us and one above our neighbour Mr Gabrah. The landlord moved in above Mr Gabrah and we had a family move in above us.

Dad's car was in front of the house, I could always see the Nissan patrol jeep a few feet from home if it was there. I was surprised that Dad was not at work, I was expecting to wait outside the house until he got home, as I had done so many times before when I had come home unexpectedly. Sometimes I had waited till past 9pm before he would finally turn up to let me in.

This time he was there, my heart began to beat a little faster because I knew I was about to walk straight into my first confrontation with Dad.

I opened the little squeaky balcony gate, and walked straight into the living room. Dad was sitting there watching TV. I could see the shock on his face; he wasn't expecting to see me for another couple of months. "I have been dismissed from college" I told him before he could even ask. He sat down with no expression on his face as I explained calmly what had happened, then to my amazement, he smiled and said "that's o.k." he told me he would travel to Ilesha to see Dr Folorunsho, however he agreed with me that no matter the outcome I shouldn't have to go back there. Instead we agreed that I would study from home for my exams.

While I stood there gob-smacked, Dad went on to explain to me. At All Saints School I had stood up against bullies, at Mayflower I got into my first fight to protect someone else, at GCK I was constantly in fights or disputes with people twice my age if I felt someone else was being cheated, basically he told me, "You always stand up for other people" he continued "you always fight for what you believe in" and then he told me how he admired me for what I had tried to do for Daniel and that I had done the right thing.

Dad had caught me by surprise! I was ready to argue with him, I was ready to be kicked out of home but I was not ready for his calmness that evening.

Later that evening after dinner I asked Dad why he wasn't at work, he explained that Nigeria's austerity was getting worse. He had been made redundant with little compensation from The United Nations; they wanted younger staff who required far less in wages than an experienced graduate like Dad.

Nigeria was now in a period of rapid decline, it had exhausted its official reserves and borrowing limits, Nigeria built up its arrears on trade credit to US$6 billion by the end of 1983 and by 1986 it was more than US$10 billion in debt.

People were losing their jobs everywhere, businesses were closing down, parents could no longer afford to send their kids to school and commodities seemed more expensive than ever. Dad had lost his job, so had my friend Jide who was only working for his dad. Uncle Tony's business Holloway Motors was also in danger of going out of business, even Aunt Lola had lost her job of over 20 years at Guinness. The depression was everywhere.

Wunmi, Dad's wife was at university completing her degree so Dad and I spent a lot of time together at home. During the day I would stay in my room most of the time studying for my imminent A-Level exams. Dad rarely drove out now, he preferred to walk and catch a bus as this saved him petrol.

In June 1986 I sat my A-Level exams, and in late August the results came through, I had scored an "A" in Physics, "B" in Biology and an "E" in Chemistry. I was most proud of my chemistry result, in spite of the years of not having teachers and then lecturers for chemistry; at least I had not failed. It wasn't a score that would get me into medicine but I was proud of myself for having not failed. I don't think Dad ever went back to Ilesha to see Dr Folorunsho.

I had a choice between two universities which had both offered me places. One was the University of Agriculture in Ibadan and the other was University of Ife which was later rechristened by the government as the Obafemi Awolowo University. In the end I didn't go to either, we just couldn't afford it.

By late September 1986 the house at Iju was more packed than it had ever been. Wunmi had moved in permanently she also brought her niece Lolade along with her. Lolade was 10 at the time, she would use Bisi's bedroom whenever Bisi was away at Aunt Lola's or college, but now Bisi was also at home, so Lolade slept on a little mat in the living room. I found her a sweet little girl.

I also had a pet, a Labrador puppy that I named "Bullet". One of Uncle Tony's dogs had given birth to a litter of 10, they couldn't afford that many dogs, especially now in austerity, so he gave all the puppies away, I went for the cute brown puppy with a black snout. I loved Bullet; he was my first dog and a very cute one too.

Dad wasn't that fond of dogs but even he spent a lot of time playing with and feeding Bullet. He still couldn't find any reasonable job so he was happy to spend time with Bullet. In fact of the five of us at home, Wunmi was the only one with a steady job.

Yemi and I still met regularly, she had also been offered admission to The University of Ife to study law, it wasn't her first choice and she wasn't sure if her parents could afford to send her there. In the end they had to focus on getting her younger brother Niyi through secondary school so like me, she stayed at home studying and looking for work.

We broke up a few months later although we remained very good friends, it was clear to both of us that we had to break up: I was far too naive in love and she had outgrown me as girls tend to outgrow boys of a similar age. I was still asking her if I could kiss her while she was ready to go a lot further than I knew how to.

We talked about it and mutually agreed that we had to move on without each other. I was naturally very sad to break up with her, she was my first real girlfriend and my first love and I was hers, we promised to stay in touch and keep a good friendship, I was determined to stay friends which we did for about four more years before we finally lost contact with one another.

CHAPTER TEN

RECESSION

For a while, life without Yemi was really boring for me, even Dad had got to know her quite well. By the time we broke up even he wanted to know why we had decided to break up when we were still so close, all I could explain was that we were still as fond of each other but we were just growing apart.

It seemed that Dad and I had found a new level of mutual respect and appreciation of one another since the day I had come home expelled from college.

Maybe he had sensed in my mood that day, that I was ready to argue and stand up to him had he been his usual self, maybe for the first time, he saw me as a young man rather than that little seven-year-old from 1973. For whatever reason it might have been, we could suddenly talk man to man a little more often than before. I still wouldn't travel in his car with him that often, I never drank beer or any alcohol with him no matter how often he offered mainly because I had tasted his favourite beer "Harp" a couple of times and just hated the taste.

I was as tall as Dad now, which was no big feat as he was only about 5ft 4 inches tall, so if I sat outside on our balcony at night it wasn't unusual to have a grown up walk by, spotting my silhouette in the dark and calling me sir thinking they were greeting Dad. I would often reply in a low growly voice imitating Dad, he had seen me do it before and saw the funny side.

I was still good friends with Jide, we spent even more time

together now that I didn't have Yemi anymore, I had also became friends with the landlord's niece a girl called Laide who was quite good looking, I fancied her but also liked her as a friend, there was no chance of us being more than friends especially as we lived so close to each other and her Uncle was quite strict anyway.

Laide lived with her Uncle permanently as did her little sister Gbemi. She later introduced me to her older brother Dipo who only came to Iju sometimes during his holidays; we became good friends as we were the same age.

Across the road from home I had met another boy called Jide, he was a skinny younger boy, probably around 16 at the time, he had seen me go out for a jog a few mornings and one day asked if he could join me on my morning run, so we became jogging buddies, we went for a 5km run nearly every morning. Then there were the boys at the shop up the road, I still went over to see them and spend hours at their shop talking about football, music and films. There was a new book and stationary shop that had just opened up 300 yards up the road from them, it was going to bring them some competition but they were pretty much running a mini supermarket by then so they weren't too worried.

I found the occasional job too, things like poultry farm work, building jobs and other odd jobs so I always seemed to have a little pocket money that I saved. I was very conscious of the fact that Wunmi was still the only one with a full time job and Dad's money was clearly drying up fast now.

One day on a walk back from an odd job that my friend Jide and I had been on all day, we decided to have a look in at the new book and stationary store. Up until that point we had consciously chosen to avoid this shop through loyalty to our friends Deji and Remi and their mini Mart.

We knew that the new shop was predominantly targeting a different kind of business, but we still felt the need to be loyal. However, on that day we decided to have a look, it was a small and very neat shop, the owners had moved to our neighbourhood just a few months ago, they had built one of the biggest houses in the neighbourhood and their shop was located at the forecourt of the house. We looked around at the various books, a little girl, probably about five years old, was sitting on a small mat listening to her older sister, who I couldn't actually see, reading a story to her. They were the daughters of the shop owner.

Both Jide and I were impressed with the store, I bought a book by Chinua Achebe called "Things Fall Apart" I had owned this novel once before, in fact it was awarded to me at Ifako International one year for being the "Most disciplined student in school" ironic now that I had been expelled from college. Anyway, the novel had gone missing so this was my chance to replace it. Things Fall Apart was a staple book in schools throughout Africa and seen as the archetypal modern African novel in English. It depicted how colonialism and missionaries impacted traditional Igbo life.

I had read it many times over and still cherished it. I went over to the counter to pay, the older girl behind the counter put the story book she had been reading down slowly and our eyes met for the first time. I stood there almost speechless fortunately for me, so did she, somehow I mumbled a few words paid and walked out with Jide.

"You like her don't you?" he asked me. Damn! He knew me far too well. "Oh my God, she is gorgeous" I told him. "Don't you think so" I asked. He agreed, but he had a steady girlfriend now who he went to visit over in Agege every evening so he wasn't as excited about this girl as I was.

In spite of the crippling austerity I had registered for a subscription of a weekly news magazine at Deji and Remi's mini mart. The magazine "Newswatch" was first distributed in late January 1985, I can't remember how I came across the first edition or why of all the newspapers and magazines I had seen in 12 years in Nigeria, Newswatch was the one that caught my attention. From its inception it was a ground-breaking magazine in a country that was being ruled with an iron fist.

Even the daily newspapers were never written with true impartiality, the editors knew they were being scrutinised so they would do their best not to upset the government.

Newswatch however was different, it was very well written, the editors were bold and they would put the topics and issues that actually mattered to the masses on the front cover of their magazine. They were not afraid to be pointed and brutally honest; they were not biased and didn't think twice about putting the blame squarely on the government whenever necessary. They wrote openly about Babangida's brutal regime, the tortures and the corruption.

I was amazed that finally someone was willing to produce a magazine of this quality and freedom of speech and opinion in Nigeria.

The magazine also had four main columnists', who were the co-founders of the magazine Dele Giwa, Ray Ekpu, Dan Agbese and Yakubu Mohammed. Dele Giwa and Ray Ekpu were my favourite writers. I picked up the magazine every Monday and pretty much read it cover to cover every week. Eventually Dad took a passing interest in the magazine too.

On October 19th, 1986, Newswatch's editor in chief Dele Giwa was killed by a parcel bomb in his home. His wife and infant daughter were upstairs when the bomb exploded, and were unharmed. The magazine was shut down for six months in 1987 because of its critical coverage of government affairs.

According to Dele Giwa's lawyer, Gani Fawehinmi, State Security Service (SSS) officials had summoned the popular editor to their headquarters just 48 hours before he was killed. Giwa was accused of planning a social revolution and of smuggling arms into the country.

According to Nigerian press reports, the government's coat of arms even appeared on the outside of the fatal package. Although this was a high-profile murder that shook the entire nation and beyond, no one was ever prosecuted.

We welcomed 1986 in, in the usual optimistic and jovial

manner. Dad was out with friends and family, his wife Wunmi and her nephew where spending Christmas at her mum's and I was up, watching our 14 inch black and white TV in the living room. I had the main door open letting the cool breeze blow through the house. As we reached midnight I could hear people shouting down the street "happy New Year" in both English and Yoruba dialects. I could hear a few fireworks going off in the distance but otherwise it was a quieter night than usual. It was clear that the economic situation was taking its toll. Dad still didn't have a job. He had done a few hours a week with Uncle Tony over at Holloway Motors but now business had dried up there too and the overheads far outweighed the need.

It was the same all over the country, people were losing their jobs and source of income everywhere and yet prices kept going up.

I couldn't find any building or farm jobs at all; Jide had even lost his job as a mechanic at his dad's! Times were really tough. Some people improvised, they set up little kiosks in front of their half-built houses and sold just about anything, the problem then was that nearly everyone had something to sell but the bigger, longer-established shops had the better prices.

I prayed that 1986 would be a turning point for the country and for Dad; I hoped that I could go on to University and I prayed that I could remain optimistic. I knew in my heart that millions of Nigerians were praying all over the country.

I was still up staring at the TV when there was a power cut. All the lights went out as did the electric fan and TV. Great, another blackout. It was not even 1am on January 1st 1986 and all my hopes and enthusiasm had been quenched by electricity supplier, NEPA.

I fiddled my way around the house in pitch darkness; I made my way to the kitchen where I easily found the matches and candles. I lit a couple of candles and then two kerosene lanterns to brighten up the house, then I grabbed an old metal garden chair and went outside to the front of the house and sat down in the dark.

I did this quite often when we had a blackout, the breeze was always cool and comforting compared to the heat indoors with no fan. Sometimes I would take a book to read under the glare of a lantern but I preferred to sit in the dark that way I didn't have to say hello to people passing by if I didn't want to and a lot of people mistook me for Dad even if his jeep wasn't there.

I could hear Dad's jeep approaching, I could usually hear it from around the corner, and I knew the sound so well. I got up and moved my chair as his lights brightened up the whole building. A few seconds later he was parked and sitting beside me outside. We talked about another year gone by and our hopes for 1986. He was glad that in spite of all the tough times Wunmi still had a job. I didn't tell him, but that was my main concern going into the New Year.

Dad and I brought in very little income now, but we could still afford to contribute towards food and amenities, my worry was that Wunmi was paying more and now I didn't have a job at all nor did Dad. I wondered what would happen if we couldn't find an income soon. We were already more than five months in rent arrears and the landlord was constantly asking me if Dad had left any money for him. He also kept giving me deadlines to pass on to Dad. The landlord himself had lost his job.

The electricity never returned that night as Dad and I folded up our chairs and went to bed.

Since first seeing the girl at the new bookstore five weeks ago I had been back in there a couple of times and had seen her once more. I still didn't know her name. I bought one more book that I didn't actually need. It was another book by Chinua Achebe "No Longer at Ease" which was the sequel to "Things Fall Apart". It was another good novel but I had only bought it because I wanted to go and see the girl again.

A few days later I decided to go there again, I didn't need anything but I thought I would buy some airmail envelopes so I could write to Mum. My main motivation was to talk to this girl and see if I could get to know her.

I walked into the shop and was relieved to find her there on her own, even better she was as pleased to see me as I was to see her, from there on it was easy, we got on from the outset. Her name was Yetunde, she had a very sweet soft voice and she looked very shy. She was 18 years old so a couple of years younger than me. I told her I was going to be 20 in a week's time on February 17th.

She told me that her family had moved to Lagos from England when she was about four. They now found the hustle and bustle of Lagos far too much and so her dad had decided to buy a plot of land and build his big house in Iju. She had just finished her A-Levels and was contemplating what to do next. She didn't feel that even her parents could afford the university fees!

I told her about how we had come to live in Iju and how, when we moved there in the early 80's, ours had been the only building on our street and at that it had been unfinished and not painted. Now the neighbourhood had a lot more houses and we even had a partially tarmac road now. I told her about Mum and how we rarely wrote to each other anymore and she told me about her dad and how strict he was. They weren't allowed to go out and visit or make friends, she told me that I could stay and chat with her at the store all day if I wanted to but I would have to leave before 5pm as her dad would be livid if he saw me there with her.

She told me that her mum was rather quiet and wasn't by any means as strict as her dad but she would rather I didn't meet either of them. Coming from living with a dad who used to be pretty strict himself I fully understood her concerns and felt very privileged that of all the boys in the neighbourhood she had chosen to open up to me.

Yetunde's little sister soon joined us at the store; she had just come back from school. She was a student at one of my old schools Ifako International primary. Like her bigger sister she was also shy and I could see the surprise on her face when she saw me there. Yetunde and I continued to talk about our lives, education and music while her sister ate her dinner and then she lay out a little straw mat and took a nap.

By the time I left the shop that evening, I was smiling from ear to ear, Yetunde had asked me if I would come by the next day and she wanted me to come over as often as I could. I walked over to Jide's house still smiling.

Jide and I lay down on his bed and we talked about music and films as we always did. I told him that I had finally got talking to Yetunde and for once I had been to the bookshop and not bought anything. He was really pleased for me and told me that he thought she was really pretty, we watched a bit of TV and then went over to my house where we played table tennis on the dining table and then played a few rounds of draughts under the weak glow of electricity that NEPA was allowing us that night.

The next day, as promised, I went over to the shop to see Yetunde again. We were both glad to see each other and once again we talked from noon till close to 5pm. When I got up to leave, she handed me a neatly folded note and asked me to promise not to read it before I went to bed for the night. She also made me buy a pack of airmail envelopes as she felt that I should write to my mum.

I promised not to read the note before bedtime and also that I would write a letter to Mum that night. As usual I went over to Jide and we watched Nigeria's Green Eagles win an African Cup of Nations qualifying match against Ghana.

Once home, I said a quick hello to Wunmi and Lolade, then went round the back of the house to feed Bullet as I did every evening. Then I went straight to the privacy of my bedroom to read Yetunde's note. It was a lovely note, beautifully written in which she told me how pleased she was that we had met, she thought I was really nice and that she liked me a lot. She thanked me for being a good friend and wanted to know what I thought of her.

My bedroom consisted of my single bed, a double wardrobe a chair and desk all but the bed were built by Dad. I sat at my desk that night and replied to Yetunde in my best handwriting which was still a scribble. I told her that I liked her too, and that she was very beautiful and also a very nice person. I thanked her for wanting to spend time with me and for encouraging me to write to my mum too.

Then I wrote a letter to Mum, it was short, but I told her that I had finished my A-Levels and that I was now trying to decide what to do next. I told her that I missed her and asked her to extend my love to Damian and Owen.

The following morning I was back at the shop and gave Yetunde the note that I had written to her the previous evening, I also showed her Mum's letter. She looked pleased and surprised that I had done what she asked me to do. I told Yetunde about the problems at home. It had been over six months since Dad last had a job and he still couldn't find one. I still managed to find the odd job and brought in some money but it wasn't much. Wunmi was still the only one with a full time job and she was now pregnant. My relationship with Wunmi had deteriorated slightly, we were never close at any stage, but now with the added stress of money at home things had got worse.

I had made a conscious decision not to eat at home anymore unless it was food that Dad or I had bought. Wunmi pretty much bought 95 percent of all the food at home and I just had this feeling inside me that I would be empowering her if I let her pay and feed me too. I didn't dislike Wunmi but it had become very clear to both of us that we were as close as we were ever likely to be.

I told Bisi as well that I had chosen not to eat any food provided by Wunmi at home and Bisi agreed with me. She wasn't home very often anyway; even now she still spent most of her time at Aunt Lola's. When she was at home, we shopped for food together with what money I had, and we ate together. We tried not to make it too obvious, especially to Dad but also out of respect to Wunmi and Lolade. Usually I would politely tell them that I had eaten while I was out or that I would cook something later as it was too early for me to eat.

Yetunde and I had been talking for hours about our respective home lives and about the note that she had written me the previous evening and we still had so much to talk about, it was going so well. I knew that I really liked her and I hoped that she liked me too, so just before I had to leave her for the day, I asked the question that had been on the tip of my tongue all day: I asked her if she would be my girlfriend, I must have looked very nervous, I didn't want her to think I was like any of the other boys in the neighbourhood, especially not the rude or rough ones who just wanted any girlfriend they could have. Yetunde smiled, walked over to me and gave me a huge hug. "Yes" she said "Yes I would love to be your girlfriend" We both knew it wasn't going to be that easy, we were under no illusions of the tricky road we were about to travel; for one, her dad was a very strict man and his reaction would not be a favourable one should he find out that his daughter had a boyfriend, then there was the fact that Yetunde was rarely allowed to leave the premises of her house on her own. This meant I could only see her at the shop whenever she was there.

None of this deterred me though, I really liked her and I hoped that with time things might get easier. We talked about the disadvantages and about the trials and tribulations that we might face and about how careful we had to be, Yetunde was understandably more nervous than me but I promised her that I would be careful not to talk to too many people about us and that all I really wanted was for us to be a couple.

Over the next couple of months we stayed true to our promises, only Dad, Bisi and my friend Jide knew that I had a new girlfriend and Dad didn't even know who she was or that she only lived a few blocks away from us. Yetunde did her best to be at the shop as often as she possibly could without arousing her parents' suspicions by looking too keen. We wrote lots of little notes to each other, Yetunde always had a little note for me when I left her in the evenings and I would usually have one for her when I saw her in the morning. It was our way of staying together, and being a part of each other's lives from the distance of our respective homes.

Sometimes she would give me something that was precious to her like a watch or hair band that I could just keep under my pillow at night or she would take one of my shirts or drawings or wristwatch and smuggle it into her house and keep it overnight.

In spite of the fact that our only privacy was at the little book shop which was open to the public, I was having an amazing time, I was as happy as I could possibly be, I didn't let the negatives put me off. It was true that Yetunde and I had never seen each other off of her premises as friends would later point out, but as far as I was concerned, they didn't understand the pure joy and contentment we had found in one another.

To help me with the eating situation at home, Yetunde in her typical selfless and ever-caring manner had started cooking food for me! One morning I walked into the shop as usual, gave her a folded note that I had written the previous night and went to sit down when she handed me a present. It turned out that she had insisted on cooking dinner at home and had saved some rice and fish cooked in a lovely pepper sauce for me; she was now handing me a small covered Pyrex dish which she had carefully wrapped in some cloths to keep it warm and then put into a carrier bag. She handed it to me and told me that it was my dinner, she told me how she had been worried that I wasn't eating much and how she wanted to help. I hugged her and thanked her as she told me she would try to save some dinner for me as often as she could. I tried to tell her what a big and unnecessary risk she was taking, I tried to assure her that I was eating OK which was true most of the time but she knew the risks that she was taking much better than I could tell her.

Bisi and I had talked on numerous occasions over the years about having a little brother or sister, we both agreed that while we loved each other's company, it would have been cool to have had a little sibling to look after. I had seen lots of boys with bigger families at boarding school; I loved the thought of playing big brother. So when Dad told us in April 1986 that He was going to be a father again, perhaps I should have been more enthusiastic than I actually was.

To be honest I was genuinely pleased for him, I felt that he deserved it and I also hoped in my mind that this would be an opportunity for him to make amends for some of the wrongs that I felt he had done to Bisi and me as kids. I was also pleased for Wunmi, I wasn't close to her, but at least I could still talk to her or share the occasional joke and I didn't dislike her. Bisi on the other hand could not stand her at all. I know she was pleased for Dad and Wunmi just like I was, but her relationship with Wunmi was typical of women who felt threatened by each other.

I wasn't as happy as I had once thought I would have been at Dad's news because so many years had passed since I last dreamt of having a little brother or sister, their baby wasn't due till October of that year and I was already 20. The irony that I was old enough to be the baby's dad hadn't escaped me either; after all I knew a lot of my old school classmates who were already parents when we were still in secondary school.

There were also a few other issues on my mind, for example, we were nearly into mid-1986, Dad still hadn't found any permanent work, I was rarely working myself and I still had no plan of any sort for going on to university, it was looking like an unaffordable luxury. We were still in arrears at home and I knew that the landlord would have kicked us out but for his long term respect for Dad and the fact that we were his first tenants.

It was clear as daylight, Bisi was nearly 18, I was close to 21 and we were both still living at home with Dad and his wife who wanted nothing more than to start a family of her very own with her husband, she didn't need us around anymore than we needed her in our lives. So Bisi stayed away at Aunt Lola's because it was by far the more sensible situation for her.

As for me, I hated staying at any of my uncles or aunts but I would be out from morning till very late; come home to feed

Bullet, sit down outside on the balcony and chat with Dad then go to bed.

Just after Bisi's 18th birthday in June 1986, I started hearing rumours Bisi might be heading back to England permanently. I knew there was no way Dad could afford the fare for her flight so I didn't believe it could be true, that was until Bisi told me that Aunt Lola was going to book and pay for the flight. At first I was sceptical about Bisi going to England on her own, after all it was Bisi who had struggled to adapt much more than I had the last time we were in England. Of course that was now nearly four years ago and a lot had changed since that surprise trip.

Bisi confirmed what I already knew, which was that there was nothing left for her to do at all in Nigeria, what she needed was a change in her life and she needed to be in control of her own destiny.

I was surprised that Aunt Lola had offered to spend so much money on a flight for Bisi. she was, in my opinion, the most generous, open and probably the most caring of all Dad's siblings, so perhaps I shouldn't have been surprised but times were very hard in Nigeria for most, Aunt Lola included, she no longer had her lucrative Guinness job, instead she was running her own small shop from which she sold crates of beer and a few household accessories. Aunt Lola also had three children of her own to worry about, so this was a magnanimous gesture even by her standards,

By the time this idea arose, I had a poor relationship with Aunt Lola partly because of my reluctance to accept her as anything more than an aunty. I think she took my reluctance to refer to her as "Mummy" as part arrogance and part lack of appreciation for her generosity and kindness. I remember her once confronting me during a difference of opinion between us and saying "all that glitters is not gold". To this day, I don't know why she felt the need to aim that quote at me, I never asked her or any of my other uncles and aunts for anything. I was usually reluctant to ask Dad for anything! I wouldn't knowingly show any kind of rudeness nor was

I the kind to show a lack of respect to any of my uncles or aunts, however, Aunt Lola did feel insulted by my actions in this instance. So I decided that it would be best all round if I visited Bisi and my cousins Yomi, Funmi and Bukki less frequently at Aunt Lola's. I also tried to avoid communication with Aunt Lola where possible, which meant I would leave just before dinner even though I loved her cooking and had previously always waited until after dinner before I left.

Bisi had her problems and issues with Aunt Lola too, hers were understandable, for one there was the young girl who had now grown into a young lady having to debate her opinions with an experienced woman who had seen it all before, then there was the fact that Bisi pretty much found herself having to live with Aunt Lola because of the situation at Iju, she had all but officially vacated her bed and eventually her bedroom to Lolade. Her relationship with Wunmi was worse than mine and I don't think Dad had a clue how to bring up a teenage daughter anyhow.

At first I was disappointed that Bisi was leaving me and going back to England, we came to Nigeria together nearly 14 years ago and over that period of time we had shared our roller-coaster adolescence together, we had grown into young adults together and it didn't seem right for one of us to leave without the other, in truth my disappointment was short lived, I knew that if I could have saved the money up to pay for her flight myself, I would have. I was really happy that she could finally try to re-build her life in England without Mum or Dad.

There was still eight months of planning to do before Bisi would leave; the plan was for her to fly out to London some time in December, where she would then spend some time with the youngest of Dad's siblings Aunty Yinka who was already in England.

The inevitable question that friends and the few members of our extended family who knew about Bisi's imminent trip was "what about me, was I leaving too"? I hadn't thought about it much but when Yetunde asked me the same question a few days later, I realised that I wasn't ready to go back, I had just started a meaningful relationship with this beautiful girl and I did not want to leave her right then! I don't know if she believed me or if she was just as shocked as I was at my own revelation but for whatever reason, she never asked me again. I did tell her also that strangely enough, in spite of his married life and the imminent birth of their child, I felt that Dad needed me around at that moment, again I surprised myself.

In July that year, I stopped talking to Wunmi and Lolade completely. I came home from Yetunde's shop early one afternoon, usually I wouldn't show up at home till much later but Yetunde had to go to some university induction meeting with her parents, so we only had the morning to ourselves that day. I walked into our living room muttered a hello to them both, Dad wasn't in. Much as I liked Lolade, she had been trained by her aunt that I was not to be trusted, so now I barely spoke to her anymore.

I went round the back of the house to take Bullet out for an early walk, I noticed that he had just been fed, someone had given him some left over traditional food 'eba' and some meat, I was surprised because it was an unwritten rule that no one but me and on the rare occasion Dad feeds Bullet, even more surprising for me was that Bullet hadn't finished the food!

I was annoyed that he had been fed because it was now common knowledge to all but Dad that I did not eat any food at home unless I bought it and neither did my dog. Neither Wunmi nor Lolade admitted to feeding the dog although it was very obvious that Lolade was not allowed to speak. Once again I politely requested that no one feed Bullet and then I proceeded with my original plan of walking Bullet.

The next morning I popped round the back to take Bullet for his morning walk only to find him lying flat on his side, he was stone dead! He had died overnight, I didn't hear a sound from him during the night and apart from not eating much, he hadn't looked poorly.

I sat down on the cold concrete floor beside Bullet for a while pondering on how to play my next card. There was only two things that could happen now, I could either keep my calm and announce to everyone that Bullet had died in the night or I could go in all guns blazing and point the blame squarely at Wunmi and Lolade because I was sure even though I had no concrete proof that they had fed my dog something which they had never done before that day to my knowledge.

In the end, I buried Bullet quietly in a little patch of soil round the back, and then went back indoors. Dad was awake now and was wondering where I was, usually I would have been outside washing his jeep. Wunmi and Lolade were also in the living room, so I told Dad calmly, but clear enough that everyone could hear me that I had found Bullet dead this morning.

Dad was shocked, he knew I took good care of my dog, he knew that I always made sure it was well fed even if I was hungry for food, I can't recall what kind of reaction my news brought from Wunmi and Lolade because Dad was already asking me lots of questions. Later that evening I told him how I had come home early the previous evening and seen that someone had fed Bullet a lot of food. Dad was surprised at my revelation just as I had been when I first saw Bullet's food bowl.

Apart from the fact that it was unusual that anyone at home would have fed Bullet aside from me or Dad, I didn't jump to any conclusions straight away, but by the time Jide, Yetunde, and a few other friends had asked me if I thought Bullet could have been poisoned, I began to realise that that was what I did think but could not believe nor comprehend. Why would they poison the dog? Why? It just didn't make sense to me; did Wunmi hate me that much? I know we didn't talk much but I didn't dislike her, so why would she want to poison my dog?

On my next visit to Bisi I told her what had happened, then Aunt Lola overheard the news and she advised me to be very careful at home, especially with what I eat. So I told her that I didn't eat anything at home that I hadn't bought or cooked myself. A few days later, one quiet evening, I was sitting down in my favourite folding chair outside the front of our house, Wunmi and Lolade had gone to bed, and Dad was out at Agege. N.E.P.A had struck again, so the neighbourhood was dark and quiet. I had a candle near me which was flickering slowly in the wind, it was attracting a few insects as I sat there deep in my own thoughts while quietly gazing at the moon and stars. As usual, I could hear Dad's car approaching from about a street away before the lights from his jeep illuminated the whole house, temporarily blinding me as he drove up the drive. We exchanged hello's he went inside to get changed and I could hear him talking to Wunmi, then he came back outside, I had already got his folding chair ready, so he sat down, after a few minutes he leaned over to me and whispered "Yemi, I don't want you or Bisi to eat anything that Wunmi cooks any longer".

I sat there quietly for a further 10 seconds or so totally surprised by his request, wondering what could have brought it on and pondering how best to respond. Then I looked him straight in the eye and told him that I hadn't eaten any food cooked or bought by her for over three months and neither did Bisi whenever she was here. Dad shook his head and smiled, "I should have known better" he said, "trust you to foresee these kinds of situations". Dad knew well enough by now that I had rebelled all my life when necessary, he knew that I wouldn't knowingly give anyone a reason to feel that they had power over me or that they could influence my life but even he hadn't anticipated this revelation.

I used to keep a little notebook in which I wrote quotations that I had either read or heard in the news on TV at college or elsewhere. One of my favourite quotations was a very simple one that I still use quite often, many people have heard me say "If knowledge is power, then secret knowledge is secret power" ironically, I can't remember who this quote was attributed to. I recited this quotation to Dad explaining that although I never told Wunmi outright not to cook for me, she must have been fully aware that I didn't eat anything that came from her and I knew that this must have really irritated her.

Dad explained to me how having discussed the incident of Bullet's death with some of his brothers they had all concluded that he most likely had been poisoned, so he had come home a few days ago and asked her if she had indeed fed Bullet and could she have given him something that had gone off for example. A big row developed between them and in her outrage she boasted about being the main breadwinner in the house, and how if it wasn't for her we would all be starving, and how she was fed up of having to cook for someone else's grown up children who had no respect for her in her house and so on. So Dad told her that he would ask us not to eat food provided by her anymore; which brought about our chat that night.

This still didn't tell me if Bullet had been poisoned or not and if he had been, was it intentional or accidental? But what had become abundantly clear to me, and now to Dad, was that I had made the right decision three months ago.

The punches just kept hitting me in 1986. One day in August my relationship with Yetunde came to an unexpected and abrupt end. I hadn't seen her for about a week mainly because she hadn't been in the shop much but also because I was trying to spend more time with Bisi now before she left. On this day I walked up more in hope that she might be in the shop, I had a feeling that something was wrong. She was there alone and my heart began to race with excitement but when I walked in smiling and said hello then saw her sad face I knew that she had bad news for me.

"Someone told my dad that they keep seeing a boy with me in the shop" she told me. Her dad had then searched through her room and found all our love letters. He was livid; she had been in all sorts of trouble and had been told to break off the relationship at once. She hadn't been allowed out of the house for days but today she was allowed to be in the shop so that she could break up with me. I could see in her eyes that she must have done a lot of crying but right at that moment, she was almost too efficient in her delivery, she showed almost no emotion and as soon as she had delivered her bombshell to me, she was trying to get me to leave the shop. "Please bring my watch back and I will go and get your things right now" she told me.

I walked back home trying not to let the water that had now filled my eyes trickle down my face; I swatted away the annoying buzzing flies around my ears with such annoyance that I could have punched myself in the ear. I walked in to my bedroom, got her watch and walked back to the shop where she was now waiting with my jumper. "I am so sorry Yetunde" I told her "is there anything at all I can do?" I asked, I even offered to apologise to her dad directly but she made it clear that there was no alternative to our situation, there was no chance for negotiations.

She asked me to kindly walk on by should I see her in the shop in future although it was highly unlikely that she would be allowed to manage the store on her own for a long time. I took my jumper and a few cards that she handed me and I once again told her how sorry I was and then I walked away. I felt like everything had collapsed around me, I couldn't believe it. I spent the rest of the afternoon with Jide; he even offered to drop a note from me to Yetunde if ever I wanted.

About three weeks later Jide and I had noticed that neither of us had seen Yetunde even once at the book store, she still hadn't been allowed back downstairs to the shop! Her dad seemed to have given up his job and now ran the shop himself. I felt so bad for her, because she really loved the responsibility of running that shop and the freedom it gave her. So after a long debate with Jide about the pros and cons I left his flat and walked up the store.

I had never met her dad before, but I could see the resemblance immediately as I nervously walked in to his shop. He was shorter than I expected, perhaps about 5ft 6 inches tall, he wore a thin pair of glasses and his eyes had now wandered away from the book he had been reading he was now staring at me from just over the rim of his glasses as I walked in, he looked like a very serious man but still I hoped that this was just a front.

I think he might have already half guessed who I might be, but I walked up to him and introduced myself. "Sir, my name is Yemi" I told him, "I live just a couple of streets further up from you, I have come to you to apologise for getting Yetunde into trouble" he sat there now looking sterner but didn't say a word, "Sir, I really like Yetunde, we have never been outside of your shop, I only ever saw her here, I am not looking to get her into any kind of trouble and I am not a trouble maker myself" I continued, "Sir, I understand now that you are very annoyed, but if you would be kind enough to let Yetunde come back to the shop and do the things that she enjoys, I promise that I won't disturb her again if that's what you want".

Yetunde's dad took a deep breath, I continued to tell him how Yetunde had tried to warn me off, telling me that she could get into trouble, I explained that it was all my fault and apologised again.

Finally, he spoke, it was brief, but I remember him telling me that he hasn't brought his daughters up to start gallivanting with men when education is their priority, he thanked me for coming by and said he would deal with Yetunde in his own time. As I walked back over to Jide's, I wondered what I had set out to achieve and what I had actually achieved.

I think Jide was surprised to see me back in one piece, no cuts, no bruises, no tears or anything of that sort. I told him what had happened and he commended me, saying he would never have felt brave enough to do that.

A week later, Jide told me that he had seen Yetunde back in the shop for the first time, I was pleased and as much as I wanted to see her or send her a note I thought it was best that I didn't. The next day Jide came over to see me at home and had a neatly folded piece of paper in his hand, Yetunde had seen him walking by and asked him to hand me a note, he was beaming, I was excited too, I opened the note and read the contents. I can't remember it all, but she thanked me for coming to the shop and talking to her dad, but she then went on to say, that it was the last thing she would have wanted me to do and that she never wanted to speak to me again!

In October 1986 my brother Lekan Jnr. was born. It was a very happy time for us all as a family. Bisi and I were truly pleased for Dad and it was nice to have a little brother in spite of the fact that I was now 21. The extended family was also very proud and most of Dad's siblings paid a visit at some point, many of them had never visited us at home in Iju in all our years there, before the birth of Lekan.

The cracks in Dad's relationship with his wife however, had grown and were now irreparable. Wunmi moved out just a few weeks after Jnr. was born. Not much was said, I came back home from a weekend in Ibadan at Femi's to find the house a little bare. Wunmi had moved out with Lolade permanently.

Dad didn't seem too upset, within a few days he was back to his bachelor ways, even though we had little income between us he was still able to come home with different women he had picked up in the course of his travels.

Towards the end of October I went up to a small beer parlour about a ten minute walk from home, I wanted a couple of bottles of Pepsi, we had so many empty glass bottles at home and I knew that most small shops wouldn't let you take your bottled drink away from their premises unless you had an empty glass bottle to swap for it.

I went in and realised that the owner was a familiar face, her name is Ranti and she was Uncle Tony's ex-girlfriend, she was a very beautiful woman whom I had always found polite and kind, before she parted with Uncle Tony she had given birth to a daughter named Keji. Aunty Ranti as I called her and Keji had moved to Iju. It was nice to see her. We sat down and talked for a while and when I offered to pay for my drinks she refused to take the money. I asked her if she still wanted the empty glass bottles and to my surprise she offered to pay for them.

I turned down her offer of payment and gave her the two empty bottles but asked her why she wanted to pay. She then explained that glass bottles are obviously recycled for repeat use and that the breweries and bottling companies charged nearly double to shops who didn't have empty glass bottles to swap. I told her that we had at least ten crates of empty beer bottles at home which I could carry over to her a crate at a time on the odd day when I had time. She offered to pay me 30.00 naira per crate which was a lot more than I imagined, I was happy with her proposal and assured her that we had a deal.

The next morning I took a crate over to Aunty Ranti and true to her promise she paid up, she also asked me for old newspapers offering to pay a little fee for them too. Over the next few weeks I started bringing home a lot of money, suddenly we could afford to buy good food at home again, I explained the deal that I had made to Dad, and although Uncle Tony was no longer on speaking terms with Ranti, Dad didn't mind and offered to help me find more bottles. I offered to buy bottles at a small cost from friends and family, I also picked up bottles that I found on the streets, took them home washed them and collected them.

One of Dad's best friends was a man called Ola Ogunjobi, I got to know him better in the weeks and months following Dad's split from Wunmi. Uncle Ola, as I called him even though he wasn't an actual uncle of mine, was great fun, he loved the a lavish lifestyle and even though he was out of work, with little or no income, he still drove a Mercedes Benz C Class, it cost him a lot in petrol but in his opinion, he had worked far too hard in his lifetime and he had to have one memento. He would come to the house every weekend and until he started running low on cash, he would always say goodbye to me, handing me a 10.00 naira note.

He was a good laugh, a very jolly man who always wore a smile, he was a bit taller than Dad, and like most of the Yoruba men in Nigeria he carried his protruding belly with pride.

Uncle Ola was pleased and intrigued when Dad told him he

had to come round more often as we now had plenty of good food at home. I told him about my new project with Ranti and how good it had been; and how unfortunately I was now running low on bottles and newspapers.

The next morning Uncle Ola rolled up in his white Mercedes Benz as usual beaming, "Yemi, take a look in my trunk" he said. In his boot were at least four crates of beer and soft drinks bottles. We were back in business. I sold the bottles on and brought nearly 60.00 naira back home. That night Dad sent me out to one of the local bukateria's to buy some takeaway food. As usual I took two big glass Pyrex dishes to the shop where I bought one of the traditional meals "iyan" which is a food made purely out of mashed yam. The lady filled one of my dishes with the pounded yam and the other with a selection of meats, okra and Dad's favourite pepper soup commonly called "Obe Ata". I paid the lady 10.00 naira and carefully carried the dishes in a plastic bag as I headed back home.

While Dad and Uncle Ola enjoyed their feast I went to Jide's house, I then took him out to Aunty Ranti's shop where we ate jollof rice with fish and fried plantains. This was the life! We both thought so at least.

For the next few months Uncle Ola would turn up every Sunday with a boot full of bottles and newspapers. It was amazing to think that those bottles could feed us for so long.

In December 1986 Bisi was back at Murtala International Airport. She was about to board a plane to England. She was going back for good. We were both sad because we had never lived so far apart but we both knew it had to be done. Her life in Nigeria had become stagnant and boring. There was no money for her to further her education and she wasn't ready to settle down and get married.

The plan was that she would go to Camberwell in South East London where a family friend of Aunt Yinka a gentleman called Akin had a three bedroom house; he was a bachelor and didn't mind the company. Aunt Yinka was already in England and lived with him. Bisi would stay with Akin for a few months while she tried to find her feet, get a job and earn some income. Then she would look for a place of her own. There was no plan to rely on Mum for any help but Bisi would meet her at some point.

We hugged and wished each other all the best, I looked at my sister with pride, here she was, this grown woman heading out to start a new life all on her own. Soon she was gone.

Over the next few weeks I began to appreciate more and more the self-sacrifice that Aunt Lola had taken in funding Bisi's trip back to England. We were in the middle of austerity, she only had a small business now and she had three kids to feed, still she found it in her heart to help Bisi and she didn't even want the money paid back!

The more I thought of it the more I found a new level of respect for her, she had acted like a mother to Bisi, although I still knew I would never call her "Mummy" as she would have preferred. I felt that I had to do something to help her in return and show our appreciation, so over the next few weeks I would visit her store occasionally. I would help her carry crates of beer from her car to the shop, I gave her spare empty drinks bottles sometimes, I would go with her to Guinness to buy beer and help her load it into her car, sometimes I even managed the shop for her while she went to pick up Funmi and Bukki from school. It was the least I could do.

Christmas 1986 passed by quietly, but it was better than Dad and I could have hoped for, thankfully we had money from my drinks bottle business and other small jobs Dad had found. We didn't celebrate in any big way, but we cooked some good food and had a few drinks with Uncle Ola and Uncle Muda.

One day mid-1987, I got up early as I always did, I had just finished washing Dad's car and was about to walk up to the shops to get bread and milk. Uncle Muda had stayed the night at ours; he was now awake waiting for me in the living room.

"Yemi, come and sit down" he said. We had been talking all

night on Christmas day so I knew this had to be important. Dad was still asleep. I sat down beside him. What I loved about Uncle Muda was that he was always straight to the point. I don't think he knew how to warm you up to a hot discussion point or he just didn't see the need to. So as usual he was direct. "You have to go back to England like Bisi has."

I sat staring at him, it took a few seconds to comprehend what he was saying, and so before I could say anything he continued. "You are a very clever man; you can do so much with your life but the opportunities you need do not exist here in Nigeria". He was right, in my heart I had known this even before I found out that Bisi was going back. I explained to him my concerns that I had now spent 14 years of my life in Nigeria and I had never had a better relationship with Dad than we had developed over the last four or five months. I felt that he needed me, there was no real money coming in for him and anyway how could I now afford a flight back to England? "Look Yemi, you don't belong here, your dad does" he could see the confusion and hint of anger in my eyes so he carried on. "Your dad is a Nigerian, he belongs here, he will survive, you are British, and you have a passport that millions of kids would kill for. You need to go back home; you can help your dad one day from there".

It was clear that Uncle Muda had gone over this time and time again in his mind, all his arguments made perfect sense and before I could ask. He said "We can raise the money for your flight, the family will contribute." Dad was in the living room by now; he assured me that it would be no trouble for him and a few Uncles to pay for a one way ticket. I stood up, hugged Uncle Muda and shook Dad's hand. "I had better go and tell Jide" I said as I ran out of the house.

My run slowed down into a walk as I headed to Jide's flat. The plan was for me to leave Nigeria on the 19th of February 1988 which would be two days after my 22nd birthday. I knew that I wanted Jide to be the first to know, he had been my best friend for so many years and I knew I would miss him, I also knew that I had to let Yemi know and most importantly of all, I wanted to tell Yetunde although I didn't know if that would be possible at all.

CHAPTER ELEVEN

GOING BACK HOME

Jide took my news well, he wasn't even all that surprised. If he'd been in my shoes, with the opportunity to go to England, he would have grabbed the opportunity, just like Uncle Muda had said. Jide also had news of his own: he had decided to move out of Iju by June of that year, he was going to live in the heart of Lagos where he had been offered a job.

I asked him if he thought I should speak to Yetunde, he agreed that it was only fair that I try to let her know. A few days later I walked up to Yetunde's shop, she was in there alone, I knew she had seen me walk by on countless occasions, sometimes taking a sly glance to see who was in the store, most of the time I would be doing my best not to look at all. This time I turned right at the shop, walked over the plank of wood that bridges the stinking gutter and continued towards her. If she was surprised, it didn't show.

She smiled when I walked in, I said a quick hello and asked how she was. We didn't have much to say to each other, so I broke my news to her. She smiled again, wished me good luck and said goodbye. I walked out of her shop feeling sad, but glad that we had spoken, albeit very briefly. I knew that part of my heart was still with her, but I also knew that what we had was now over. I walked away without looking back.

Yemi was both elated and sad when I sat down in her living room and told her my news. We both promised to try to keep in touch. We hugged and talked for hours before I finally went back home.

February came round very quickly. My flight had been paid for in January, I had my new British passport, and I had long since packed the few things I wanted to take with me and was now counting down to the 19th. One of my few regrets was that I couldn't say goodbye to some of my favourite cousins, especially Tunde & Femi because, although my dad comes from a big family, there was very little trust amongst the siblings and Dad could not trust anyone to know except for Uncle Tony & Uncle Joe in Agege. I was under strict orders not to discuss this with anyone else, amazingly not even Aunt Lola who he had again fallen out with.

A few days before my 22nd birthday, I bumped into an old and very welcome face. It was Nike Sobowale; the very pretty girl who a few years ago back in 1983 was the young girl at GCK who became my school daughter. She was now a very cute 17 year old. I had gone to a part of Lagos called Yaba to do some last-minute shopping for my trip back to England. By sheer coincidence Nike approached a small shop where I was looking at a pair of shoes. Our eyes just met and we instantly recognised each other. We hugged for a long time, we had never seen each other nor did we keep in touch since I left GCK back in 1984.

We had so much to talk about, she was now studying A-Level literature and economics she wanted to become a teacher, her family had moved to a slightly bigger house but she was the only one her family could afford to give an education to. None of her brothers or sisters went to school so she was expected to get a good job and help educate her siblings.

We spent 2 or 3 hours catching up on old times, we still adored and admired each other and best of all, now we were both old enough to date. I realised what a shame it was that it had taken so many years for us to finally make contact again. I wished that I had kept my promise of writing to her or that she had kept hers when I left GCK. But now it was too late as I told her, I couldn't commit to or promise her anything. I was leaving for England in just a few days and I didn't know where my life would take me from there.

I remember Nike being really disappointed, she wanted me to promise that I would at least keep in touch with her from England and perhaps she could still be my girlfriend; after all, people do have long distance relationships she explained. But I was adamant, I knew from past experience, we hadn't kept the promises we made back in 1984, my mum rarely wrote to me from England and I knew how much that hurt. Worse still, we hardly knew each other anymore, we hadn't seen or spoken to each other in over four years so I was not sure that we could possibly build a long-distance relationship while I was trying to settle down and start another chapter in my life, thousands of miles away.

In retrospect, I did feel bad that Nike and I never had a chance, but I know that I made the right decision.

∞

On February 19th, 1988 two days after my 22nd birthday and just over 14 years and 4 months since we were first taken away to Nigeria, I landed at Heathrow airport in England as a young man about to make a fresh start in life. I took a taxi from the airport to Camberwell, where I stayed with our family friend Akin for a few months. I would later move on to Streatham to rent my first flat with my closest friend at the time, a guy called Steve who I met while working at McDonald's.

There was no longer a dad to go to for support and although I was back in England, I had no immediate plans of making contact with Mum.

The plan was to get a job as soon as possible, get enrolled into a university; to find a place of my own and then, once settled, contact Mum.

I did various jobs over the next few years, the first being a 6 month stint at McDonald's on the Strand near Charing Cross in London, which at the time was rumoured to be the busiest branch in the world. From McDonald's I went on to work at the Royal

Mail sorting office in Nine Elms, Vauxhall, London for a few months then, for the next three years, I worked the night shift at a Sainsbury's supermarket in South Ruislip, just outside London. It meant I was able to do a full time job whilst also studying for a degree in Civil Engineering.

With the first 2 jobs, I couldn't wait to move on. At McDonald's I did everything from serving at the tills, to cleaning the restaurant, to flipping burgers. Lunch times were incredible: we would have queues all the way out of the restaurant and we would shorten those queues in no time at all. I worked hard but knew I didn't want to be there, so I never accepted a single star.

I remained ambitious when I joined Sainsbury's too, but I did realise that it paid well and that it allowed me to go to Southbank College in the daytime. I met and made some good friends at Sainsbury's on the night shift, Peter Smith was my closest friend, but there was a rebellious group of us that also included Neil, who we called Frosty because his night shift was always to do with stocking up the big storage freezers when deliveries arrived, then there was Chris who we called "Pikey" and later on another Peter who joined us and introduced union membership to us all. That didn't go down well with our management because we suddenly learned that we had so many rights and we were prepared to demand them all. Eventually in 1993 all of us left, one-by-one, some were shown the door, while others like me, just felt it was time to move on.

Steve and I lived in Streatham and then Balham for about a year before I decided that I wanted to move outside of London. I eventually found a one-bedroom flat in a village called Northolt situated in Middlesex. I spent the next 3 years there from late 1990 to early 1994. There I finally felt at home, I lived on a housing association project in Gauntlet Close where my first friends where a young couple who lived downstairs. Sharon & Mike, I was good friends with them and their daughters Sarah & Rachael, I later made friends with a few more of the neighbours.

I didn't know another black person in Northolt. For a while it seemed like I was the only black person in the village, but it was easy to make friends and settle down.

One of the things I was finally able to do now that I was in England was play football without being questioned by my dad anymore, so I bought a football and would take it to the park in my spare time, sometimes I would be invited to join on-going kick-a-bouts, other times I would just practice on my own. At the time I was already playing as a winger and a striker for Peter Smith's Sunday League side in Windsor, previously I had played for teams in Putney and Roehampton before joining a local team in Northolt called "Northolt Panthers".

In 1992 I injured my ankle, damaging ligaments while playing for one of Peter's teams at Bisham Abbey Sports Centre. It was such a bad injury that I was unable to play again for over 15 months. I missed football a lot, so whenever I was awake during the day I would walk my Belgian Shepherd dog "Anfield" to the park in Northolt where I would play "fetch" with him, he loved chasing anything that I kicked or threw, I had him from when he was just 4 months old, he was now a big dog at 3 years old. He was so fast; I remember back when he was a puppy, we would go jogging and I would race him to the top of the hill always beating him. That didn't last long; soon Anfield would be at the top of the hill waiting before I had even started the climb!

One summer day while at the park in Northolt, I watched some young boys playing against much bigger lads from my team Northolt Panthers, I was impressed at how these teenagers confidently handled the tackles and pushes from the bigger lads, they didn't even seem to be intimidated by the size and age difference and they could also play some good football. Eventually I met one of the lads, Michael Webb; he was a local boy about 16 years old at the time. I told him he was a good player and asked him if he and his friends played for a football team. He told me that they were just a bunch of school friends who played football together but didn't have a manager or a team. As luck would have it, I was still injured and was interested in helping them, so I got them all together and started training them every Saturday that summer while looking for a way to get them into a football league.

Then a second stroke of luck came along: my good friend Marvin, the boyfriend of my neighbour Lisa, managed a team that had just folded near Hayes. He had the kit and everything else but just 2 or 3 players left. So, through Lisa we met and formed a team called Conway United Football club, the name of the area where Marvin lived in Hayes. We registered into Ealing Youth League as an Under 18's team. Michael had invited a few more of his friends from Northolt High School to join us so we had a squad of about 15 with some very good players like Kevin Lewsey, Mark Isaacs, Ian Philps and Gary Boreham, with Gary Harkins in goal. Then there was Mark and Ivan Shears, Chris Green who joined later and many more. We also had players like Jeffrey Bare who could hardly kick a ball, but that was the beauty of training a youth team, we were there to enjoy football, everyone deserved a chance to play if they wanted to.

We lost our first match of the league season, then drew the 2nd one at which point, Kevin brought his friend Marc Thorpe, a goalkeeper, along for a late trial. Marc at 17 was a year older than any of the other boys.

Gary was a good goal keeper no doubt, and the team was just about settled, I felt that Marc was going to have to be very good to make it into our squad that season but I agreed to give him a trial. I took a few free kicks, penalties and in general gave him a hard time, but he was brilliant. He was pretty tall too, I think close to 6ft at the time. In the end, I had no doubt that Marc would be an all-round better keeper and would have to be my new no.1 goal keeping choice; I just had to break the news to Gary and the rest of the boys.

Fortunately, Gary could also play on pitch as a defender but he much preferred playing in goal. He didn't take the news very well and nor did some of the boys initially but I stuck to my guns and thankfully, Marc was the final jigsaw piece that we needed.

We went on to win all of our remaining League matches including a 26-1 demolition of one team. We won the Division Youth League and narrowly lost our League Cup Final to a team we had beaten home and away in the league that season.

The following season a couple of the boys including our new goalkeeper Marc, were already 18 years old and wouldn't qualify to play in the youth league, we had to make a decision. Collectively, we all agreed to stick together. This meant leaving the youth league and playing in an adult's league, and for me it also meant that I could now be player/manager for the team.

Although I knew that the boys had experience playing against men much bigger than them, I was still apprehensive about the prospect and even more so when North Hillingdon & District League council put us straight into division three of their football league based on our records from the Youth League. I wanted us to start from Division five to give the boys a chance to get used to playing against adults every weekend but we stayed in division three.

So in our second season together a few things changed, we were now playing against men every Sunday, we changed our name from Conway UTD to Northolt Sports Football Club as we were all local lads from Northolt and once again I was able to play football. We had a good first season and won promotion to division 2 as runners-up, we then went from strength to strength and within four seasons we were playing in the premier division.

We were a very good side but the boys were now in their 20's, they had discovered women, late Saturday nights and beer, so some players would turn up late, some would be sick on the field of play and I was unofficially promoted to manager/player/linesman/the kit cleaning man and so on. We became a kamikaze team, really good on a good day and pretty bad when we were bad. In the 1996/97 season, we finished as runners-up once again to our arch-rivals Park

United. They were a very dominant side with an aggressive manager, they could play and they could brawl, they hated playing against us but the best result we had ever achieved against them was a couple of draws in four seasons. This season was no different, we had lost to them at home and away in the league and this time we both made it to the League Cup Final.

We were the clear underdogs; we knew that we had never beaten Park United. It had also been a while since we last made it to a cup final, so there was an extra air of excitement around Northolt Sports. Most of the boys invited their friends and family along, I remember Darren Welsh who I had played mainly as a substitute that season inviting his family and his boss and colleagues from work. He asked me if he was going to be in the starting 11 especially as he had so many supporters there with him, I smiled but kept quiet.

Finally, in the changing room with a rare full squad to pick from, I named my squad. I didn't name myself on the bench; there were no major surprises other than the fact that in spite of the pressure on me, I named Darren or Welshy as we called him as a substitute. He couldn't believe it, some of the boys were initially surprised but boys being boys they soon saw the funny side and kept taunting Darren.

I can't remember who scored our equaliser but Park United had led for most of the first half, we were playing our best ever football against our arch rivals, I could see that we were tiring under the scorching sun but so were they. The match tightly poised at 1-1 went into extra time. I had had to endure over 90 minutes of Welshy in my ears, "Yem, put me on" "Please let me come on, everyone's here to watch me" "Please Yem," and so on. A couple of minutes into the first half of extra time, I finally called "Welshy" and he approached me beaming. I made the substitution, giving him his instructions and telling him he would have to be one of my penalty takers if the match went that way, he nodded and on he rushed to the loud cheer around him, I can't quite remember exactly what happened next so I sent Darren a message recently to ask for his recollection. In Darren Welsh' own words, "Park United's goalie kicked the ball out and Steve headed it to Kevin down the left wing, I burst through the middle, skipping past the two Park United Centre halves, Kev crossed the ball in along the ground about 5 yards from goal and with the outside of my right boot I slotted it into the corner… I think" We stunned Park United 2-1 and won the cup, our most memorable victory. One of which we still talk about fondly today.

I managed the team for a couple more seasons but then moved to Luton and stepped down as manager. Occasionally, I turned up to play for them if they were short of players. In 2001 whilst playing for them, I got a very bad knock on my fragile ankle, causing minor fractures and ligament damage. I was out of football again and soon afterwards I lost all contact with the boys. That was until 2011 thanks to Facebook which I joined after the publication of my book. Through Facebook, Kevin found me, then I found Mark Isaacs and one by one we all connected. Around August 2011, Kevin kindly invited me round to his house for a barbeque; he and Mark kept it a surprise. It was so good to see some of the boys. I now meet them on Tuesday evenings to play 5-a-side football.

I moved to Luton after I met Lisa, she lived in Luton and I worked in Milton Keynes so it made perfect sense to move. I had gone through a few jobs before I finally settled for a career in IT Sales. When I left Southbank University, I worked as a temporary assistant site Engineer on a project for Taylor Woodrow, but the project went into receivership and I was left jobless. After a lot of soul searching, I realised that the building industry was struggling so I switched careers, initially working for 2 years as a financial advisor, a job I was good at but didn't enjoy. Eventually, I decided to leave financial services and look at IT. I love gadgets and technology but I had no background experience. I had an interview at a company called Technomatic in North London where I got a job in telesales. All we had to do, was take incoming purchase enquiries and take the customer's order, the cleverer sales people would suggest accessories and other add-ons for more profit. I bought myself a computer dictionary, I needed to understand the jargon and understand why customers where buying certain things. Within a year, I was very competent, so I decided to move on from telesales.

My next job was at an IT components distributor called Karma UK in Wembley, I learned a lot there and stayed for three years before eventually joining Ingram Micro in Milton Keynes after Karma went into administration.

At Ingram I met and made a lot of friends who I still keep in touch with today. I stayed there for four and a half years before finally moving on to my current job in June 2004. Today I still work for Western Digital, nowadays better known as WD. At the time I joined them they were the world's third largest manufacturer of hard disk drives. Today we are the number one.

∞

Mum and I did make contact, this time it was more mutual, we both realised that this was a fresh start and an opportunity to get to know each other all over again; I didn't know her any more than she knew me. I had decided that I would visit her and her family Owen and my brother Damian regularly but not too often, I felt we needed time to get used to each other and I didn't want Mum to think that I would need any support morally or financially from her.

For moral support and advice I relied on our old family friends Uncle Charles and Aunt Erika. Uncle Charles is a Nigerian by birth and came to England in the late 50's, he and Dad have been lifelong friends. I knew that both he and in particular Aunt Erika were very disappointed in Dad and how he had taken us away.

We were so close with Uncle Charles and his family that we

were practically family, to the extent that their two children Ricarda who I knew very well from my childhood days growing up in England and her younger brother Oliver who shares the same birth date as me are cousins as far as Bisi and I were concerned. Ricarda was only a couple of years younger than me so we were very close, while by the time we left England Oliver was still a toddler. To this day I still see my Uncle and my Aunt as well as my cousins Ricarda & Oliver.

It made sense that if I needed any help or advice that I visited Uncle Charles. When I needed a reference for a job application I went to Uncle Charles who duly wrote me a good reference. As it turned out, I mainly visited them just to reminisce about old times, let them know I was doing well and occasionally to stay for Sunday dinner. I rarely saw Ricarda who was now a mother.

In 1992 I moved to a small town near London called Perivale, it was pure coincidence that Mum lived no more than half a mile away from me also in Perivale. It was a useful coincidence because once Mum knew that I lived around the corner, she made more of an effort to invite me round every Sunday to join them for lunch. I realised how much I had missed rice and peas and curry goat amongst other meals.

It gave me another opportunity to get to know Damian & Owen as well as Mum and we all got along fine. Mum came round to my little studio flat a couple of times too and when I decided that I could no longer keep my black Belgian Shepherd dog "Anfield" in my small flat while I had work commitments, I gave him to Damian who had always loved the dog.

In 1993 Mum told me that they had sold their house and were going back home to Jamaica permanently. Mum always kept her cards close to her chest, so here she was telling me that they were going to Jamaica in less than a month. I offered to help them pack, however all but a few small things had already been packed and shipped. I wanted Damian to stay, but they had checked on schools and found him a good local school out there in Jamaica. So once again just as we were beginning to open up, we were going to have to live thousands of miles apart again. Mum and her family soon left for Jamaica, I still didn't know her that well…

CHAPTER 12

(THE ORIGINAL
EPILOGUE)

I recall it being one of the heaviest downpours I had ever seen in England at the time, it was almost torrential rain; it was just before 5am on the 3rd of July 1999 that my daughter Shaya Jada Olive was born. I was there at Northwick Park Hospital near Harrow to witness little Shaya come into the world fast asleep. I knew from that very moment that she was going to be a good baby, just like my mum had always described me. I was now 33 years old.

Shaya was born into a broken relationship, the one thing I had sworn that I would never let any child of mine go through. I had already broken up with her mum by the time she was born but the experiences in my life had given me more than enough determination to make sure that I had a good bond with her from the outset. I was the first person she saw when she eventually opened her pretty sleepy eyes whilst still in my arms and I knew that I had to be a good father in spite of the separation.

I started out by having Shaya every other weekend from the time she was born until she was about 3 years old. At age 3, my girlfriend Lisa and I realised that the fortnightly stay with us was too much for Shaya so we eventually agreed with her mum to have Shaya every 3rd weekend from Friday evening to Sunday night.

We also have her for longer periods during school holidays and we take alternate times with her mum for birthdays and Christmas.

When I came back to England in 1988 the first phone call I made was to my dad to let him know that I had arrived safely, I thanked him and the family for helping me to return and I promised that I would keep in touch with him. I kept in touch for only 3 months after which I realised how angry and confused I still was with him. I realised that Bisi and I still had no explanation as to why Mum and Dad had fallen out of love and why he had subsequently smuggled us away. I tried to blank a lot of this out of my mind but it lingered there.

I didn't like some of the advice Dad was constantly giving me, especially the part where he would ask me to stay close to Bisi. Bisi and I were still very very close, yet he himself only spoke to perhaps 2 of his 8 living siblings, not even to Aunt Lola who had looked after Bisi for so many years and had paid for Bisi's return.

I felt that he was at fault for the lack of any kind of bond between me and Mum and I felt that I needed my own time away from Dad so I stopped all contact with him for over 11 years until the afternoon of the 3rd of July 1999.

It wasn't a deliberate ploy out of spite not to communicate with Dad, I just found that I was angry and upset within myself I also felt that he had no regrets whatsoever and this annoyed me more. Bisi on the other hand, remained very close to him, calling him regularly while I neither wrote nor called him.

After Shaya's birth, I rang Bisi, Aunt Yinka & Aunt Lola who now lived together in South East London, my cousin Tunde who was now married with 2 kids and also lived in South East London near Peckham, and then I rang my closest friends to tell them my happy news.

I went home showered and kept thinking of the first moment Shaya opened her eyes and saw me, I still couldn't believe that I was now a dad. I had waited for this moment all my adult life and now it was finally here. My best friend Jay came round with some cigars, neither of us actually smoke but we held one each and laughed, his girlfriend was pregnant too and was due to give birth in August, we both knew that we had really become men.

When I finally got some quiet time I kept looking back at my life and how I had grown from that little kid in England, through teenage life in Nigeria to now a father and I realised that my dad who I had only seen as a man was himself once just a little boy. In fact he had lost both his parents before he had even turned 10 and I realised that I had to call him to tell him that he was a grandfather again.

Bisi had wed her husband Bola in December 1994; I was there as the father figure in the absence of Dad, to give her hand in marriage, their son Oliver was born in March 1998. She had always kept in touch with Dad and had even been back to Nigeria with her husband to visit him in 1992 but she rarely made any contact with Mum and even less with Uncle Charles and Aunt Erika. She understood my resentments and I understood hers so we rarely spent our times together talking about Mum or Dad.

What we did do though and still do today is reminisce on our years in Nigeria, the various schools we had been to, the house at Iju and our favourite portable radio cassette player, the friends we had made along the way. We always wondered how much Dad really understood our feelings and thoughts in those days.

We often call each other today after listening to an old music track which brings back some memories; it's amazing how much we can laugh about those days now. We call them "the good old days." That's the amazing thing in my mind, I hated a lot of my time in Nigeria, yet I grew up wanting to prove that I could survive in that world just as well as any kid born and bred in Nigeria. Bisi and I had many highs and lows yet when we reminisce, we smile, we laugh, we cringe at some of the memories and we still call them the good old days.

When I rang Dad that afternoon of July the 3rd, I started the conversation with "Hello Dad" and he replied "Hello Yemi" I asked him how he had been and apologised for not keeping in touch I then told him that I felt more relaxed and that I had matured as a man, I told him that I felt we had both wronged each other and that I was old enough to let bygones be bygones, then I told him that he was a grandfather again. Dad seemed happy enough for me; He didn't sound any different, he still had the same deep growly voice although it was no longer intimidating to me, he congratulated me then asked me how mother and child were doing, I told him they were both fine and well then he said "Listen to me Yemi, it's been 12 years since you last spoke to me, so I am now banning you for the next 12 years" at which point I stood staring at the phone in my hand in amazement, I didn't say another word, in fact I couldn't, I didn't know if he was still on the line by the time I put the receiver down.

I was furious, I had tears in my eyes and my whole body was shaking with rage, I knew I hadn't called him in actually 11 years and 5 months but what effort had he made to contact me? It wasn't as if he had written and I hadn't replied or he had called and I had refused to take his call, I felt that the man was so proud that he still couldn't see his failings as a father, he still had no idea how much he had hurt me and scarred me and now he wanted to ban me? I must have stood inside the public telephone booth for an age just steaming up.

It took a couple of days for me to calm down enough to be able to tell Bisi and my Aunt Lola about my conversation with Dad. They both wanted me to give him another try, they both knew that Dad was proud and wouldn't back down that easily but I was determined that I would never speak to him again and no one could convince me otherwise. I felt that I had tried to break the ice, I had apologised for my faults and now he had let me down again.

Nine years after Mum and her family had left England, I was about to see them all again. My partner Lisa and I went on a three week holiday to Jamaica late in 2001. It was a nervous trip for both of us for different reasons, for me it was yet another reunion with Mum, I was also going to my mother's land for the first time in my life and for Lisa it was her first time on an airplane.

Owen met us at the arrivals hall in Sangster International airport in Montego Bay; we arrived on a late flight so it was already pretty dark. We shared a big hug, Lisa got an even bigger hug, Owen then carried her luggage to the small car driven by a family friend of theirs nicknamed "Smoker". It was a good couple of hours drive to St Elizabeth, Lisa and I slept most of the way.

It was my first trip to Jamaica, I had heard a lot about the beauty and poverty of the Island but I still didn't know what to expect. I was impressed at the stark contrast between Nigeria and Jamaica, the roads in Jamaica were much better and cleaner, and things seemed a lot better organised than the chaos of Nigeria. My first impressions of Jamaica were already very good.

We got to the house just after 1am, it was good to see Mum who was still awake and had been waiting excitedly for us to get there. It was also great to see Owen and especially Damian who was now a teenager he was taller than me and also had a deeper more masculine voice; he was still cute and quiet. We spent one and a half weeks at Mum's house and then spent the rest of our holiday like tourists in Montego Bay.

It was easier than my experience of 1984 living with Mum this time, I was a very mature man, I had learned from our experiences of '84. It still had its moments of difficulty but this was mainly because I had my girlfriend there too and she didn't know anyone and of course she had never been outside of England before this occasion. So it made sense that we only spent a short time at Mum's house.

Mum did have one of her closely kept cards to play before we left St Elizabeth. One afternoon Mum called me in from the front of the house where I had been sitting with Lisa who was sunbathing. She had her home phone off the hook and looked into my eyes. "there is someone I want you to talk to" she said, I continued to listen; "You have another sister, her name is Sandra, she knows about you, but I didn't know how best to introduce you to one another" she went on "however I think it's important that you get to know each other and stay in touch."

I drew in a deep breath, picked up the phone and spoke to Sandra who lives in New Jersey, United States, she sounded anxious on the phone, there wasn't much we could say to each other but we both agreed that we had to meet one day somehow. On our way to Montego Bay I just kept wondering how Mum had managed to keep Sandra a secret from me, Bisi and even Dad.

Lisa and I stayed at the "Sandals Holiday Resort" in Montego Bay, we went out on various tours and we enjoyed a lot of the local delicacies and watched the sun set on the beach most nights. I also called Mum a couple of times to let her know we were having a good time. It had been good for me to visit Jamaica, I learned a lot about the Island and it had served as a step in the right direction towards a better relationship with Mum and Damian.

∞

On Friday the 13th of July 2001 I got a phone call from one of my cousins Deji, he was Tunde's younger brother and he also now lived in the UK. I was very busy at work that afternoon, I took his call in a hurry, I heard him call my name twice and then say something to me in Yoruba, I replied saying "ok" and then I put the phone down. A few seconds later I realised that he had just told me that Tunde had died!

Tunde and I had remained very close from our days back in Nigeria. We used to spend the occasional weekend at each other's house in England before we became family men, but we still spoke to each other regularly. He had called me a week before he died to tell me he would be visiting a friend of his very near to me in Luton, unfortunately he had suffered a stroke that same evening.

He had seemed to be recovering when I visited him in a London hospital a couple of days earlier. His left side was paralysed and he had lost his speech, but he recognised me, he waved and then whispered in my ear "thanks for coming". On the morning of July the 13th I rang his brother Deji to find out how Tunde was getting on at hospital, all the news was positive, Tunde looked more energetic than at any time since he had suffered the stroke. That afternoon he died. He was the first truly close family member I had ever lost. I was devastated for weeks.

One lesson that the loss of Tunde brought home to me was that life is short; I still knew that I would never want my daughter to be so mad at me that she would choose not to communicate with me in the way that I had chosen not to communicate with my dad. It had been two years since our last conversation so I decided to give him one final try. I knew that there was no turning back this time; if he was still determined not to talk to me then we might never talk again. This time Dad was a lot calmer when I rang him, it was clear to me that some of his family members had spoken to him too, also Tunde's death was still lingering on everyone's mind and he knew how close Tunde and I were.

We spoke for about 5 minutes and agreed to keep in regular contact. It was a start, over the next three years I rang Dad almost fortnightly on a Sunday after I came back from playing football. I had even started sending him money occasionally.

In 2004 on one of my calls to Dad I asked him how he would feel if I decided to go to Nigeria to visit him. He was truly ecstatic even though he kept calm, he told me that he would really love it; he wanted me to think about it and to tell no one but Bisi of my thoughts. I told him immediately that I would come.

So in April 2004, sixteen years since I had left Nigeria, I was on a flight back into the unknown. I saw it as something of a homecoming. Dad had sworn me to secrecy and only some of his very closest friends and family had any idea I was coming to Nigeria.

Once again here I was outside Murtala International airport Nigeria; I had booked a 12 day holiday. I travelled to Nigeria with just hand luggage so I was one of the first on the plane. I soon understood the check-in attendant's surprise at Heathrow when I confirmed that I was indeed travelling to Nigeria with just one piece of hand luggage. It took a long time to get everyone boarded because most people had hand luggage the size of what I would have packed as a suitcase, the so-called hand luggage came in all shapes and sizes, every single overhead cabinet was packed to bursting point.

I stood there in the bright sunshine outside the airport reading the sign "Murtala International Airport" I was trying to convince myself that I really was here in Nigeria. A few touts kept coming over to pester me, some wanted to offer me a taxi ride, others wanted to loan me their mobile phone so I could call Dad and pay them for the use. I politely declined and waited patiently in the baking sun as Dad had asked me to do over and over again. I wasn't going to question his wisdom here; this was his country after all.

I continued to wait and decline the touts while I wondered if Dad would recognise me at first sight, there was no doubt I would recognise him, but I had changed a lot since he last saw me. I was a lot more muscular, weighed at least 2 stone more and now had a clean shaven head. I spotted Dad from a few hundred yards away, he had changed but not much, he still sported his trademark full beard but it was in a neat trim and it was all grey now as was his hair. He had also lost some weight; he still had a bit of a belly on him but nowhere near what I remembered.

He still had that smile that would fill a room, as we got nearer to each other I could see he was dressed in a native dashiki top, light trousers and leather slippers, he still wore his wrist watch on his right wrist as did I. He was also a lot smaller in stature than me. We shook hands and then hugged. He then introduced me to Mr Amodu his good friend and local neighbour who had chartered a kombi bus for the trip. One of the first questions I asked Dad was if he had recognised me immediately; Of course he had.

On the trip back to Agbado a small village on the outskirts of Lagos where Dad now lived, we talked about my flight while I looked out the window at some vaguely familiar places and some that I did not recognise at all. It didn't take more than 5 minutes into the journey for me to say what Dad was waiting for. "Wow! This place has changed, it's worse than I remember it" I said. He nodded. It was probably 5 times worse than I expected. Nearly every single house I saw had a little shop; it seemed everyone had something to sell.

∞

There were motorbikes everywhere, every street seemed packed with people hurrying about either with something to sell or somewhere to be, those familiar gutters and their little planks of wood that served as foot bridges were every-where too. Drivers all seemed to be in a hurry, with some driving on the wrong side of the road, it was clear that the walk paths were not the pedestrians' right of way. You had to have your wits about you or you could easily get knocked over by one of those motor bikes carrying three or four passengers.

I recognised the central part of Ikeja where I had frequented quite often all those years ago. It was busier than I had ever seen it, it was just as run down as everywhere else we had driven through but I recognised it and wasn't surprised to see the Guinness factory where Aunt Lola had once worked as we continued through Ikeja.

We continued to talk, once in a while I might recognise a landmark but, to my utter disbelief when Dad told me later, we drove right through Iju without me realising it, I didn't recognise one part of the quiet little village I had lived in and loved!

Dad's house was one of the bigger ones on the much eroded clay street in the small village where he lived. It had big red iron gates but was not painted. Still it looked impressive in comparison to the squalor all around it. I wasn't surprised; Dad had spent his life designing building plans for his family, friends and clients so he was bound to have a nice house. As we walked through the gates I noticed he also had a nice little garden in front of the house including a coconut tree which provided much-needed shade from the unforgiving sun.

The inside of Dad's house showed me, once again, how tough it was to live in Nigeria. It was very bare; none of the rooms were painted. We went upstairs to the living room, a sparse room which had a three-seater sofa, the leather was ripped in various parts and I could see the sponge from the sofa, there was a small cupboard with a 14" black and white television on top of it, and there was a reasonable sized dining table with four chairs.

Dad showed me the room that he had prepared for me, the first thing I noticed was the mosquito net in the window and the metal bars that served as a deterrent to would-be thieves, then the flimsy mattress, but the room looked nice. Then I saw a portrait that Dad had put against one of the walls, I went over and took a closer look. "Oh my god"! I remember this, I drew that a long time ago didn't I?" I asked in bewilderment that he still had it. He smiled as he nodded. It was a self-portrait of me, I knew that I had drawn it many years ago but I had long since forgotten all about it and all the other drawings I had made.

Back in the living room I now noticed a photo clock on one of the walls on which Dad had a photo of his parents, one of Shaya sitting on a beach which I had sent him, one of Bisi and her family and an old one of me still with hair.

We had a small shower room; Dad explained that one of the young kids across the street would bring me a bucket of water for my shower every morning. Dad's room looked the most familiar to me. He had the same kind of set-up that he had always liked.

The first person to visit me was an ecstatic Uncle Muda, he had made the trip from Ibadan in a little car as he no longer rode motorcycles. We hugged while he thanked God that I had come back to see him, I was so pleased to see him; it was hard to tell who was more ecstatic.

Over the next few days I saw so many old faces, Tunde Ogunro who I used to call Tunde Jnr visited with his wife and kids, Uncle

Tony visited regularly with his wife Funmi, he also picked us up one day and took us back to his house which hadn't changed too much from the old days but he had now finished most of the building work that used to be in his sparse compound. My favourite cousin Abake visited with her young son, her older sister Bolanle also called in as did some other uncles some of whom I had almost forgotten about.

One of my favourite moments was seeing Uncle Ola, he hadn't changed much, and he still had his huge shiny smile, if anything he looked like he had put on more weight around the belly. He had built his house on the same road as Dad just a stone's throw away. It was great to reminisce about those good old days of gathering and selling bottles.

I also went to Agege with Dad and Uncle Tony to visit Uncle Joe, he still lived at the same house that Bisi and I first slept in way back in 1973, it seemed a little smaller now but the street hadn't changed too much except for every house also having a small shop. Uncle Joe had lost his sight now, but he remembered me clearly as he shook my now much bigger hand and then gave me a hug. We all sat down in the living room and I took a photo of the three brothers. I wondered when they had last sat down together like this.

I was sad to hear that Maami had passed away a few years earlier, she was one of the people I most looked forward to seeing on my return to Nigeria, so I took time to visit her final resting place, a small grave which was right outside the front side of the house. I sat down beside it alone in my thoughts for about half an hour as I whispered a little prayer to her.

I would have liked to see Jide and definitely Yemi on my return to Nigeria but it wasn't to be. I had lost contact with Yemi a long time ago and Jide who had kept in touch with Dad while he lived in Iju had now lost contact since Dad moved to Agbado.

Most evenings Dad went across the road to one of his friends, he just called him "The Old Man". They drank beer or wine while they either played cards or draughts under the moon and stars long into the night. They would also use that time to talk and reminisce about life in general. Dad must have told him about his kids in England on many of those nights but now finally, I was there, drinking a bottle of Guinness while showing them that I still could play a good game of draughts, although Dad was a bit too canny for me and always found a way to beat me.

I sat there one night listening to them talk, they were so happy, everything they spoke about was positive as if they didn't have a care in the world. Yet we had stopped playing cards that night as it was too dark, N.E.P.A had struck again. The old man lived in a small bungalow with his family which had no electricity or water of its own; the whole family slept on the floor as they had no beds and the roof was only partly finished. Across the road from him to the left were some even worse looking houses and to the right I could just make out the silhouette of Dad's house under the stars.

The one thing that struck me that particular night as I sat there sipping a drink from my bottle of Pepsi; while they were busy talking to some young man from the neighbourhood, was how comfortable Dad was in these surroundings. I now realised what I had never seen in him before. He was as much a Nigerian, as much a Yoruba man as anyone else in the neighbourhood. For him this is home, this is where he belonged and where he was happiest. Dad in Nigeria fit like a hand to a glove, he had lived in the UK, he had travelled to many parts of the world but there was no place like home for him. I smiled and continued to enjoy the fresh breeze on my face while I admired the stars.

I travelled with Dad to Ibadan by public transport which brought back a lot of memories. I was particularly surprised at how big and squashed I now felt in the kombi bus which they still packed tight. It was still seated in rows of four passengers per row. Ideally it was made for three passengers. We still had to sit at the bus garage for nearly two hours until the bus had all of its seats filled.

It was a very rickety old bus, it seemed even worse than some of the ones I remembered. Just as we were about to leave, a woman in the back called out "Let us pray" everyone bowed their head while she screamed "Jesus, bless this driver, Jesus give this driver peace, Jesus wash his tyres in your blood, Jesus please give us a safe journey". Now that never used to happen! As soon as we were out on the open Expressway and I saw the rickety old bus trying to reach speeds of up to 80mph I realised why they pray so much, I realised that our lives where now in the hands of a driver who wanted to complete the 80 mile trip as quickly as possible so he could pick up his next fare and we were in the hands of his rickety old bus which would have been obliterated completely on any form of impact.

The house in Ibadan still looked the same as I remembered it. It was packed with kids, I still don't know exactly how many children Uncle Muda has but his grandchildren also lived there as did the oldest living member of Dad's family "Alhaja". She was Uncle Muda's mum and Dad's aunt.

On the eve of my departure from Nigeria Dad and I invited a few of his friends including Mr Amodu and Uncle Ola over to their local club house where we wined and dined about 12 people in total. It was a good night, to me it was a small cost, but I could see the pleasure and gratitude for one nice free meal on everyone's face.

Three months after my visit to Nigeria I got the sad news that Uncle Ola had died after suffering a stroke. He was never taken to hospital, instead his family tried to care for him at home. He never had a chance.

On October 29th 2004, at 11pm I noticed that I had missed three calls from Bisi and one from Mum. It was unusual for Bisi to try to ring me more than once on any single occasion so I was worried, I was worried that her daughter, my niece Antonia who had been born with a heart condition may have taken a turn for the worse. It was too late to call Bisi back and I didn't want to hear any bad news that night. The following morning I tried to call Bisi but she was out, so I rang Mum. I told her I had missed her call last night, then she explained that she had tried to call me a few times to tell me that Damian had been killed in a car crash in Kingston Jamaica!

I last read an email from Damian just a week earlier. He was about to graduate from The University of West Indies at last. They were planning a graduation party and he wanted to know if I was planning to visit Jamaica soon. I was so busy at work, I decided to reply the next day and then the day after that… now it was too late. Damian and a fellow graduate friend Ricardo; had gone out to town in the friend's new graduation present a performance car.

They were going to pick up their graduation cloaks in Kingston. Ricardo lost control of his wheel, no other car was involved but Jamaica had lost 2 more graduates on its notorious roads, Damian "Chisel" Powell and Ricardo "Jigga" Harris; I had lost my brother, Owen had lost his son and Mum had lost the only child that had ever lived with her from baby to adult.

Bisi and I decided for financial reasons as well as for the sake of the fact that she could not travel at such short notice given Antonia's condition that I would go to Jamaica on behalf of both of us. So on the 7th of November 2004 I flew out to Jamaica, Mum and Aunt Winnie met me at the airport.

I was in Jamaica a week before the funeral so that I could help around the house but most of all so that I could give Mum a shoulder to cry on. Any mother would be inconsolable at the loss of a child, let alone more than one. At times I wasn't sure that Mum could survive yet another cruel blow by fate, so I was determined to be a rock for her.

I was right, Owen was inconsolable himself, so he didn't have the motivation to be able to put his grief to one side and comfort Mum, he had his sisters and close family there to support them both, most had flown in from England and I had never met them before.

I knew this would be the toughest thing that Mum would have ever have had to get herself through, she felt that she was cursed in life when it came to her children because Bisi, and I had disappeared from her life when we were just 5 and 7 respectively, then her oldest daughter Dawn had died from terminal cancer 11 years ago at the age of 34 whilst Mum nursed her through her last days in Jamaica. Then there was Sandra, who I was about to meet for the first time, she had been a well-kept secret until we spoke in 2001.

∞

Damian was the unique one of Mum's five offspring, he was the only one of us who really knew Mum as a mother, he was the only one who had lived with her for all of his life, from baby to young adult, the more I realised his unique standing in her life, the more I knew that I would have to hide my emotions and grievances for Mum's sake. I knew she would struggle to survive and move on past the loss of Damian.

It was unfortunate that it was in the circumstances that I finally met my sister Sandra, she had flown in from New Jersey USA where she lives, she looked so much like Mum and their voices where almost identical, they had both heard this many times before. Sandra was now 39, I was 38 and we were Meeting for the first time in our lives, under these circumstances. We both knew that it was at least fortunate that Mum had introduced us to each other by phone three years earlier otherwise this could have been a very very awkward scenario for all of us.

Most of the family took time before the funeral to visit Damian where he was laid out for viewing, I opted not to, I felt that I couldn't bear to see him like that and I didn't want anything to break me for Mum's sake. Instead I worked around the house and in the garden, I drove up to Junction a few times to buy some of the things we would need for the wake and I spent hours with Sandra as we tried to catch up on so many missing years.

The day before the funeral a car turned up to deliver a wreath and a large bouquet of flowers for Damian. Mum, Sandra and I went outside to accept them. Up until that moment I had managed to keep my emotions locked up inside, I hadn't been to the funeral parlour in spite of plenty of encouragement from my cousin Lorraine and Damian's ex-girlfriend Maschelle who had both also flown in from England. But the flowers changed it all for me, they brought the reality home to me, now I knew clearer than ever that we were here to bury my brother the next day.

I excused myself hastily and walked round to the side of the house to the little bushes where I sat down and cried uncontrollably for the first time since I first got the news.

I was probably gone for no more than 10 minutes but Mum had noticed how upset I was at the sight of the flowers. So once they had taken them in, she went around the house searching for me calling out my name. I heard her approaching so I quickly cleaned my eyes and tried to pull myself together, I didn't want her to see me in that state, I smiled as I approached her, we hugged and walked back into the house, I knew that she could read through my smiles. The one time I was weak, she was there for me.

Later that day I decided that I needed to go to the funeral parlour to pay my last respects to Damian, if the flowers had upset me so badly, how could I possibly be strong for Mum? I asked myself. So I spoke to Lorraine and Maschelle, and they agreed to go with me.

I was the last of the three of us to approach Damian, once I had stood with him for about 10 minutes I realised I was completely relaxed, I told Lorraine that I now knew I would be fine at the funeral, I seemed to have found the strength that I needed and now I was sure that I would be a rock for Mum.

The funeral service was held in the assembly Hall of Munro College in St Elizabeth, Damian's old college. Because the accident that resulted in the loss of these two young men was big news across Jamaica, the service needed to be held in a big hall.

Mum was terribly inconsolable, she had cried a few times on

our way to the college in our limousine, each time I had cuddled her and tried to calm her as quickly as I could. Sandra needed comforting too as did Lorraine and Owen. All I could do was focus on Mum.

I have heard and read a lot about the way mothers would wail and scream over the death of their child, Mum had broken down on numerous occasions before the funeral but nothing that I had ever read or seen beforehand could have prepared me for Mum's loud screams the moment we walked into the hall and she spotted the open mahogany coffin lying to the left of the hall's stage, she screamed and yelled and cried while I held her tight and tried to keep her from collapsing on the floor.

Throughout the service, Mum sobbed, sometimes the sobbing would get louder and people around us would try to calm her down. Sometimes she would suddenly scream out loud having taken another glance to the left at the coffin, I knew that she had to cry, that she had to let all her emotions out, so I knew that all I could do was support her, cuddle her, keep offering her tissues and keep swallowing the lumps in my own throat.

Lorraine broke down whilst reading a sermon, but with a little help from Aunt Dorothy, she made it through. A few of Damian's friends either read sermons or said a few words as did his old college head teacher, then a group of his friends and old colleagues sang a moving rendition of "It's Hard to say Goodbye to Yesterday" by Boyz II Men. One of the boys cried through the entire song and had to be helped off the stage at the end of the song.

It was a very moving service that left hardly a dry eye in the college hall. I was impressed and amazed by how many people of various generations who all wanted to say something positive about Damian and distraught as I was, I could still feel pride in how much this young man had moved so many people.

The mother and family of Ricardo, the other boy killed in the accident came over to express their sympathy; they had buried their own son just a day earlier. Ricardo's mother wanted to speak to

Mum immediately after the service but Mum couldn't even walk without my support at that point. I knew that there was some resentment between both families at that moment, so I quietly asked Mum if she wanted to talk to Ricardo's mum Mrs Harris. She declined, so I spoke to Mrs Harris and explained that Mum was in no state or mood to talk. She countered loudly that she knew exactly what Mum was going through and kept asking for Mum to at least talk to her, so I calmly thanked her for attending the service in spite of her own loss, I apologised for Mum and told Mrs Harris that Mum had lost more than one child in her life, I asked her to respect Mum's need for privacy and I assured her that Mum had no intention to ignore her but this just was not the right time or place; so instead I took her phone number.

We followed the hearse in our limo, as it headed to the family resting place, as we drove down the road it was incredible to see the hundreds of ordinary families who were now waving or throwing flowers from either side of the road, the tragic event had clearly touched everyone, young and old.

A short prayer was said at the side of the grave then we sang a couple of hymns as the casket was lowered into the ground, Mum screamed, wailed and fought, but I held her tight and kept comforting her. The family threw a little dust on to the coffin; some stood there and watched it being buried while some school girls sang more hymns.

I walked Mum to the limo after the burial where she had time to sit down and gather her thoughts, I then went about thanking some of Damian's friends and colleagues as well as the pastor who had somehow made the service a little more bearable for me.

∞

The limo took us back home where we hosted a small celebratory wake in memory of Damian's life. As soon as we pulled up to the house, I realised that I had a severe headache, I couldn't do anything and I suddenly felt tired and dizzy, so I told Mum that I had to go and lie down, I took a couple of paracetamols and must have slept for over 4 hours in spite of the music and voices in the vicinity.

When I finally woke up, the headache had cleared, I still felt a little tired but that was understandable. I rang Bisi to tell her about the funeral service; then I rang one of my friends and colleague in England Jermaine, to tell him about my tough day, he commiserated with me and then gave me the one piece of good news for that day, November 14th 2004: he and his wife Zola had just given birth to their first child Noah.

Jermaine's news made me smile for the first time that day as I headed outside to join the party. I listened to the music ate some food and got to know some of Damian's friends. They were all humble and had nothing but the very best memories of their friend who I realised they knew much better than I did.

The night before I left Jamaica, I lay down in bed quietly and reminisced about the events that had taken place, I felt sad that although there was no question as to the strength of the bond between Damian and me, the fact was that we did not know each other well enough and now we never will.

I met Damian for the first time when he was a four-year-old back in 1984, then I saw him a few times between the ages of 8 and 11 before they moved back to Jamaica. The contact between Mum and me hadn't really improved that much, which meant that I only visited them in Jamaica once before Damian's untimely death.

Although we did communicate by email, it wasn't consistent, we admired each other, we respected each other and we loved each other but the fact that Mum and I had very little contact meant that Damian and I were restricted too.

If I had learned one lesson from this tragic event, it was that I needed to build a relationship with both my parents. I knew that I would never have the kind of bond that a son should have with his father but we could try. For my part I was going to make a bigger effort to keep in touch with him and to help him financially in

Nigeria. For Mum, I owed it to myself and to Damian to let the past go and to be there for her. We are still getting to know each other today, it's hard as we live in different countries but we have kept in touch more regularly since 2004.

Letting the past go and letting bygones be bygones has been the hardest thing for me to do. For over 30 years I have been searching for answers to the same questions I had been asking since I was a confused seven-year-old kid.

Why did Dad take us away? Why did Mum and Dad's marriage fall apart? Why didn't Mum even try to come and get Bisi and me from Nigeria? Do my parents realise how much psychological and mental stress their actions caused their five-year-old daughter and their seven-year-old son? I guess they thought we were far too young and would not be impacted by their actions.

The birth of my daughter Shaya helped me. It made me stronger and more determined to talk to her and to explain anything to her that I did, which would have a bearing on her life.

The passing of Damian helped me to finally put an end to the questions that I had asked Mum and Dad as well as numerous uncles and aunties over and over again.

I don't know how or why Mum and Dad grew apart to the extent that we had to be taken away, but now it just does not matter anymore. Time has helped me to heal the scars. In writing this book, I have found peace within myself; my sister has found peace and happiness too. We remain close and laugh quite often when we look back at those years in Nigeria. It has left us with a lot of good memories.

Did my experience in Nigeria make me a better or stronger person? I don't know. What I do know is that it made me appreciate life and what I have, it has helped to make me a tough person and a person determined to keep smiling. Jimmy Cliff was right; time has certainly developed into a story for me.

Before I left Jamaica a week after the funeral, I made Mum promise to make more effort to stay in touch with both Bisi and me. I told her we all had to learn from this tragedy and I knew this was our last chance to have a relationship. Mum understood my concerns and she was so appreciative of the efforts that Bisi and I had put in at such short and sudden notice to make sure at least one of us could be in Jamaica when Mum needed us the most.

Sandra and I also promised to keep in touch too and we hoped to get to know each other better over time.

My journey back to Montego Bay Airport was a fairly quiet one. In my hand luggage I had a couple of VHS videos of the funeral service for Bisi and me. Lorraine and some of the family had either left Jamaica before me or gone on to visit friends and family in other parts of Jamaica. I was sad to say goodbye to Sandra but I knew that we would stay in touch and perhaps one day I could visit her and get to know her side of the story better, who knows, there could be a whole new book to write.

Once I had hugged, kissed and waved goodbye to Mum and Owen at the airport, I checked in quickly and was soon seated on the Jamaica Airways flight.

The next thing I remember was being woken up perhaps an hour into the flight by a stewardess who wanted to know if I wanted any dinner! Clearly I had fallen asleep as soon as I had buckled myself into the seat, I never heard any of the safety check announcements, nor did I hear or feel the plane take off. It was only the second time in my entire life that I could say I don't even remember taking off in an airplane. The first time was way back in September 1973.

CHAPTER 13

TIME DID TELL

Just before 6 am on the 5th of January, there I was once more outside Murtala International Airport in Lagos, Nigeria, this was only the second time I had visited the country and it was nearly eight years on from my previous journey. It would actually be the third time that I had seen Dad in those eight years because Bisi and I had sent him tickets in the summer of 2010 to visit us in England and get to finally see his three grandchildren. I remember telling Bisi that we had to get Dad to visit us in England now or never, he was 70 years old when he came to England in July 2010.

That was the first time he had set foot in the United Kingdom in 37 years. It was a significant experience for all three of us but especially for Dad. He had finally for the first time seen all his grandchildren. He had seen Oliver, Bisi's son once before when he was a baby, but he had never met Oliver's sister Antonia who was eight nor my daughter Shaya who was 11 at the time.

It was also the first time that he had seen Bisi and me together in more than 23 years.

Dad also spent a lot of time with Uncle Charles and Aunt Erika; time had healed a lot of old wounds and it seemed as if they had never been apart. Uncle Charles took Dad into London a few times visiting all the places they had once frequented as young men, Dad was amazed at how much the city had changed in those 37 years.

He stayed in England for exactly a month but he had become home sick after the third week of his holiday. The one thing I did notice at the time was that he still suffered from the same old chest pains that he had experienced when I had seen him in Nigeria back in 2004.

The trip was too short to get him any detailed medical check-up but we made sure he went back with some good medication and all the things he needed. He arrived with just hand luggage and went home with two large suitcases.

He was a very happy man when he finally left England, he had achieved his most important ambition of seeing his children, their partners and his grandchildren in his lifetime and he even saw us all under one roof at Bisi's. He also took away with him a copy of my manuscript which a year later became the published book "Time Will Tell".

So here, 2 years later, I was in Nigeria visiting Dad once more. Just as on the previous occasion, my cousin Gani picked me up from the airport in the same old kombi bus which he still managed to keep on the road for work.

The roads looked like they hadn't been repaired in the last eight years, there were more potholes than ever and there was so much clay dust in the air. I have no idea why the conditions of the country and the resilience of the people still amazes me but it does. The population of Lagos seemed to have continued to increase too. Rickety vehicles of all shapes and sizes, motorbikes commonly called "okada" some carrying as many as 3 adults and a child with none of the passengers wearing helmets. All that commotion plus ordinary pedestrians going about their daily life all seemed to be using the roads at the same time.

As I took in the sights and conditions in awe, I took time to reflect on the reason why I was in Nigeria this time. Dad had been ill for a little while. In fact he had spent almost a month in a small local hospital called "Sarabis Hospital" which was owned by the son of one of his best friends Mr Amodu. His son the doctor, Femi specialised in psychiatric treatment but had a lot of experience in prostate problems and had done his best to help dad.

During numerous telephone conversations that either Bisi or I had with him, he had sounded very well and jolly, he did admit that he had been ill but kept reassuring us both that the concerns aforementioned to us by some cousins and in particular by Aunt Lola who lived in Ohio were all exaggerated. I had asked him back in October 2011 if either Bisi or I needed to visit him in Nigeria, "No, I am in good hands, they are looking after me well, all I need is your financial support" he would counter time and time again.

My suspicions started to grow firmer when he missed a couple of family weddings, events that he wouldn't normally miss, then in December when Aunt Lola rang again from Ohio to tell me that she had just seen a very recent photograph of Dad and he now looked thinner than when she had seen him just a couple of months earlier. She sounded very convincing and she was spot on when she advised me not to use the strength of Dad's voice as a guide. He had always had a strong enthusiastic voice and could easily disguise his illness on the phone to us.

I did a lot of thinking in bed that night after my conversation with Aunt Lola, by the next morning I was convinced that either Bisi or I needed to visit Dad to see him and make the judgement on his state of health for ourselves. I rang Bisi that morning and after a short discussion we were both in agreement but we knew that Dad would probably object. I told Bisi that we had to take the initiative, so we made a conference call to Dad who was now back at home recuperating. He sounded as jolly and lively as ever and reassured us both that he was improving significantly. "Dad" I said, "Bisi and I have had a long talk and think, I have decided to come and visit you in Nigeria next month, I have booked my flight and will arrive on the 5th of January." Then I paused, Bisi and I both waited for his protests, we knew he would try to dissuade us from spending money. "That's fantastic he said," once again, his reaction had shocked me. "I am really pleased that you have taken the initiative, I look forward to seeing you, we will have your room ready" I think Bisi and I just listened to him in bewilderment as he continued to express his joy. Once we had dropped Dad from the conference call, Bisi and I laughed at how easy that call had turned out to be.

I only had about two weeks before I had to travel to Nigeria, I spoke to Dad a few times including on Christmas Day; he still sounded keen and kept telling me what visits and trips he had planned for us. He told me that he wouldn't be able to travel too often on this occasion and I reassured him that I was specifically coming to spend some time at home with him.

I had half expected Dad to meet me at the airport with Gani but I wasn't surprised to see Gani on his own, after all, I could imagine that Dad needed to rest and picking me up at six o'clock in the morning meant that they would have had to have left home as early as four o'clock.

The sights began to look familiar as we bounced our way over the heavily eroded roads in the village of Agbado, the roads looked more worn than ever, the bus squeaked and made a racket over the bumps, a few seconds later I could see Dad's house just ahead, it stood out as it was one of just a few two storey houses on the street, it still wasn't painted but looked majestic in comparison to a lot of the shabby buildings around it. Gani jumped out of the bus to open the now very rusty big gates, then he drove into the familiar compound and parked.

I lived in Nigeria for over 11 years as a kid, yet the lack of development and the poverty I see still amazes me every single time.

∞

I think that I just about managed to hide the huge shock that I felt when I first set my eyes on Dad, he was really happy to see me "A Yem Yem" he called out as I walked over to give him a hug, I felt his frail body on my grasp and noticed how his legs where close to just flesh and bone. I told him it was good to see him, he hadn't lost his wit or his big smile, but it was hard to see him this way.

Dad had some good support around him at home as he needed it, he could barely move in bed without some assistance. He had Gani who had lived with him and helped him at home for so many years, Gani was married now, so his wife also lived there. He also had a couple of ladies who he paid to visit him daily, they helped with his daily needs such as bathing, cooking his meals and general cleaning of the house. There was also a physiotherapist who helped him exercise his joints and legs in general, a nurse named Talani who visited weekly to check his blood pressure and heart rate among other things, she also used intravenous drips to help pump more fluids into his body. Then he also had lots of friends from the village and the regular visits of one of his childhood friends, I called him Uncle Desun. I saw them all on this first day back.

Later that evening I supported Dad while he stood on a scale so we could keep track of his weight and see if he was gaining any. He weighed a shocking five stone. He was finding it very difficult to stand upright and couldn't stand without support for more than a few seconds but it was only when I later helped him from his bed to the toilet that I truly realised the extent of his frailty, it made me shed a few tears in private, I felt so sorry for him, yet he was going through it all with a smile on his face, so it was important that I didn't show too much fear.

I sat with Dad in his room for quite a few hours that night; he lay in bed where he had been all day, throughout the day he had nodded off a few times, sometimes he would be awoken by the sound of his mobile phone ringing, on other occasions it was when NEPA suddenly gave us a short burst of power supply, so the ceiling fan would come to life, otherwise he would sleep for about an hour and then wake up and we would continue our various chats. Whilst he fell asleep for the night after a very small dinner, I sat there in near darkness deep in my own thoughts. As usual, we had no power supply so we relied on a small kerosene lantern and a couple of small flash lights that I had sent him in the past. I had my iPad with me so I began updating my memoirs.

I witnessed four power cuts on my first day in Nigeria; the last one lasted right through to the following morning. In a changing world, I realised that some things just don't change quickly enough in Nigeria.

Visiting the market the following day was an experience, the traders easily outnumbered the prospective shoppers, Agbado Railway Station market was chaotic and congested, it ran along the very busy main road which had the main village bus garage, basically a long queue of kombi buses waiting their turn to fill up with passengers, as you walked past the buses, the conductor would try to usher you in, "Agege; Agege" I heard them shout as we battled our way past them. You could easily get hit by vehicles from either direction as the road was so narrow. Along either side of the road were the familiar gutters and just across the gutters were traders and motorcycles used as taxis, as usual it was noisy. The market itself got busier as you left the main road and made your way further inside. The ground was muddy and you had to hop over various puddles as you also wriggled your way around other people who were far more efficient than I was. We bought 24 bottles of drinking water, some fruit, peanuts and a Bible. Dad wanted a new bible and he needed one that was interpreted into modern English, so I bought one in the market called "The Good News Bible." I put about 8 bottles of water straight into the small freezer which was in Dad's bedroom, I needed these as I was always hot and thirsty.

When we first realised that Dad was ill and needed some basic amenities to help facilitate his day to day life, Bisi and I had sent him money for the small refrigerator that he had in his bedroom, he had also bought an orthopaedic mattress which he now found too soft and wanted to replace with a firmer one and we had been sending him regular income so he could pay the various people who came to look after him during the day.

I slept well that night, it was hot and from time to time a mosquito would buzz about around my ears but apart from getting up a couple of times to go and have a quick check that Dad was alright, I slept well. The next day I began to get a clearer idea of Dad's condition. He was certainly quite frail and very tired, he didn't eat much and he had a prostate problem. He had tried to get himself diagnosed at one of the general hospitals in Ifako before he fell very ill. He was still complaining of chest pains and was having a lot of prostate pain.

So one early morning at the age of 71, dad caught a bus to Ifako, a half an hour bumpy bus ride away, he then made his way to the hospital where he completed an out patient's form after which he was told to take a seat. Dad told me that he waited from 8:30am till 4pm at which time he concluded what he had known all along, that going to any of the general hospitals would be a waste of time. So over the next few months he tried more local remedies but as his condition worsened, his good friend Mr Amodu recommended that he visit his son Femi who ran Sarabis Hospital. Thankfully, Femi's knowledge of prostate problems was good enough to save Dad who had a very swollen and twisted prostate.

Now out of hospital, he still had regular check-ups from Dr Femi who would call round to the house to check on Dad's urinal aid and general health and a lady who called round every day to look after him, wash him and cook for him while Gani was at work.

Because of his current situation, Gani had decided to take a month off work, so we had to make sure that we compensated him for his financial losses. I spent the whole day in Dad's room playing on my iPad, listening to music, chatting with Dad and his regular stream of visitors or doing some of my writing, he spent most of his time in bed, occasionally moving across to the armchair in his room when he felt like sitting upright.

My second night's sleep was the worst I had ever experienced in my two visits to Nigeria. We had endured another five or six power cuts the previous day, the last one stretched from 4pm through to 2pm the following afternoon. It was a very hot night with no fan to keep the mosquitoes away and to compound my misery that night, a local church was holding an overnight vigil service. The service went on from around 9pm till 4am the following morning.

The noise was unbelievable; there was drumming and singing all night, then there was also a lot of very loud preaching and praying via loud microphones and megaphones that carried for miles in the night. The next morning while I looked like I had been out partying all night long, Dad and Gani looked fresh; they had slept right through the racket! Of course they were used to it, it was just part of normal life to them so much so that they hardly noticed the noises in their environment. Apparently, it's actually illegal to make that kind of noise at night even in Nigeria but no one seemed to care and it seemed no one would confront the powerful churches.

The following day, I went out with Gani to visit Uncle Joe at the house in Agege where we had stayed for that first night so many years ago. The kombi bus trip brought back a lot of old memories, but it did seem as though the days when you would have had to push and fight your way onto one of those buses had gone. Now there were buses and taxis in abundance. It was still a tight squeeze inside the bus which still wouldn't set off until every single seat was occupied; each row of seats which was actually one long bench, could comfortably sit three passengers but they still had to squeeze four on each row. All the buses still looked and sounded as rickety as ever. As we travelled over some unbelievably bumpy clay roads we heard a loud metallic bang underneath us, Gani who was also a bus driver, told me that one of the rear shock absorber springs on our bus had snapped. It was a common occurrence and clearly nothing to worry about as the driver carried on his journey only pausing to moan about the cost of fixing the broken spring.

Although he had lost his sight many years ago, Uncle Joe's memory and wit remained sharp as ever. He was nearly 83 years old but he still looked very well. He reached out for my hand grasping it between both his hands as he said a short prayer and thanked Bisi and I for making the emergency trip to visit Dad. Once again I looked around the small living room and recognised a couple of ornaments that were still around from way back when I lived there in the 70's, I even picked one of them up and placed it in my uncle's hand, reminding him how I used to play with that ornament, he laughed and commented on how much I remembered from so long ago, then he reminded me that he still wanted a copy of "Time Will Tell" which one of his grandchildren would read to him.

After leaving Agege, Gani insisted that we go on to Ikeja in Lagos State, he wanted to show me a new complex where he was sure I would feel at home shopping, so we took another kombi bus on to Ikeja driving past the old Guinness factory and a few other buildings that I vaguely remembered, we then took one of the little moped-tricycles popularly called "keke marwa" further on to the complex called "ShopRite. It was indeed impressive, the first of its kind that I had ever seen in Nigeria, I saw the "KFC" sign from a distance and immediately got my camera out, Gani was so excited because he knew that I was surprised.

It was a nice shopping mall which had only just opened to the public on the 14the of December 2011. It was fully air-conditioned and there were quite a few shops inside, including a massive supermarket full of very familiar products. Gani was right, I did feel at home. I bought lots of fresh fruit for Dad as well as some soups and chocolates such as "After Eight" and Cadbury's "Fruit & Nut" which I hoped would help him to regain weight quicker.

One of the things I had noticed on this particular trip and could see again as we headed back to Agbado on another kombi bus was the amount of anger in the air. All the way from the airport to Dad's house I would see heated arguments and near fights going on by the roadside and at bus stops. Everywhere I went and even outside Dad's house in the neighbourhood there were arguments. Frustration was clear to see and one of the biggest reasons for the added tension this time around was the new tax subsidy which the government had recently removed from the price of fuel just before

I arrived in Nigeria. It meant that the cost of petrol would rise an unprecedented 150% meaning a rise from #65 per litre to #141 per litre of petrol in a country where most of its population was already on their knees, this latest government policy seemed to be one step too far. That evening Dad had a few of his friends at the house, we all sat in his bedroom, they saw me physically lift dad out of bed and then sit him in the armchair beside his bed so that he could sit upright for his dinner. While he ate a small portion of food, we all discussed the fuel subsidy, it wasn't often that I heard people outside politics vehemently question or dispute the government, usually, they would grumble amongst themselves about how tough it was to live in Nigeria but this time the whole country was going to oppose this subsidy, they made their feelings very clear but the government failed to respond in any form so an a national strike was agreed by the various unions and set to start from the following Monday which was the beginning of my last week in Nigeria, I sat there hoping that the strike wouldn't last more than two or three days, I definitely didn't want to be stuck there in uncertainty.

Bisi rang to talk to Dad later in the evening, and then I talked to her and told her about the imminent strike, I wanted to be there to help Dad as much as I could but I was also homesick, I wasn't getting much sleep, wasn't eating much and had so many itchy mosquito bites. All I did throughout the day was sit in Dad's room and watch him sleep and wake up while I either wrote my notes or played games on the iPad which I also used to play music. She promised to keep her fingers crossed for me and as I had no 3G or internet access, she would also have to keep me informed on all news related to the strike and my flight which was booked for the following Sunday the 15th of January.

∞

The indefinite national strike as it was later termed, started in the morning of Monday the 9th of January, an ultimatum had been proposed to the government, with no response or reaction from the president or his ministers the strike commenced.

Pretty much everything came to a standstill between the hours of 5am and 7pm each day, there was absolutely no public transport available, this included flights, trains and all the Kombi buses, taxis, motorcycles "keke Marwa" and tricycles which by the way, were all privately owned. All the shops and markets were closed; some of the airports did run restricted flights but in general, the country was almost at a complete standstill even good old NEPA seemed to be weighing in, we had even less power supply than usual, so I constantly left my iPad and phones plugged to the sockets for any burst of power supply we got, this eventually burned out the circuit of my brand new Blackberry phone.

Around six o'clock each evening during the strike period, the village of Agbado in Ogun State where Dad lives would come to life; it seemed almost unbelievable that the whole place had looked almost deserted just an hour or so earlier. The buses and all other forms of public transport would have taken over the roads, most market stalls would be operational and the Agbado Railway market would look like it had never been on strike at all. The only tell-tale signs being the deserted train left parked on the track which kids used for hide and seek.

With no reaction from the government the strike carried on into the next day as the unions and people had threatened. My concerns about getting out of Nigeria by the weekend began to deepen. Dad's condition wasn't improving rapidly and now the risk of attempting to get him to a hospital had tripled. Before the strike I was concerned about the bumpy and uneven roads being too tough on his frail body and the fact that the hospital could keep us waiting for any number of hours. Now we had the additional risk that any form of transport could be attacked by thugs in the street thinking that the passengers were violating the strike. We had no choice but to stay in and give Dad the best treatment we could.

One of the good things about being there was that, unlike all the people he had there to support him, I could be strict with Dad. This meant that I made him attempt to eat three meals a day instead of next to nothing, then throughout the day, whenever he was awake, I would offer him some chocolate or other snack, sometimes he would even wake up and declare himself hungry! I also reduced his salt intake significantly, then I showed his physiotherapist how to perform sport physio on dad's legs, which made Dad do some exercise as he now had to try to use what muscle he had left rather than simply having his legs massaged. Dad liked the idea of exercising and although it was tough and tiring for him, he insisted on trying twice a day and within a couple of days, he started to feel his muscles responding better. He knew I had taken training in various sports related exercises especially as I had been a football coach and now a referee, a point which he repeated to anyone who visited including the physiotherapist who was happy to learn these new methods.

On Tuesday night I spoke to Bisi on the phone again, this time I went out onto the balcony while Dad was asleep for the night. As usual, we had no power supply, I could hear the buzz of a few generators in the neighbourhood and some distant music which seemed to be coming from the streets which were alive again after the day's strike. I told Bisi that I was very concerned about Dad's condition and suggested that she apply for a visa immediately, she had to see him now or it could be too late. I suggested that as much as he had been excited to see me, his joy of seeing her would be more than be doubled and that this could give him an even bigger boost of energy and enthusiasm for life. For the first two or three days of my visit Dad had a twinkle in his eye, he found some new energy and could move about in his room with some support, three or four days later, the initial boost of energy was gone and now he could hardly turn himself over in bed without help but he still did his exercises and even reminded me on days when I had tried to skip it thinking he was too tired.

Bisi agreed to apply for her visa and book a flight as soon as she got it approved, we agreed that it was best that we didn't tell Dad until everything was confirmed then she gave me an update on my flight circumstances, so far the flight wasn't cancelled but there was no additional information.

The strike itself continued to run for a further two and a half days. The government had finally responded and set up meetings to talk to heads of unions and other agencies, so in the afternoon of Friday the 13th of January the strike was temporarily suspended for 2 days. This allowed people to get around and re-fuel, while also giving time in the on-going negotiations between the unions and the government.

The next day was a Saturday, it was the first full day since the suspension of the indefinite strike and it seemed like everyone wanted to make up for lost time and also get their errands done in case the strike recommenced on Monday. We took a Kombi bus for the 20 min trip to Agege for another visit to Uncle Joe; the trip was interesting because every single passenger including the driver, young, old, man or woman all had the same topic on mind. It was all about the president who they had now nicknamed "Badluck" and his regime. They wanted him out, it was the same conclusion I had heard time and time again, the fuel subsidy argument was certainly fuelling the anger of Nigerians who had already been pushed to the edge.

I listened to the on-going debates all around me on the bus, even Gani joined in, everyone was annoyed, everyone had a story and ultimately it all came down to the same conclusion, life was certainly tough in Nigeria.

At Agege, I gave Uncle Joe an update on Dad's health, Uncle Joe rarely left the house nowadays due to age and loss of sight, but he made sure that my cousins visited Dad regularly. Still he was shocked to hear my analysis of Dad's health, I was optimistic, after all Dad was eating more than before I visited Nigeria but he had a long way to go to get back to good health.

That evening, I spoke to Bisi once again, there was still no additional information regarding my flight schedule, so I just had to hope that all would go to plan at the airport the next day. I wanted to be with Dad because he was so poorly, yet I knew there wasn't much more I could do for him there and on the other hand I was feeling really homesick.

That night, I sat with Dad in the usual darkness relying on the lights from little lamps and torches I had brought with me, we had a heart-to-heart, I told him that he would have to write out his will, and that I would need to take any important documents that he wanted to keep safe back home with me, he was too weak to write but he understood the importance of what I was telling him, he looked at me weakly and now I understood what he had been saying to his friends in jest all the time I was there. He would say it in Yoruba to them but it translated as *"eventually the old man becomes the kid and the kid becomes the man"* I felt so sad but he wanted me to be the man, to encourage him and to guide him, he knew how weak he was even if his mind was still sharp and active.

We agreed that he would take a few days to think about it then he would either dictate his will to me or Bisi or if he had the energy he would write it and get it sent to us. I still didn't tell him that Bisi was coming the following month as we didn't want to get him too excited before Bisi got her visa.

I could see that Dad had a lot on his mind as he lay in bed shaking his head occasionally, "yes I will make sure I get the will sorted out next week" he said, "Before I write my will I have some things to ask you and to talk to you about" he continued. "Yemi, you are the oldest of my three children, we haven't always seen eye to eye and I find you a bit of an enigma, I read your book, it was very interesting indeed. I did enjoy it and I am glad that you wrote it" I sat there waiting for the bombshell "You got some dates and locations wrong, I have some notes that will help you with that. Here's the thing that worries me about you, I don't know how you feel about Nigeria, you live in England and I know you feel you belong there but if I was to ask you where you are from, what would you say?" I looked him in the eye and said "My Dad is Nigerian, My Mum is Jamaican, I am British by birth but I descend from an Afro-Caribbean background. I am part Nigerian, part Jamaican and that will never change, my name tells you that I am Nigerian" He smiled and breathed a sigh of relief then I continued, " I know we had our differences all those years ago but now hopefully through reading my book you understand why I was angry, that said, since I came back to Nigeria in 2004 and you made me feel so welcome in your home, I learned a lot about you, I realise how much you love this country, I saw how homesick you were in 2010 when you visited us in England and I knew that you were fiercely proud of being a Nigerian, that you belong here and want to live the rest of your life here, I am proud of what you have done in this village, everyone respects you, they love you, they all know you and they respect me because I am your son" with a lump in my throat, I carried on "I respect you for never forgetting my birthday, or Bisi's or any of our children's birthdays, you always rang or sent a text message, I also know and see your undying love for your children, when you visited me in England, everyone thought that you were a lovely man, I have to tell you that I agree with them, I am proud to be your son." "That's all I wanted to hear" he said. "Well in that case, I know how I must write my will."

"Oh about your book" I took a deep breath and listened, "you said you didn't know why I took you away" I nodded "Well, here goes" and this is what he told me...

Dad arrived in England in September 1962 to further his education. His goal from the outset was always to return to his fatherland once he had achieved his degree so that he could utilise his education and skills in Nigeria a developing country at the time.

He met Mum three years later on a Monday in London way back in 1965, I don't know the significance of it being a Monday but he remembers it vividly. They aimed to marry on February 17th 1966 but had to put the marriage back two days to the 19th due to the birth of their first child who they named AdeYemi after his father.

Mum knew that one day she would move to Nigeria with him, so late in 1966 he travelled to Nigeria with some of their belongings and savings to start work, find a home and begin settling down. Unfortunately his dreams didn't go to plan, Nigeria was tougher than he had left it, so by the time he went back to England, it seemed as though he had squandered all their money. Mum found it hard to trust his intentions and the logic of relocating to Nigeria; this along with a few other small misunderstandings may have been the first signs of strain in their relationship.

Dad went back to Nigeria in March 1968 so he missed the birth of my sister Bisi in June. He went with enthusiasm but describes the trip as a sad adventure. He returned to England in August of that year.

This time around, as Mum would later tell me, she was furious at the thought of most of their life savings having been wasted in Nigeria due to one reason or the other, she said that at that point, she asked for a divorce. Dad told me that by then he knew that Mum no longer wanted to go to Nigeria but for him, there was no place like home. His only dilemma was the message that his family had given him back in Nigeria, they told him that he would still be respected as a man even if he returned to Nigeria with no degree or qualifications but not if he returned without his children. So on the 11th of September 1973 dad left Britain with his Carpentry & Joinery degrees as well as with his two children, we flew out on a Ghana Airways flight via Ghana, eventually arriving in Nigeria on the night of 13th September 1973. He concluded, "For what it's worth, I am sorry for what I did to you" "Apology accepted that's all I have ever wanted to hear" I told him. I was grateful that he had given me the answer to the biggest question in my life.

One day before my 47th birthday, Saturday the 16th of February 2013, Mum, my Step-Dad Owen and my Uncle Derrick came to meet me at Norman Manley International Airport in Kingston

Jamaica, I had travelled for a short holiday with my daughter Shaya. The next day, Sunday the 17th would be the first time my mum and I had seen each other on my birthday in just over 40 years.

It was the half term holiday period for a lot of London schools, Shaya and I had planned to visit mum back in July of the previous year for a two week break but due to unforeseen circumstances we had to cancel at the last minute. So now we were making up for lost time with a six day whirlwind trip for her to finally get to know her grandma properly and for me to make some final notes for the revised edition of my book.

Mum had previously watched my BBC News interview and then read the copy of *"Time Will Tell"* that I had sent her. She read it early in 2012 while she was spending some time with my sister Sandra in America. Mum was actually there to have some much needed specialist treatment on a troublesome injury to her leg. She told me back then that she had gone through the book page after page with a towel around her neck which she used to wipe away the tears, she found the story gut wrenching but she could not put the book down. She couldn't believe the amount of schools we had gone through, the number of places we had lived in and the amount of spankings I had endured but she said "I must give him (Dad) credit for one thing; he made sure that you got a good education." I agreed.

Once we had settled in at the big house in Southfield St. Elisabeth, I read Dad's explanation of how he had come to take us away to Nigeria. "In general, that's exactly what happened, but I can also explain the significance of that Monday to you" she said.

Mum had learned her trade of dress making as a young lady back home in Jamaica, She worked at Smith's Crisps in England while trying to find a job to match her career. She was finally invited to her big interview in London on that Monday morning of 1965. She said she wasn't confident on the train routes back then, so when she got to Hammersmith train station she decided to ask the young Nigerian man she saw on the platform if she was going in the right direction. He assured her that she was and that he in fact was heading in the same direction, so they travelled together, mum promised to call him at some point but she didn't until they bumped into each other again a few weeks later in Shepherds Bush, London, His name was Lekan, he went on to become my dad.

With the age old burning question of why Dad had taken us away finally answered, there was just one equally major question that I needed to ask Mum and which many left behind parents had asked me. At what point did she realise that we were gone? I asked her if she could take me down memory lane from the moment of realisation to how she managed to get her life back on track. Mum had agreed to help me with the missing parts to my book while I was with her in Jamaica. She told me that she recalls giving Dad a parcel to post for her that morning on his route to work, when she got back home that evening, she went straight upstairs to Mrs Brown to collect us. Mrs Brown informed her that Dad had been back and had taken us out for the day.

On getting back indoors, Mum noticed the parcel that she had asked Dad to post earlier that morning on the coffee table, she says at that point alarm bells began to ring for her. She then went into the bedrooms and saw scattered clothes all over the bed and floor, the possibility and realisation of the improbable began to play on her mind. Hysterically she rang her best friend Aunt Winnie who came over to console and help her. Then she rang Uncle Charles and Aunt Erika to ask them if they knew where Dad had taken us, she became suspicious of all his close friends and family as she made call after call.

Later on she called the NSPCC (National Society for the Prevention of Cruelty to Children) who then advised her to immediately contact the airports authority, they also tried to reassure her that her kids must be in the UK somewhere and that it was unlikely that he could have got them out of the country so quickly.

The airport couldn't help her with outbound passenger

information, for one she didn't know what time, what airline nor which destination we may have been heading to if in deed we had even been to the airport at all that day. Next the NSPCC advised mum to travel to Nigeria and try to locate us, there was no evidence yet that we had even left England let alone our destination. Mum was a 26 year old Jamaican who had never been to any country in Africa, yet she was being advised to get onto a plane in 1973 and travel to one of the largest countries and the most populated nation in Africa to locate her two children.

Over the next couple of weeks, life was unbearable for her, she cried every day, she trusted very few people and everywhere she went, she hoped that she would bump into us. Then the confirmation came in form of a letter with no contact address from Dad that we were in deed in Nigeria and that we were both fine. Her worse fears had been confirmed. She says over the next few years she continued to hope that we were actually in England somewhere but the facts were clear because I had started to write to her from Nigeria. She also recalls that she never moved out of Norland House because I knew the address and she hoped that maybe one day we could find our way back, also because she feared that we might lose contact entirely should she move.

The NSPCC, the police and the Foreign Office all reiterated that if Mum could get into Nigeria and locate us and then somehow get us to the British Embassy building in Lagos that they would then be able to help her bring us back home. "How could I travel to Nigeria to find you?" "I feared for my life, I knew he would not harm you but for me it would have been too dangerous" she carried on "In a country where I don't know who to run to, I would have had to try and find you both and then bundle you both away somehow and find my way to the British Embassy with you two on tow." I understood the enormity of the task that was being laid out before her. In the 70's the cost of a flight alone would have been astronomical.

Mum also told me that Dad didn't want her to write to us and she thought that he probably confiscated some of my letters to her, I wasn't so sure about this especially as I posted the bulk of my letters from my various boarding schools and she did in fact reply occasionally which I had to remind her.

I don't know how she really coped day by day and year after year, but she did tell me that with her work, she could drown away her problems and worries. She loves the work she does, she still designs and makes lovely clothes today and her shop "Jazzy Lady Fashion Designing & Dressmaking" is very popular around Southfield in Jamaica for her professional work. While in front of her sewing machine at home she can clear her mind and throw her focus into work she told me. Whenever she stopped for the day or took a break, she would cry and cry. Sooner or later she would be back working again once again burying her thoughts away to the tune of her Singer sewing machine.

About six years later, she met my Step-Dad Owen a Jamaican, he had to move into Norland House with her as she wouldn't move away, then in 1980 they had a beautiful boy who they named Damian, Bisi and I would meet him four years later during our surprise holiday to England.

Some time after we left Mum and went back to Nigeria in 1984, Mum and her family finally moved out of the flat in Norland house and bought a house in Perivale just on the outskirts of London. They moved back to Jamaica in 1992 four years after Bisi and I had finally settled back in England. The visit of February 2013 was only my third to Jamaica, I had also been to Nigeria just three times since I left in 1988.

CHAPTER 14

THE NEW EPILOGUE

On Sunday morning, the 15th of January, Gani drove me back to the airport, I had spent the early hours with Dad, encouraging him to keep strong and making him promise that he would keep trying to eat well and reduce his salt intake while I was gone.

We were all still all apprehensive as to whether I would be able to fly out on schedule after all the delays that had occurred during the national strike. I had rung the airport information desk the night before and I was pretty sure that the lady I spoke too had done no thorough checks. "Everything is fine and on schedule" she reassured me. Once past the security police at the main entrance to the airport at just after six o'clock, I headed straight for the information boards which also showed the flight back to Heathrow still on time for 11am but I had my doubts, how could it be so easy and so smooth even after such a big strike in a country where hardly anything goes to plan on a normal day?

I had breakfast with Gani while I tried to contact Bisi. Eventually I decided to ask at one of the information counters. "Your flight is delayed" that's all she could tell me, so I countered, "it still says on time for 11am on the information board, why isn't it being updated there?" She stared at me almost exasperated "your flight is delayed" "for how long?" I asked, "Your flight is delayed that's all" so I smiled as I walked off expecting a long day. Bisi found out online that my flight had been delayed for twelve hours so I told Gani to go back home to Dad. We still had fears of the national strike recommencing, so it wasn't safe to stay out too late. I knew that I would have to stay at the airport however long it took.

In the end I spent 19 of the most stressful and most chaotic hours at Murtala International Airport. The airport was packed to its rafters with angry people trying to catch flights, the information boards were never updated, there was no organisation, whenever a check-in desk opened for a flight; there was no announcement. Which resulted in tempers rising further, so many people tried to jump queues resulting in fights. I watched on as men fought other men, women fought each other and of course there was angry women fighting equally angry men. The police were nowhere to be found. Not once did the police intervene to break up a fight or restore order.

After several hours of wait, I noticed a queue for London Heathrow, so I joined and watched on as arguments over queue jumping broke out all around me. My luggage was checked manually as none of the scanners were working, once checked in I was advised to go straight to passport control as the flight was well behind schedule. I chuckled to myself as I dashed over to a very disorganised passport control. There were about 15 queues which all merged into one; it took over an hour to get to the passport desk. "So how are you going to warm me up today?" the customs lady asked me. I glared at her "I have been here over 15 hours" I replied. "Well I have been here for a long day too you know" she said. The audacity I thought, "You get paid to be here." Well why don't you go to the kiosk and buy me some food and drink" she asked, her questions continued to irritate me so I just asked if she was done checking my passport. "You see the kind of thanks I get?" she announced to the angry queue of people behind me.

Once past the starving customs lady, it was back into yet another chaotic queue, this time for hand luggage scanning; once again the conveyor belts and scanners were out of order leaving about 3 or 4 customs staff to do manual checks while the area filled to its brim with angry passengers. The passengers for Detroit started to panic knowing they were about to miss their flight, so they started pushing forward, then the London passengers realised that we were about to miss our flight too and so it went on, suddenly there were more than 200 angry passengers pushing and punching their way past the hapless customs staff, I initially stood there with my jaw wide open, Wow! I thought, and then I quickly joined in the chaos and squeezed my way past customs into the waiting area.

Once again, after all the pushing and barging, the flight was delayed. This time it was because our plane didn't have enough fuel a member of staff risked his life to announce to us at the top of his voice. He continued "So the plan is a two hour stopover in Ghana for refuelling" he announced to a hoard of angry passengers. He looked like a man about to be stoned. It was eventually decided that the plane would go to Ghana without its passengers for refuelling while we waited another couple of hours.

So, in the early hours of Monday morning, just over 19 hours since arriving at the airport, I finally boarded my flight from Lagos to head back home.

The next month, around the time of my 46th birthday, Bisi went to visit Dad, I always knew that her visit would bring the sparkle back to his eyes and hopefully along with all the gifts, goods, medicine and other foods she too took with her, there was a chance that he might find his willpower to fight for life again.

"Thank you for everything you have done, I can see you really want me to live" he told me during our phone call that night, I had sent lots of torch lights and lamps, batteries for all the devices, as well as an electronic photo frame loaded with memories from all aspects of his life, we sent lots of packets of soup, and vitamins along with all the other things he had asked for.

Indeed he did respond very positively to Bisi's visit, he began to eat better especially as his meals were now being prepared by his "only daughter" his voice sounded stronger and all seemed positive once again.

Bisi stayed in Nigeria for two weeks just like I had done, we spoke every evening and the good news was that Dad was actually gaining weight. By the time she had left Nigeria the news was still good even if he had slowed down a little just like he did in the second week of my visit.

By April, Dad was walking around his bedroom by himself, he was cooking his own food and Gani was telling me how Dad couldn't stop eating. At last Bisi and I could begin to contemplate the probability of bringing him back to the UK for a thorough medical check-up.

By mid-June as Dad continued to improve, there was more good news, Gani's wife had delivered a baby boy who they eventually named Raquib. Dad was overjoyed and wanted to host the naming ceremony at his house where Gani also lived. I wired him some money through Western Union for the small party and some extra pocket money for him and we had a long conversation about how he needed to split the money, he was in a very jolly spirit even if as I told Bisi that night, his voice sounded very weak.

Sadly, Dad never got to cash the money I had sent him, the next day July 1st 2012 Dad passed away just after 3:45pm.

On the 11th of July, Bisi and I boarded a flight together for the first time since 1973 and ironically back to Nigeria. Dad was laid to rest on the 13th of July.

Resources for Families Affected by Child Abduction

United Kingdom

Abducted Angels
25 Martindale
Martindale Trading Estate
Cannock
WS11 7XN
www.abductedangels.org
Tel: 01543 571 818

Child Rights International Network (CRIN)
East Studio
2, Pontypool Place
London, SE1 8QF
United Kingdom
www.crin.org
E-mail: info@crin.org
Tel: 0207 401 2257

Children and Families Across Borders (CFAB)
CFAB
Canterbury Court, Unit 1.03
1 – 3 Brixton Road
London
SW9 6DE
www.cfab.uk.net
Email: info@cfab.uk.net
Advice Line: 020 7735 8941

Children and Family Court Advisory Service (CAFCASS)
6th Floor
Sanctuary Buildings
Great Smith Street
London
SW1P 3BT
www.cafcass.gov.uk
Email: webenquiries@cafcass.gsi.gov.uk   Tel: 0844 353 3350

Children's Legal Centre
Coram Children's Legal Centre
University of Essex
Wivenhoe Park
Colchester
Essex CO4 3SQ
www.childrenslegalcentre.com
Email: clc@essex.co.uk
Tel: 01206 877910

Citizens' Advice
Myddleton House
115-123 Pentonville Road
London
N1 9LZ

www.citizensadvice.org.uk
Tel: 0844 111 444
Families Need Fathers **(FNF)**
134 Curtain Road
London
EC2A 3AR
www.fnf.org.uk
Tel: 0300 0300 363

Foreign and Commonwealth Of ce
Child Abduction Section
Consular Directorate
King Charles Street
London SW1A 2AH
Tel: 020 7008 0878 (or the FCO Response Centre on 020 7008 1500
outside of office hours) www.fco.gov.uk/childabduction

Mothers Apart From Their Children (MATCH)
BM Box No. 6334
London
WC1N 3XX
www.matchmolthers.org
Email: enquiries@matchmothers.org

Reunite International Child Abduction Centre
PO Box 7124
Leicester
LE1 7XX
www.reunite.org
Email: reunite@dircon.co.uk
Tel: 0116 255 5345

Resolution
PO Box 302

Orpington
Kent BR6 8QX
www.resolution.org.uk
E-Mail: info@resolution.org.uk
Tel: 01689 820272

USA

Association of Family and Conciliation Courts (AFCC)
6525 Grand Teton Plaza
Madison, WI 53719
Phone: (608) 664-3750
www.afccnet.org
E-mail: afcc@afccnet.org

Children's Rights Council (CRC)
9470 Annapolis Road
Suite 310
Lanham, Maryland 20706
Phone: 301-459-1220
www.crckids.org
E-mail: info@crckids.org.

Family Law International
1942 Broadway St, Ste 314
Boulder, CO 80302-5233
USA
Phone: (303) 323-1938
www.family-law-international.com/
E-mail: info@familylawint.com

The International Centre for Missing & Exploited Children (ICMEC)
1700 Diagonal Road, Suite 625
Alexandria, Virginia 22314
United States of America
www.icmeg.org
Telephone: +1 703 837 6313
E-mail: information@icmec.org

National Center for Missing & Exploited Children (NCMEC)
Charles B. Wang International Children's Building
699 Prince Street
Alexandria, Virginia 22314-3175
USA
Phone:703-224-2150
www.missingkids.com
Supervised Visitation Network
3955 Riverside Avenue
Jacksonville, FL 32205
Tel; (904) 419 7861
www.svnetwork.net

EUROPE

Committee for Missing Children
PO Box 1252
63502 Lagenselbold
Germany
www.kinder-nach-hause.de
E-mail: findthekids@kinder-nach-hause.de
Tel: +49 6051 7009292

Hague Conference on Private International Law
Permanent Bureau
Hague Conference on Private
International Law
Scheveningseweg 6
2517 KT THE HAGUE
Netherlands
www.hcch.net